D1612428

PROFESSIONAL NEGLIGENCE IN THE CONSTRUCTION INDUSTRY

DISPUTE RESOLUTION GUIDES

Practical Guide to Litigation
second edition
by Travers Smith Braithwaite
(1998)

What is Dispute Resolution?
by Peter L. d'Ambrumenil
(1998)

Professional Negligence in the Construction Industry
by Neil F. Jones & Co.
(1998)

PROFESSIONAL NEGLIGENCE IN THE CONSTRUCTION INDUSTRY

BY

NEIL F. JONES & CO.

|L|L|P|

LONDON HONG KONG
1998

LLP Reference Publishing
69–77 Paul Street
London EC2A 4LQ
Great Britain

EAST ASIA
LLP Asia
Sixth Floor, Hollywood Centre
233 Hollywood Road
Hong Kong

First published in Great Britain 1998

British Library Cataloguing in Publication Data
A catalogue record for this book is
available from the British Library

ISBN 1–85978–828–9

Text set in 10/12pt Plantin by
Selwood Systems, Midsomer Norton
Printed in Great Britain by
WBC Limited,
Bridgend, Mid-Glamorgan

PREFACE

As practitioners in the field of construction law we are all aware of the risks which professionals in this area face and the liabilities, both potential and actual, which they can encounter. Construction law appears to retain its particularly contentious aspect, a fact which has been recognised by sections 104 to 117 of the Housing Grants Construction and Regeneration Act 1996 which have been in force since 1st May 1998.

The aim of this book is to focus upon the liabilities of construction professionals and it is written in a manner in which construction professionals themselves, as well as lawyers and insurers, should readily understand and appreciate.

Chapters 1 (Liability of Professionals), Chapter 2 (Insurance Implications), Chapter 5 (Liabilities of Arbitrators, Mediators, Adjudicators and Experts), Chapter 6 (Bonds and Warranties) and Chapter 7 (Causation, Ascertainment of Liability and Quantum) have been written by Jeffrey Brown. Chapter 3 (Architects and Engineers), Chapter 8 (Professional Negligence, Litigation and Arbitration) and Chapter 9 (Dispute Resolution under the Housing Grants Construction and Regeneration Act 1996) have been written by Ian Yule. Chapter 4 (Quantity Surveyors and Claims Consultants) has been written by Mark Arrand. In dealing with topics of this nature there is inevitably some overlap of material between chapters. However, it is hoped that this is not excessive and that, where it occurs, it is of benefit to the reader.

The authors acknowledge the benefits of the general references made from time to time to Jackson & Powell, *Professional Negligence* (4th edition), published by Sweet & Maxwell. Mark Arrand's thanks go to Kenneth Wall of Quest Building Consultants for his assistance with his chapter. Thanks go to Alan Nugent of Lambert Fenchurch for the permission to reproduce the APIA/95 wording and to the Royal Institution of Chartered Surveyors for their kind permission to include the SURVIS-PI policy wording, both included as appendices. The CoWa/F and CoWa/P&T Warranties which also appear in the appendices do so with the kind permission of the British Property Federation. Katrina Bevan, Susan Bickerton and Yvette Coates are to be thanked for their assistance with the careful typing of the text. The law is as stated at March 1998, but the publishers have also kindly allowed specific amendments to the text which have arisen subsequently, particularly in reference to the Housing Grants Construction and Regeneration Act.

Needless to say, the views contained herein are those of the authors, who bear full responsibility for the contents.

JCB
IRY
MRA
6 July 1998

CONTRIBUTORS

Jeffrey Brown LLB, FCIArb, ACII

Jeffrey won an Evan Morgan Scholarship to read law at the University College of Wales, Aberystwyth.

He joined the practice in 1984, became a partner in 1986 and in 1993 became the Senior Partner. Throughout this time he has developed his knowledge and understanding of construction law and has had the conduct of substantial disputes both in arbitration and litigation. Latterly also, he has become involved in insurance law particularly professional indemnity claims. He speaks regularly at construction and insurance law conferences.

Ian Yule MA (Oxon), FCIArb

Ian joined the practice in 1990 having had several years' experience of conducting commercial litigation actions. He became a partner in 1992. He specialises in construction and engineering law. He also advises on non-contentious matters such as drafting of contracts, bonds and warranties, and on non-construction standard forms e.g. MF/1, the IChemE forms etc. He has lectured for a number of commercial and professional organisations, as well as preparing and running specially-tailored workshops for clients.

Mark Arrand FCIArb

Mark joined the practice in 1992 after extensive experience of commercial and other litigation to specialise in construction litigation and arbitration, becoming an associate in 1995 and a partner in 1996.

Mark's principal areas of practice are those involving construction and professional negligence disputes, upon which he has lectured and published articles.

CONTENTS

TABLE OF CASES

TABLE OF LEGISLATION

CHAPTER 1

LIABILITY OF PROFESSIONALS

1.1. CONTRACTUAL LIABILITIES

Clients of professionals may feel that professional fees are substantial. While the level of fees charged should have no direct bearing upon the legal duties and responsibilities, the existence of the obligation to pay substantial fees will often have a bearing on the mind of any client as to what his expectations are of the professional and will influence those remedial steps, if any, which he takes if he is dissatisfied or disappointed with the net result.

Clients also are discerning and will instruct specific professionals for specialist tasks, taking into account expertise and perhaps cost implications. Where a client does not have inherent loyalty toward one single or group of professionals, there will be a greater willingness to go to law in the event of any dissatisfaction with the quality of service. Unfortunately also for the professional, while it is a brave individual who practises without the benefit of insurance cover (and it is indeed mandatory for many professionals), any would-be plaintiff has the comfort of knowing that any claim made for damages is most likely to be honoured if liability is established, given the presence of such cover.

Professionals working within the construction industry have in the past been identified as giving rise to particular risks. "Construction industry professionals", which were defined as architects, building services engineers, building surveyors, civil engineers, quantity surveyors and structural engineers, were the subject of a distinct fact-finding study the findings of which were comprised within the report produced under the chairmanship of Professor Andrew Likierman in April 1989. Further, the non-construction surveyors were the subject of another fact-finding study the findings of which were also included within the same report. Professionals working within the construction industry have complicated responsibilities which are not only independent of but are also inter-dependent on each other. The professionals will owe contractual responsibilities to a number of different parties, many of whom exist as a consequence of the execution of collateral warranties. These responsibilities are in addition to those owed in the tort of negligence. If one also takes into account that the failures of any buildings may often be due to a number of complicated factors, it is not surprising that multi-party disputes are a well-established feature within the construction industry.

The classic statement on the standard of care that may be expected from a professional is provided by McNair J. in *Bolam* v. *Friern Hospital Management Committee*[1] when he stated as follows:

> "The test is the standard of the ordinary skilled man exercising and professing to have that special skill. It is well established law that it is sufficient if he exercises the ordinary skill of an ordinary competent man exercising that particular art."

The requirement to exercise the ordinary skill of the ordinary competent man exercising that particular art may well form the basis of the contractual relationship between the professional and his client as a consequence of a written contract which may make reference to such a duty. Professions often publish standard terms of engagement and a term will be included to this effect.

The aforementioned test as set out by McNair J. in *Bolam* v. *Friern Hospital Management Committee* has been cited with approval in very many cases. The test of the skill and care has not since this time been seriously challenged. However, reference needs to be made to the decision in the Court of Appeal in *McManus Developments Ltd* v. *Barbridge Properties Ltd and Blandy and Blandy (a firm)*.[2] This decision related to the conduct of a firm of solicitors having the conduct of a conveyance of property. It was argued on behalf of the solicitors that the test should be based upon whether or not the individual was "reasonably competent" or "reasonably well-informed". Reliance was made upon the earlier comments of Lord

1. [1957] 2 All E.R. 118.
2. [1992] E.G.C.S. 50.

Diplock in *Saif Ali* v. *Sydney Mitchell & Co*,[3] when he made reference (at page 220 C, D and E) to the words "unless the error was such as no reasonably well informed and competent member of that profession could have made". This argument was, however, rejected since the Court of Appeal rightly identified that to import this test would be to reduce the standard required to something lower than the lowest common denominator. It stated that one could always find, in this instance, an apparently reasonably competent solicitor who could say that he would probably in similar circumstances have done the same.

In the absence of any express condition, however, the law will always imply a term that the professional man will use his reasonable skill and care. The implication of such a term can always be justified on the basis of the requirement for business efficacy and also the clear but unexpressed intention of the parties to the contract.

A difficult question arises when one is asked to consider the practical application of the test of the exercise of all reasonable skill and care. Is it the case that a particular individual's experience and expertise need to be taken into account when assessing the requisite standard to be expected or, alternatively, is it more appropriate for the individual to be adjudged by the standards of his profession generally? In the past, the courts have tended to favour the latter approach: see, for example, *Andrew Master Hones Ltd* v. *Cruikshank and Fairweather*[4] in which Graham J. stated:

> "The degree of knowledge and care to be expected is thus seen to be that degree possessed by a notionally and duly qualified person practising that profession. The test is, therefore, if I may put it that way an objective test referable to the notional member of the profession and not a subjective test referable to the particular professional man employed."

In practice difficulties would arise in applying any other test, since it could give rise to problems in ascertaining the manner of deciding this subjective test. The courts would find difficulty in differentiating between standards of skill and care and how these would vary given age and experience. How could an expert witness viewing the actions of a fellow professional assist the court otherwise than by assuming an objective view? There would also be the danger if a subjective test were to be applied of the courts favouring a strict

3. [1980] A.C. 198.
4. [1980] R.P.C. 16.

liability approach, i.e. if there has been a mistake then there has to be an inference that a breach of the duty of reasonable skill and care exists. However, the converse argument could be put forward. Clients of professionals, quite correctly, could expect to pay a larger fee to an individual, which would reflect his skill and experience if he has, for example, spent 20 years in a particular field and is a renowned authority. Why then should this individual be judged by the same criteria as would a person with one year's experience? The dilemma was discussed by Megarry J. in *Duchess of Argyll* v. *Beuselinck*,[5] a claim for negligence against a solicitor. He stated:

"No doubt the inexperienced solicitor is liable if he fails to attain the standard of a reasonably competent solicitor. But if the client employs a solicitor of high standard and great experience, will an action for negligence fail if it appears that the solicitor did not exercise the care and skill to be expected of him, though he did not fall below the standard of a reasonably competent solicitor? If the client engages an expert, and doubtless expects to pay commensurate fees, is he not entitled to expect something more than the standard of the reasonably competent? I am speaking not merely of those expert in a particular branch of the law, as contrasted with those practising in the same field of the law but being of a more ordinary calibre and having less experience. The essence of the contract retainer, it may be said, is that the client is retaining the particular solicitor of the firm in question, and he is therefore entitled to expect from that solicitor or firm a standard of care and skill commensurate with the skill and experience which that solicitor or firm has. The uniform standard of care postulated to the world at large in tort hardly seems appropriate when the duty is not one imposed by the law of tort but arises from a contractual obligation existing between the client and the particular solicitor or firm in question. If, as is usual, the retainer contains no express term as to the solicitor's duty of care, and the matter rests upon an implied term, what is that term in the case of a solicitor of long experience or specialist skill? Is it that you will put at his client's disposal the care and skill of an average solicitor, or the care and skill that he has? I may say that Mr. Arnold advanced no contention that it was the latter standard that was to be applied; but I wish to make it clear that I have not overlooked the point which one day may require further consideration."

The view presently taken by the courts is, whatever a client's expectations may be when instructing a professional, in terms of experience and expertise, which will no doubt be mirrored by the fees charged, and whatever the level of performance obtained in return, the standard of care required of the professional should not thereby be affected and remains fixed.

5. [1972] 2 Lloyd's Rep. 172.

However, to date, the prediction of Megarry J. in *Duchess of Argyll* has not been implemented, although it may yet form the basis of future judicial precedent.

Thus, the effect of this statement must be that ignorance of precise areas of practice cannot be relied upon as a defence—a general knowledge will be assumed. One assumes that this would occur with increased experience of that particular speciality. It must be however that the answer to this question is of no relevance to the issue of determining the standard of care. Recent years have seen a relaxation of the professional rules which allow for the publication and distribution of brochures to clients and potential clients, and individuals within the profession now freely market themselves as having specialist skills in specific areas. In these circumstances, would it be wrong to expect the same standard of care from such individuals as would be expected from individuals professing to have those specialist skills, as opposed to the ordinary skills which may exist within the profession at large? The argument that a higher duty of care is owed in such circumstances may be based on estoppel. If a professional has held himself out as having specialist skills, a court may prevent him from denying that he was a specialist in a given field, and hence a greater measure of expertise could be expected. It should be noted, however, that the estoppel argument can only apply to deny the existence of an obligation where one already exists. It cannot of itself create the obligation. If a representation is made on the expertise of a professional, either orally or in writing and this is relied upon by the client, then it may be incorporated as a term of the contract. In *Gloucestershire Health Authority and Others* v. *Torpy*,[6] His Honour Judge Bowsher Q.C. had to consider the liability of engineers who had been engaged in connection with the installation of an incinerator at Gloucestershire Royal Hospital. One of the issues in the case was whether or not the standard of care to be expected of the engineers should be that of specialists as a consequence of their professed experience and knowledge of incineration matters. The engineers added that they considered themselves to be "uniquely qualified to fulfil" the objectives of the project. Thus, were Torpy to be judged as building services engineers professing to have the ordinary skill and care of that profession or, alternatively, were they to be judged by some

6. (1997) 55 Con. L.R. 124.

higher quality, being that of specialists? The judge indicated that stating they were experienced in such matters did not of itself make them specialists. The judge stated "there is considerable difference between saying 'I have extensive experience in field X' and saying 'I am a specialist in field X' ". Thus, unless there is clear evidence from the terms of engagement of that professional that "specialist" skills are being offered, the court will not introduce a higher standard of care. Against this, however, consumers show an increasing awareness and appreciation of any specialist skills, and thus they may seek to introduce terms into the contracts of engagement which expressly refer to these specialisms.

Many professionals within the construction industry work within multi-disciplinary practices. Large consultancies have many disciplines. Thus, terms of engagement must make clear at all times precisely what are those services which the client will obtain. Without this, which standards of which particular profession(s) will be applicable in each case may not be clear.

It is important to note that it is not every error of judgement that gives rise to a claim for a breach of the requirement for all reasonable skill and care. For example, see *Whitehouse* v. *Jordan*.[7] The facts in this case, which was a decision of the House of Lords, related to a claim against a medical practitioner. To equate an error of judgement with negligence is a dangerous precedent indeed and would substantially extend the professional's liability for claims.

In the Court of Appeal decision of *George Hawkins* v. *Chrysler (UK) Ltd and Burne Associates (a firm)*,[8] the requirement of reasonable skill and care only was affirmed as being the test by which a professional would be judged when producing a design only. The court in *Hawkins* concluded that the earlier decision of the Court of Appeal in *Greaves & Co. (Contractors) Ltd* v. *Baynham Meikle and Partners*,[9] in which a firm of consulting engineers responsible for the design only had been judged by the application of a test of fitness for purpose, should not be considered as general authority for such a proposition and should be restricted to applying to its own facts.

Difficulties can occur if a professional initially takes on a specific responsibility and then seeks to delegate it to others. It is important

7. [1981] 1 W.L.R. 24.
8. (1986) 38 B.L.R. 36.
9. [1975] 1 W.L.R. 1095.

to recall that any party to a contract—and the professional can be no exception—cannot unilaterally seek to alter the terms of the contract, i.e. the terms of his engagement. If a professional seeks to engage specialist help this cannot affect his responsibilities to his client. For instance in *Moresk Cleaners Ltd* v. *Hicks*[10] it was held that the defendant architect had no authority to delegate the function of design without the express agreement of his client. This issue has particular relevance when one is considering the liability of professionals involved in a construction project where a certain consultant may seek to provide a "package deal" for his client and then seek to delegate the tasks to other specialists. It is clear that he still remains liable for all of his own prime liabilities in the absence of his client's agreement to release him from such. The comments made by Sir Walter Carter sitting as an Official Referee[11] are informative:

> "In my view, if a building owner entrusts the task of designing a building to an architect, he is entitled to look to that architect to see that the building is properly designed. The architect has no power whatever to delegate his duty to anybody else, certainly not to a contractor who would in fact have an interest which was entirely opposed to that of the building owner."

He then added[12]:

> "In my view, an architect cannot escape his responsibility for the soundness of the design of the structure by delegating his work to any other person, still less to a contractor who is seeking to obtain the contract.
>
> If the defendant was not able, because this form of reinforced concrete was a comparatively new form of construction, to design it himself, he had three courses open to him. One was to say: 'this is not my field'. The second was to go to the client, the building owner, and say: 'this reinforced concrete is out of my line. I would like you to employ a structural engineer to deal with this aspect of the matter'.
>
> Or he can, whilst retaining responsibility for the design himself, seek the advice and assistance of a structural engineer, paying for his service out of his own pocket, but having at any rate the satisfaction of knowing that if he acts upon that advice and it turns out to be wrong, the person whom he employed to give the advice will owe the same duty to him, as he, the architect, owes to the building owner."

This decision was cited and approved by the Court of Appeal in

10. (1996) 4 B.L.R. 52.
11. At p. 53.
12. At p. 54.

Investors in Industry Limited v. *South Bedfordshire District Council.*[13]

Thus, applying this same logic, it is easy to see why the attempt by an architect to reduce his liability to that of a quantity surveyor failed to impress the Court of Appeal in *Nye Saunders & Partners* v. *Alan E. Bristow.*[14] Stephen Brown L.J. said:

> "Of course it was a very sensible and prudent step for Mr Nye to take to consult a quantity surveyor who is an expert in computing costs. But in my judgement, he cannot avoid responsibility for the fact that he did not draw the attention of his client to the fact that inflation was not taken into account. The duty rested fairly and squarely upon Mr Nye and it cannot be avoided by, as it were, seeking to move the responsibility onto Mr Parker."

A cautionary tale was illustrated by the decision of His Honour Judge Newey Q.C. in *Richard Roberts Holdings Ltd and Another* v. *Douglas Smith Stimpson Partnership and Others*[15] where the defendant firm of architects was found to be liable for negligence in the design of effluent tanks where it genuinely did not believe that it was so liable. The court however found that the terms of its agreement with its clients was to act as architects for the creation of the Hinckley Dye Works, which included the design of the tanks. If the architects had wished to limit their role they should have done so expressly and in writing. Had the architects felt that they could not form a reliable judgement about the linings of the effluent tanks they should have informed their clients of this and advised them to take other advice, probably from a chemist. This decision illustrates the importance of identifying with certainty the terms of a professional's engagement.

In deciding whether or not a professional has exercised the requisite standard of reasonable skill and care that may have been expected of him, courts of law have increasingly referred to the professional rules which govern the conduct of the professions themselves. There has been a tendency to regulate the performance of their members by professional bodies who have argued that, in codifying expected standards of performance, their members are in turn assisted since they are able to observe exactly what is and what is not required of them in stated situations. The value of any such rules of conduct were appreciated by Oliver J. in *Midland Bank*

13. [1986] 1 All E.R. 787.
14. (1987) 37 B.L.R. 92 at 107.
15. (1988) 46 B.L.R. 50.

Trust Co. Ltd v. *Hett Stubbs & Kemp (a firm)*[16] when he stated:

"The extent of the legal duty in any given situation must, I think, be a question of law for the court. Clearly, if there is some practice in a particular profession, such accepted standard of conduct which is laid down by a professional institute or sanctioned by common usage, evidence of that can and ought to be received."

In *P. K. Finians International (UK) Ltd* v. *Andrew Downes & Co. Ltd*,[17] allegations against a surveyor were considered to be unsustainable in view of the terms of guidance note 6 of the RICS "Guidance Notes of the Valuation of Assets". While the judge made clear that these guidance notes were not to be regarded as having the force of statute, and mere failure to comply with the guidance notes did not constitute negligence, the guidance notes were nonetheless to be considered as being powerful evidence of the conduct that may reasonably have been expected of the surveyor. The position of chartered surveyors may be regarded as being special on the basis that, until 31 December 1995, chartered surveyors were under a professional duty to comply with all practice statements published by the RICS as published from time to time by the Assets Valuation Standards Committee of the RICS. As from this date, however, they have ceased to be mandatory, albeit that the RICS has warned that departure therefrom should only be made for a good reason. Care should, however, be taken at all times to distinguish the standard of performance by the professional from the responsibility or the duty *per se*. This is a matter for the court to determine. This inference was clearly drawn by Oliver J. in *Midland Bank* v. *Hett Stubbs & Kemp (a firm)*.[18]

In *South Australia Asset Management Corporation* v. *York Montague Limited*,[19] the House of Lords has dealt with allegations made against valuers who had negligently overvalued a number of properties. In deciding that the valuers could not be held responsible for the subsequent fall in the property market, the court distinguished the provision of information and the giving of advice on what course of action had to be adopted. It was only in the giving of advice that the adviser had to consider all the potential consequences of that course of action. A person providing information was liable only

16. [1979] Ch. 384.
17. [1992] 1 E.G.L.R. 172.
18. [1979] Ch. 384 at 402E.
19. (1996) 80 B.L.R. 1.

for the consequence of that information being wrong.

1.2. LIABILITY IN THE TORT OF NEGLIGENCE

In the famous decision of *Donoghue* v. *Stevenson*,[20] a decision which is now over 60 years old, the House of Lords by a majority of three to two held that a manufacturer of ginger beer owed a duty of care to its ultimate consumer irrespective of any contractual connection. The leading speech for the majority was delivered by Lord Atkin who referred (at page 580) to the duty being considered as an obligation to take "reasonable care to avoid acts or omissions which you can reasonably foresee would be likely to injure your neighbour". He further considered who was a neighbour by referring to those persons "so closely and directly affected" that one ought reasonably to have them in mind as being so affected. Lord Atkin was careful to distance himself from any attempt to create an exact formula which could be applied to each and every case, stating that "to seek a complete logical definition of the general principle is probably to go beyond the function of the Judge". This fact, which Lord Atkin considered to be self-evident, has during subsequent years often been overlooked by the courts as they have struggled to devise some form of universal magic formula. However, in giving his judgment, Lord Atkins set about defining the limits and parameters of modern tortious liabilities.

The law has always looked at the duty of care in the tort of negligence as giving rise to a remedy in cases of injuries to persons and damage to property. Further, in so far as any financial or purely economic loss arises as a consequence of that injury or damage this sum is recoverable. Thus, in *Eckersley* v. *Binnie & Partners*,[21] consulting engineers who had been employed by a water authority to design and supervise the construction of a water tower and associated valve house were found liable in negligence to 31 plaintiffs who were or were representatives of members of a visiting party injured or killed in an explosion at the valve house. This was caused by the ignition of methane gas. Neither at first instance nor on appeal was there any dispute that the consulting engineers owed a

20. [1932] A.C. 562.
21. (1988) 18 Con. L.R. 1.

duty of care, although there was some dispute whether or not the presence of methane gas was reasonably foreseeable.

The issue of damage has to be contrasted with that of defects. Time and again, the courts have considered that a duty of care exists in relation to the former but not the latter. In *Londonwaste Limited* v. *Amec Civil Engineering Limited*,[22] the defendant was a main contractor who had been engaged in the performance of road improvement works. During the course of his performance of the works, some electricity cables were severed, thereby causing physical damage to a nearby electricity generator and also purely economic loss. It was conceded in this case that the plaintiff could recover for the physical damage caused to the plant itself. However, the court found that no damages could be awarded for the purely economic loss comprising the loss of income derived from the sale of the electricity while the plant was out of action. This was due to the plaintiff's inability to prove that this economic loss arose from the damage to the electricity generator.

There is, in addition, an extension to the right to claim as a consequence of physical damage, and that is where monies are incurred in order to prevent physical damage occurring which would surely take place were it not for the expenditure of these costs. This category was discussed by the House of Lords in *D & F Estates* v. *Church Commissioners for England*,[23] but is however of limited practical application.

The courts have historically encountered difficulty in defining what may be considered to be "damage". Sound sense and logic would dictate that this should mean damage to any third party's property and thus should not include the defective component itself. However, the effect of the decision of the House of Lords in *Pirelli General Cable Works Ltd* v. *Oscar Faber & Partners*[24] was that a claim in respect of defective work was indeed to be considered as giving rise to a cause of action. The facts related to the use of an unsuitable material (Lytag) in the construction of a chimney to factory premises. Cracks developed at the top of the chimney and the primary issue before the House of Lords was when the damage came into existence. In the tort of negligence, a cause of action accrues on the date that the damage occurs. This is in contrast to

22. (1997) 83 B.L.R. 136.
23. [1989] A.C. 177.
24. [1983] 2 A.C. 1.

a cause of action for a breach of contract where the relevant date is the date of the breach of the contract. In proceeding to consider that the damage occurred when the cracks near the top of the chimney came into existence, the House of Lords was confusing the issue of defective work, i.e. the use of the unsuitable material giving rise to the cracks in the work itself, i.e. the chimney, with damage to third party property. This has to be incorrect. It should be suggested that there was a remedy in the tort of negligence in respect of the latter but not the former. The simple fact that the issue of what was meant by "damage" arose within the determination of the issue of limitation of action did not give cause to justify this error.

More recently, the House of Lords in *Murphy* v. *Brentwood District Council*,[25] stated that the *Pirelli* case was one dealing with a claim for purely economic, i.e. financial, losses on the basis that it was the defective component itself, i.e. the chimney as designed, which proved to be the cause of the difficulty. Thus the error in logic of the earlier decision would appear to have been identified and addressed. Nonetheless, Lord Keith, with whom all the other Law Lords agreed, explained the *Pirelli* decision as a case based upon negligent advice falling within the principle of *Hedley Byrne & Co. Ltd* v. *Heller & Partners*[26] (see *post*).

In considering the issue of damage, the courts have considered in the past whether or not a building is to be perceived as one complete entity or whether, in the alternative, it is to be perceived as comprising a number of different elements, each of which may be perceived as being an item which may be damaged as a consequence of the failure of another separate component within the building—to choose an obvious example, where defective foundations prove inadequate, giving rise to cracks within other parts of the superstructure of the building, e.g. walls and roofs. This issue was first raised by Lords Bridge and Oliver in *D & F Estates* v. *Church Commissioners for England*.[27] In this decision Lord Bridge described it within the context of "one element of the structure [which] should be regarded for the purpose of the application of the principles under discussion as being distinct from another element, so that damage to one part of the structure caused by a

25. [1991] 1 A.C. 398.
26. [1964] A.C. 465
27. [1989] A.C. 177.

hidden defect in another part may qualify to be treated as damage to 'other property', and whether the argument should prevail may depend on the circumstances of the case".

This argument, which has since become known as "the complex structure theory", received further judicial discussion in *Murphy* v. *Brentwood*, when each of the Law Lords considered the circumstances in which the theory might apply for the future. Lord Bridge in this case, when commenting further (at page 478), suggested that it may be possible to bring a claim in negligence against the manufacturer of a defective central heating boiler if it were to explode and damage the house but not in the situation where, due to the inadequacy of foundations in a building, differential settlement and consequential cracking were caused.

"The complex structure theory" has been applied once only in England and Wales. In *Jacobs* v. *Moreton & Partners*,[28] which involved a case against defendant engineers who designed and supervised the remedial foundation works to a house, the judge, Mr Recorder Rupert Jackson Q.C., set out four circumstances which he considered would necessitate the application of the policy:

(1) whether the defective item was constructed by someone other than the main contractor responsible for the construction of the building as a whole;

(2) whether the defective item had been retained by way of its separate identity;

(3) whether the defective item positively inflicted damage on the building;

(4) whether the defective item was constructed at a different time from the rest of the building.

These circumstances all are designed to emphasise the lack of physical connection between the component responsible and that which is the subject of the damage.

Thus, the complex structure theory as a theory survives, albeit there must appear to be some distinctions between the two components, and none of the judgments in *Murphy* tends to support an actionable claim in circumstances where a part of a building, i.e. foundations, which must be an inherent part of the building itself, causes damage to another.

28. (1994) 72 B.L.R. 92.

1.2.1 Pure economic or "financial" losses

Having evaluated what may be included within the term "damage", one can see that the majority of claims involving professional negligence within the construction industry will relate to purely economic or financial losses. It is here that the courts have encountered difficulties. It is one thing to owe a duty of care to avoid causing injury to the person or damage to the property of others; it is quite another to avoid causing others to suffer purely economic loss. The spectre which the courts always had in their minds was the avoidance of the opening of the "floodgates" to admit any kind of tortious liability. This may lucidly be summarised by quoting the classic words of Cardozo C.J. in *Ultramares Corp.* v. *Touche*:[29]

> "Liability in an indeterminate amount for an indeterminate time to an indeterminate class. This would confer on the world at large a quite unwarranted entitlement to appropriate for their own purposes the benefit of the expert knowledge or professional expertise attributed to the maker of the statement."

The issue of whether or not financial loss should be recovered in the tort of negligence came before the House of Lords in *Caparo Industries Plc* v. *Dickman and Others.*[30] This case involved allegations of negligence being made against a firm of accountants who were auditors of a public limited company. The allegations related to negligence in certifying the accounts. In deciding how one should approach the test of whether or not claims for financial losses were recoverable in the tort of negligence, Lord Roskill in *Caparo* stated the dilemma in lucid terms.

He relied upon *Hedley Byrne & Co. Ltd* v. *Heller & Partners*,[31] in which it was stated that Denning L.J. in *Candler* v. *Crane, Christmas & Co.*[32] correctly identified the law. It was clear that a duty of care could be owed by professional men to third parties where there was no contractual relationship between them. Subsequent attempts to define both the duty and its scope had created more problems than the decisions had solved. There was no simple formula or touchstone to provide in every case a ready answer to the questions whether, given certain facts, the law would or would

29. (1931) 174 N.E. 441.
30. [1992] A.C. 605.
31. [1964] A.C. 465.
32. [1951] 2 K.B. 164.

not impose liability for negligence, and in cases where such liability could be shown to exist, determine the extent of that liability. Phrases such as "foreseeability", "proximity", "neighbourhood", "just and reasonable", "fairness", "voluntary acceptance of risk" or "voluntary assumption of responsibility" were not precise definitions. At best they were but labels or phrases descriptive of their very different factual situations, which had to be carefully examined in each case before it could be pragmatically determined whether a duty of care existed and, if so, what were the scope and extent of that duty.

Lord Oliver followed the same logic by stating that the extensions in the law of negligence since the decision in *Hedley Byrne* to cover pure economic loss not resulting from physical damage had given rise to a considerable and as yet unsolved difficulty of definition. The opportunities for the infliction of pecuniary loss for the imperfect performance of everyday tasks upon which people relied for regulating their affairs was illimitable and the effects were far reaching.

To search for any single formula as the general test of liability was to pursue a will-o'-the-wisp. Once one discarded, as one had to, foreseeability of harm as the single exclusive test—even a *prima facie* test—of the existence of a duty of care, the attempt to state some general principle served not to clarify the law but merely to bedevil its development. Thus, the essential requirements for establishing a duty of care in the tort of negligence are foreseeability, the relationship between the parties, i.e. proximity, and furthermore a requirement that it would be fair and reasonable in those particular circumstances to impose such a duty. The three matters overlapped with each other and, as Lord Oliver pointed out,[33] were in reality facets of the same thing.

The essential requirements for establishing liability for economic loss following *Hedley Byrne* was that a statement had to have been made with the knowledge of its maker and to have been available to the recipient for the particular purpose upon which he had relied on it. The maker of the statement also must have actual knowledge or inferred knowledge that his advice so communicated was likely to be acted upon without any form of independent enquiry. Reliance upon any statement did not establish a duty of care of unlimited scope, since regard has to be had to the transaction or transactions

33. At p. 633.

for the purposes of which the statement was made. It was a loss arising from such transaction or transactions rather than "any loss" to which the duty of care extended.

Yet if Lord Oliver in *Caparo* had indicated that the extension of the law of negligence since *Hedley Byrne* to cover pure economic loss not resulting from physical damage had given rise to a considerable and yet unsolved difficulty of definition, this dilemma was not resolved by the decision in *Caparo* itself. Identifying the problem is not the same as constructing an answer, which Lord Oliver himself indicated was to pursue the impossible. Thus, in an attempt to create certainty of boundaries he indicated that the law should develop on the basis of an incremental approach, thus looking at the subject matter and concentrating upon that as opposed to some abstract formula. Thus, in so doing, he affirmed the logic of Brennan J. in *Sutherland Shire Council* v. *Heyman.*[34] He advocated the developing of novel categories of negligence by increments. However, no reference was made to the manner in which the judges should decide whether or not there should be any retreat from allowing liability in those areas already established as giving rise to causes of action. Thus, if the incremental approach were to be adopted and universally applied, existing areas of liability would inevitably become entrenched, whatever the arguments for and against their justification. However, the incremental approach of Brennan J. in *Sutherland* was approved by the House of Lords in *Murphy* v. *Brentwood District Council.* Lord Keith[35] emphasised that the correct manner of determining the existence and scope of the duty of care in novel situations was the incremental approach.

There are many examples of the operation of the incremental approach. Thus, for example, one may refer to the decisions of *Smith* v. *Eric S. Bush & Partners* and *Wyre Forest District Council* v. *Harris.*[36] These were cases involving negligent valuations performed for mortgage purposes.

A further example may be seen in the Court of Appeal decision in *Pacific Associates Inc. and Another* v. *Baxter and Another.*[37] This decision in particular raised important issues for professionals

34. (1985) 60 A.L.R. 143.
35. At p. 446.
36. [1989] 2 All E.R. 514.
37. (1988) 44 B.L.R. 33.

within the construction industry, since it dealt with the duty, if any, owed by an engineer appointed to supervise construction works to the contractor being the party responsible for the performance of these same works. The issue in this case was whether or not a duty of care was owed by an engineer to a contractor not to cause it economic loss in the process of certifying and of accepting or rejecting claims under the contract. The court emphasised in this case that no duty of care was owed, albeit that it decided that each case would depend upon its own circumstances and upon the provisions of the relevant contract. Furthermore, the court held that the contractor did have an identified remedy in the event that he was dissatisfied with any decision of the engineer, and that was to seek the appointment of an arbitrator. This must presumably also include the appointment of an adjudicator now the provisions of the Housing Grants Construction and Regeneration Act 1996 have been brought into effect, albeit that the particular facts in *Pacific* would not have brought it within the Act, since the subject matter was a construction project in the Persian Gulf.

In *Pacific Associates* there was no request to the engineer by or on behalf of the contractor for the engineer to render any service of any kind to the contractor. Any relationship between the contractor and the engineer came into being as a consequence of the contractor entering into a contract with the employer and of the engineer having been engaged by agreement with the employer to perform the functions of the engineer under the contract. The engineer assumed the obligation under his agreement with the employer to act fairly and impartially in performing his functions. He was under a contractual duty to the employer to act with proper care and skill. Such risk as the engineer could reasonably foresee of the contractor suffering loss as a result of any want of care on the part of the engineer was remote.

The distinction between statements and acts or omissions was not considered relevant in *Pacific*. Formerly, liability on the basis of *Hedley Byrne* related to statements of fact or opinion. Notwithstanding that ultimately no duty of care was found to exist in *Pacific*, the fact that liability would have followed as a consequence of acts or omissions by the engineer, in either accepting or rejecting claims, was not a consideration which featured in any of the Lords Justices' judgments.

This distinction was ignored altogether by the decision of the

House of Lords in *White* v. *Jones*,[38] being a case involving allegations of negligence against solicitors.

In this instance, a solicitor was found to have owed a duty of care to a potential beneficiary even though the negligence related to an omission to perform the instructions of the deceased testator. As the court argued, there was good reason why the solicitor should be liable to this third party in this special situation, since otherwise there was no sanction in respect of the solicitor's breach of his professional duty. The estate had suffered no loss; the only loss suffered had been on the part of the beneficiary.

It needs to be clearly borne in mind that the courts can hold that individuals also owe duties of care in the tort of negligence in their own personal capacities. In *Punjab National Bank* v. *De Boinville and Others*,[39] the Court of Appeal had to consider this issue. It took the view that the employees of a Lloyd's broking company did owe a duty of care in the tort of negligence toward their employer's client, for whom they acted. The facts were that the employees had continued to act on behalf of the plaintiff when they moved from one Lloyd's broking company to another, and thus the court concluded that the degree of proximity to the client was greater than that of the employer. While the court concluded that it was not every employee of a firm or a company providing professional services who owed a personal duty of care to his client, the court took the view that in this instance the employees had been entrusted with the whole or nearly the whole of the task which they, as employers, undertook. The portion of the judgment relating to the personal liabilities of the employees does not contain a great deal of detail. Thus, it is difficult to assess whether or not this decision will be perceived to relate to its own special facts or whether, in the alternative, it is to be considered of more general application. There may be some benefit for maintaining claims against the employees in person if they are of financial substance and the employer is either insolvent and/or, alternatively, without the benefit of professional indemnity insurance. It is submitted, however, that if this argument were to succeed there must be a stronger connection between the individual and the claimant, as in *Punjab National Bank*, than a normal relationship where the individual is a mere employee.

38. [1995] 2 A.C. 207.
39. [1992] 3 All E.R. 104.

Furthermore, one sees potential difficulties if employers seek to exercise subrogation rights against individuals or employees. Indeed many policies expressly waive any rights of subrogation they may have against the employees, e.g. General Condition 6.10 of APIA—RIBA/95 Policy.

Care should be taken against the adoption of the *Punjab Bank* decision as grounds for suggesting generally that employees of a professional firm or company owe independent duties of care in the tort of negligence to clients. The facts in *Punjab Bank* showed that the individuals concerned had a close relationship with the plaintiff so that they continued to be engaged by them notwithstanding the change of employer. If the *ratio* were to be applied generally it might mean that employees of firms of professionals or limited companies wound up would be faced with the prospect of being sued and having to insure themselves against this potential liability.

Prior to *Hedley Byrne* the limits of tortious liability were only too clear; a claim would have to be based upon either physical injury or damage to succeed. In allowing claims to be made for pure economic loss the advantage of certainty of boundaries of the law of tort has been sacrificed. Furthermore, whereas the courts have sought to define anew its limits, they have discovered, as will be demonstrated by the preceding authorities, the impossibility of so doing.

The criticism of the incremental approach is that it leaves established findings of liability in previous cases unchanged. Many of those decisions however were reached not by the adoption of incremental approaches but on Lord Wilberforce's two-tier test in *Anns* v. *Merton LBC.*[40]

Thus to summarise, one sees that in assessing whether or not a duty of care in the tort of negligence exists, one must have regard to the statements made in *Caparo* with the emphasis upon adoption of the incremental approach. It must always be recalled however that the threefold requirement of proximity, foreseeability and fairness and reasonableness cannot be considered analogous to any "test". Furthermore, as will be seen from the more recent decisions hereafter discussed, there has been renewed emphasis upon the issue of any voluntary assumption of liability.

40. [1978] A.C. 728.

1.3. CONCURRENT LIABILITIES IN CONTRACT AND TORT

There has been a traditional suspicion in the minds of the courts toward expansion of the law of tort especially where the parties have already entered into a contract. Formerly, it was assumed following the decision in *Bagot* v. *Stevens Scanlon*,[41] a case involving a negligent architect, that responsibilities were owed for breach of contract alone and there was no concurrent duty of care owed in the tort of negligence as well. It could have been assumed that the dilemma was finally resolved as a consequence of comments made by the Privy Council in *Tai Hing Cotton Mill Ltd* v. *Liu Chong Hing Bank Ltd*.[42] In this case, Lord Scarman observed:[43]

"Their Lordships do not believe that there is anything to the advantage of the Law's development in searching for a liability in tort where the parties are in a contractual relationship. This is particularly so in the commercial relationship. Though it is possible as a matter of legal semantics to conduct an analysis of the rights and duties inherent in some contractual relationships including that of banker and customer either as a matter of contract law when the question will be what, if any, terms are to be implied or as a matter of tort law when the task will be to identify a duty arising from the proximity and character of the relationship between the parties, their Lordships believe it to be correct in principle and necessary for the avoidance of confusion in the law to adhere to the contractual analysis: on principle because it is a relationship which the parties have, subject to a few exceptions, the right to determine their obligations to each other, and for the avoidance of confusion because different consequences do follow according to whether liability arises from contract or tort, e.g. in the limitation of actions."

He then continued:

"Their Lordships do not, therefore, embark on an investigation as to whether in the relationship of banker and customer it is possible to identify tort as well as contract as a source of the obligations owed by the one to the other. Their Lordships do not, however, accept that the parties' mutual obligations in tort can be any greater than those to be found expressly or by necessary implication in their contract."

This passage was cited with approval in the judgment of the Court of Appeal delivered by Slade L.J. in *Banque Keyser Ullmann*

41. [1996] 1 Q.B. 197.
42. [1986] 1 A.C. 80.
43. At p. 107.

en Suisse SA v. *Scandia (UK) Insurance Co. Ltd*[44] who added:

> "Lord Scarman's opinion contains a valuable warning as to the consequences of an ever expanding field of tort. It should be no part of the general function of the law of tort to fill in contractual gaps."

Whereas the primary obligations are defined by reference to the contract itself, there are, however, instances where it is important to establish that a concurrent duty of care in the tort of negligence exists. Consider the following four instances:

(i) The most obvious of these must be where the contractual cause of action has become time-barred. The primary period of limitation for breach of contract is usually six years, and occasionally 12 years, from the date of the breach or breaches of contract complained of. In the tort of negligence, the primary period of limitation is again six years, but this period does not start to run until the damage occurs. While the courts have experienced initial difficulty in defining what is meant by damage, and examples may be seen in the decision of *Forster* v. *Outread*[45] which may be contrasted with *Pirelli* v. *Oscar Faber and Partners*,[46] in most instances, the limitation periods for causes of action in the tort of negligence will expire later than those for contractual causes of action, even though they may arise from the same facts. Thus, for example, in *London Congregational Union Incorporated* v. *Harriss and Harriss*,[47] it was conceded that the cause of action against the architects in contract had expired, while it remained to be argued whether the cause of action in the tort of negligence remained. The prospect of the continuation of causes of action in the tort of negligence following the expiration of contractual causes of action has been enhanced by the implementation of the Latent Damage Act 1986.

(ii) The existence of a concurrent duty of care is of importance when deciding issues of contributory negligence. It has already been seen that the contractual relationship is responsible for limiting the scope of a duty of care. Conversely, by reference to contributory negligence, the existence of a duty of care can limit or reduce the potential contractual liabilities of the parties. In *Forsikringsaktieselskapet Vesta* v. *Butcher & Others*,[48] the Court of Appeal

44. [1988] 2 Lloyd's Rep. 513 at 563.
45. [1952] 1 W.L.R. 86.
46. [1983] 2 A.C. 1.
47. (1987) 35 B.L.R. 58.
48. [1988] 2 All E.R. 43.

considered the power to apportion blame under the Law Reform (Contributory Negligence) Act 1945. Even though this dispute went to the House of Lords on appeal from the Court of Appeal, the appeal did not relate to the Court of Appeal's findings on contributory negligence. The Court of Appeal had identified three categories of cases when the question could be asked whether or not the 1945 Act applied. They were:

(a) where the defendant's liability arose from some contractual provision which did not depend upon negligence on the part of the defendant;

(b) where the defendant's liability arose from a contractual obligation which is expressed in terms of taking care (or its equivalent) but does not correspond to a common law duty to take care which would exist in the given case independently of contract;

(c) where the defendant's liability in contract is the same as his liability in the tort of negligence independently of the existence of any contract.

The court held that facts giving rise to claims falling within the third category only could give rise to a finding of any contributory negligence under the 1945 Act. The principal judgment of the Court of Appeal was delivered by O'Connor L.J. who respectfully disagreed with the comments of Neil L.J. in the earlier decision of *A B Marintrans* v. *Comet Shipping*.[49] He considered that he had to consider in detail the wording of the 1945 Act. Section 1 of the Act provides:

"1. Where any person suffers damage as a result partly of his own fault and partly of the fault of any other person or persons, a claim in respect of that damage shall not be defeated by reason of the default of the person suffering the damage, but the damages recoverable in respect thereof shall be reduced to such extent as the court thinks fit and equitable having regard to the claimant's share in the responsibility for the damage...."

By Section 4:

"4. ... fault means negligence, breach of statutory duty or any other act or omission which gives rise to a liability in tort or would, apart from this Act give rise to the defence of contributory negligence."

In his judgment, O'Connor L.J. indicated that he was of the view that concurrent liability existed in contract as well as in tort. He stated as follows:

49. [1985] 1 W.L.R. 1270.

"... this is but a recognition of what I regard as a clearly established principle that where under the general law a person owes a duty to another to exercise reasonable care and skill in some activity, a breach of that duty gives rise to claims in tort notwithstanding the fact that the activity is the subject matter of a contract between them. In such a case the breach of duty will be a breach of contract. The classic example of this situation is the relationship between doctor and patient."

The crucial portion of this statement that needs to be analysed is his Lordship's reference to "general law". He proceeds to argue that there is power to apportion in contractual cases, but only in the third category as cited above where liability in contract is the same as in tort independently of the existence of any contract. Therefore, one should assume that he is, by specifying the term "general law", making reference to a contractual duty to exercise all reasonable skill and care, which arises irrespective of the existence of any express contractual provision to this effect.

(iii) The Law Reform (Married Women and Tortfeasors) Act 1935 provided a party with a right to claim a contribution from another tortfeasor but it did not provide a right of contribution between a tortfeasor and contract breaker or between two contract breakers. This situation was changed by the Civil Liability (Contribution) Act 1978 which repealed the 1935 Act. However, the 1978 Act preserves the position which prevailed before then. Thus, in order to obtain a right of contribution from a person in breach of contract where the contractual duty was assumed prior to 1 January 1979, it would be necessary to establish a concurrent duty of care in the tort of negligence which would allow the contribution proceedings to be made in the tort of negligence giving rise to a remedy under the 1935 Act. The effect and significance of the 1935 Act are diminishing, given the passage of time since the 1978 Act.

(iv) The English courts, unlike their counterparts in the USA, award exemplary damages in exceptional cases only. Reference can be made to *Rookes* v. *Barnard*[50] and to *A. B.* v. *South West Water Services.*[51] However, while there are instances when the courts will allow exemplary damages to tortious liability they will not where damages are claimed for breach of contract.

Three more recent decisions have added a new dimension to the

50. [1964] A.C. 1129.
51. [1993] 1 All E.R. 609 (C.A.).

issues of concurrent liabilities in contract and in tort and have, furthermore, considered the existence of a duty of care in the tort of negligence as being consequential on a finding of a "voluntary assumption of liability". The first decision is that of the House of Lords in *Arbuthnott and Others* v. *Fagan and Feltrim Underwriting Agencies Limited and Others*; *Deeny and Others* v. *Gooda Walker Ltd (in voluntary liquidation) and Others*; *Henderson and Others* v. *Merrett Syndicates Ltd and Others*[52] (hereafter referred to as "*Henderson*"). The main judgment in this case was given by Lord Goff. The facts in this case arose from a number of actions brought by underwriting members (known as "Names") of Lloyd's against their underwriting agents. The court had ruled that, since there were a number of common issues arising from these facts, they should be tried together. One of the main issues was whether or not managing agents who had been employed by the members owed a duty of care in the tort of negligence to the Names. The court concluded that there was such a duty of care owed, resting upon the principle in *Hedley Byrne & Co Ltd* v. *Heller & Partners*[53] whereby the managing agents had voluntarily assumed responsibility by the provision of underwriting services. This principle was not inconsistent with the existence of a contract between the plaintiff and the defendant. However, the importance of the finding of a tortious remedy was due to limitation issues. Lord Goff stated:[54]

> "Approached as a matter of principle, therefore, it is right to attribute to that assumption of responsibility, together with its concomitant reliance, a tortious liability, and then to enquire whether or not that liability is excluded by the contract because the latter is inconsistent with it."

He then furthermore added:[55]

> ". . . in the present case liability can, and in my opinion should, be founded squarely on the principle established in Hedley Byrne itself, from which it follows that an assumption of responsibility coupled with the concomitant reliance may give rise to a tortious duty of care irrespective of whether there is a contractual relationship between the parties, and in consequence, unless his contract precludes him from doing so, the plaintiff who has available to him concurrent remedies in contract and tort, may choose that remedy which appears to him to be the most advantageous."

52. (1994) 69 B.L.R. 34.
53. [1964] A.C. 465.
54. At p. 63B.
55. At p. 64D–F.

Thus, there is clear evidence from the *Henderson* decision that the duty of care in the tort of negligence can provide a remedy where no such remedy exists in contract, that is, simply, where any contractual cause of action has become statute-barred. Furthermore, it is clear that unless the duty of care is in some way limited or restricted by the terms of the contract itself, the remedy in tort may be wider than any such remedy available in contract. The court made the point that a duty in tort was imposed by the general law and that a contractual duty was attributable to the will of the parties. It was, however, not objectionable that a claimant may be entitled to take advantage of a remedy which was most advantageous to him, subject only to ascertaining whether the duty in tort was so inconsistent with the applicable contract that, in accordance with the ordinary principle, the parties must be taken to have agreed that the remedy in tort was to be limited or excluded.

This decision was the subject of further comment and analysis in a second leading case, that of *Holt & Another* v. *Payne Skillington (a firm) and Another.*[56] This case involved allegations of negligence being made against solicitors and surveyors as first and second defendants respectively. Beldam L.J., delivering the main judgment, in referring to *Henderson* emphasised that a duty of care in the tort of negligence and a duty imposed by contract may be concurrent but they need not be co-extensive. The difference in scope between the two would reflect the more limited factual basis which gave rise to the contract and the absence of any term in that contract which precluded or restricted the wider duty of care in tort.

Thirdly, *Barclays Bank Plc* v. *Fairclough Building*[57] extended the findings of *Henderson* to a building context when considering whether or not a duty of care was owed in the tort of negligence by a sub-contractor in addition to his contractual responsibilities in the performance of the exercise of skill in the use of cleaning equipment. The issues in this case arose from the cleaning of roofs by a sub-contractor who used a power hose. The pressure of the water broke down the cement bonding of asbestos in the roof, creating an asbestos slurry. When this dried out, it created a serious hazard to health. The costs incurred by the plaintiff, Barclays, for the performance of the necessary work was assessed at £3,890,572.

56. (1996) 77 B.L.R. 51.
57. (1995) 76 B.L.R. 1.

Beldam L.J., relying upon the decision in *Henderson*, stated:[58]

"a skilled contractor undertaking maintenance work to a building assumes a responsibility which invites reliance no less than the financial or other professional adviser does in undertaking his work. The nature of the responsibility is the same though it will differ in extent."

Prior to the decision in *Henderson*, two authorities at first instance had sought to establish the principle that a design professional could be liable to his client in tort for economic loss resulting from a defective design. The first was the finding of Judge Michael Kershaw Q.C. in *Lancashire* v. *Cheshire Association of Baptist Churches Inc., Howard Seddon Partnership.*[59] The second was the conclusion of Judge Fox-Andrews Q.C. *in Wessex Regional Health Authority* v. *HLM Design and Others.*[60] As a consequence of the findings of the House of Lords and the Court of Appeal in the trilogy of cases as referred to above, they must undoubtedly be assumed to have been correctly decided.

Thus, one sees in these three cases a differing approach toward the application of a duty of care albeit concurrent with a contractual responsibility. In these cases, the key requirement is that of a "voluntary assumption of liability" following the earlier authority of *Hedley Byrne*. This contrasts with the incremental approach and the approach in *Caparo* itself which imposed a threefold requirement necessary for the establishment of such a duty. The distinction may clearly be identified by reference to the assumption of liability in the former instance, to be contrasted with the imposition of liability of the courts in the latter. Thus, if the courts have, by common consensus, abandoned any attempt at a formulaic or exhaustive test to be applied and have, to the contrary, reverted simply to the *Donoghue* v. *Stevenson* principles, there has been some inconsistency in how these principles were interpreted. What, however, is the significance of these cases? A number of salient facts occur which are likely to be of direct relevance to those professionals working within the construction industry. These are:

(i) Whereas it was perceived that, following *Tai Hing*, the concurrent remedy in the tort of negligence was relegated to a much lesser and subservient role, it now appears that this role has received

58. At p. 24C.
59. (1994) 65 B.L.R. 21.
60. (1995) 71 B.L.R. 32.

greater impetus and recognition on the ground that this remedy in tort is now not only concurrent but has also been considered not to be co-extensive in each and every case.

(ii) Thus, to give an obvious example, if a professional adviser goes beyond his contract and gives any form of gratuitous advice, he will be liable if it is found that the advice was negligently given. Thus, an architect who may, in the interests of maintaining client goodwill, give advice outside his capacity and competence, say, in respect of the structural integrity of the building, he does so at his peril. This was the clear message that was the subject of comment in *Holt*.

(iii) Furthermore, if the incremental approach as discussed in *Murphy* v. *Brentwood* still holds good, it is clear from *Fairclough* that the issue of concurrent liability in the tort of negligence has been extended to the building industry, so that a duty of care is owed by a sub-contractor to his main contractor concurrently with that of contract. As has been seen, however, this duty is not necessarily co-extensive.

(iv) You need have no clearer example of how a tortious claim can create greater liability than *Henderson* itself. In this case, the parties must be deemed to have decided what was to be the relevant period of limitation in contract, by deciding the manner in which the contract should have been executed. If, contrary to merit but perhaps in keeping with comments made in *Tai Hing*, the remedy in tort was not only concurrent but also co-extensive, one would assume that the contractual limitation period would have cut down the remedy in the tort of negligence. However, this was not the conclusion reached by the court.

1.4. CONTRIBUTORY NEGLIGENCE

There has been reference in the preceding section to section 1 of the Law Reform (Contributory Negligence) Act 1945 which entitles the court to apportion damages giving rise to a reduction where the person suffering injury has done so partly as a consequence of his own fault. Furthermore, as may be seen from *Vesta* v. *Butcher*, this remedy can apply in circumstances where the contractual remedy is analogous to the remedy in tort. Thus, even where the professional may have been considered culpable, there may be compelling arguments in certain instances where the quantum of damages may properly be reduced. It will have been seen from the discussion in *Vesta* v. *Butcher* that contributory negligence in cases involving contract can only be effective where the claims in contract and in the tort of negligence are effectively the same. It is doubtful whether O'Connor L.J. had the situation of a tortious liability greater than that in contract in mind when he delivered his judgment. However, as has been readily appreciated from *Henderson and Others* v. *Merrett and Others,* the tortious and contractual duties, while concurrent, may not necessarily be co-extensive. In a situation such as in *Holt & Another* v. *Payne Skillington,* where the extent of any liability in tort was considered potentially more onerous than liability in contract, the existence of a potential remedy in contract should not prevent the operation of the Act. Consider the following:

(1) In *Kensington & Chelsea & Westminster Area Health Authority* v. *Adams Holden & Partners and Others,*[61] His Honour Judge Smout Q.C. at first instance had to consider the effect of the appointment of a clerk of works in relation to any findings of negligence by the architects. The architects were responsible, *inter alia,* for the supervision of building works which were subsequently proved to be defective. The architects' appointment included a term for the provision of "such periodical supervision and inspection as may be necessary to ensure that the works are being executed in general in accordance with the contract". The appointment of a clerk of works by the employer was not sufficient to abrogate this responsibility. The degree of supervision to be required of the architects had to be governed to some extent by their confidence in the contractor. The judge considered that there had been a failure properly to supervise the works. The court nonetheless took the view that the measure of damages should be reduced in order for there to be a finding of 20 per cent contributory negligence on the part of the clerk of the works. As the judge indicated:

> "I have reached the conclusion that the Clerk of Works' negligence whilst more than minimal is very much less than that of the architects. If I may adapt the military terminology: it was the negligence of the Chief Petty Officer as compared with that of the Captain of the Ship. I assess responsibility as to Clerk of Works 20%, as to the Architects 80%. By reason of the vicarious liability of the Plaintiff, I make a finding of contributory negligence of 20%."

61. (1984) 31 B.L.R. 7.

The conclusion reached by the judge on the negligence of the architects was taken notwithstanding the authorities, which suggested that they could not be present at the site at all times to ensure that the work was being properly performed. To this extent, the learned judge was reminded of the well-known comments of Lord Upjohn in *East Ham Corporation* v. *Bernard Sunley & Sons Limited.*[62] Architects and engineers are naturally very reluctant to assume any liability for supervision as a consequence of the significant risks which are created in the event of there being any defective work. Similarly, employers, if they are to seek to engage a clerk of works, will often insist that this person is employed by the architect and not themselves, thus avoiding any risk of any finding of contributory negligence.

(2) In *Barclays Bank* v. *Fairclough*[63] ultimately the Court of Appeal had to decide upon the relative liabilities of Carne, whom Fairclough had appointed as its sub-contractor to perform the roofing works, and its own sub-contractor Trendleway, to which the responsibility for the performance of the work itself had been sub-contracted. The court had earlier concluded that Trendleway in performing the work owed to Carne a concurrent duty in tort to avoid causing economic loss and that it had failed in the exercise of this duty. Further, the court reached the view that Carne itself knew of the risks and Fairclough had indeed warned of the precautions that needed to be taken. While it is true that Carne did rely on Trendleway to advise, no steps were taken by Carne to inform itself of the problems that could arise. Thus the court ultimately concluded that it could see no basis for distinguishing the degree of Carne's responsibility from that of Trendleway, on the ground that the fault of one was a greater cause of the damage than the fault of the other. They both ought to have appreciated the risk of contamination from asbestos dust, and thus the loss was to be borne equally between them.

Within the context of the liability of professionals, one can see the possibilities of findings of contributory negligence arising in situations where design of a structure is assumed by one party and subsequently either the whole or a part of the design responsibility is sub-contracted to another party. This process would be performed

62. [1966] A.C. 406 at 443.
63. (1995) 76 B.L.R. 1.

without change in the primary responsibilities owed by the party sub-contracting to its own client. In such a situation where the person performing the design may be found to be liable, there may nonetheless be arguments for reducing the amount of damages on the ground of contributory negligence by the person who has sub-contracted the liability to him.

CHAPTER 2

INSURANCE IMPLICATIONS

Note: Throughout this chapter, reference is made to the APIA—RIBA/95 and SURVIS policy wordings. These wordings are reproduced in full at Appendix 1 (p. 227) and Appendix 2 (p. 237) respectively.

2.1. RIGHTS OF INDEMNITY

It is usual for professional bodies to insist upon their members holding professional indemnity cover up to a specific financial limit. Often, the professional bodies in addition indicate precisely the policy cover which is to apply to their members by producing with specific insurers a standard policy wording. By entering into contracts of insurance, professionals are seeking to be indemnified by their insurers up to specific defined policy limits and subject to the policy conditions. It is important to note that the professionals are insuring against their liabilities which may exist either for breach of contract, breach of a duty of care in the tort of negligence and/or, alternatively, under statute. No liability will exist on the part of insurers until and unless the extent of the professional's liability to any third party has been established by judgment, arbitration award or settlement. The policies of insurance also inevitably cover not only the insured's own costs of defending claims but also any liabilities which are incurred for paying an opponent's and probably also the arbitrator's costs. In *Callaghan and Another* v. *Dominion Insurance Company Limited and Others*[1] the court defined indemnity insurance as an agreement by the insurer to confer on the insured a contractual right which came into existence immediately when loss was suffered by the happening of an event insured against. Thus, the insurer was to be put into the same position in which the insured would have been had the event not occurred. In the context of liability insurance, this right of indemnity arises only once liability has been established. Those claiming against professionals will

1. [1997] 2 Lloyd's Rep. 541.

know of the requirement imposed by the professional bodies themselves to insure against liabilities, and often it is this knowledge that any judgment will be satisfied that acts as a catalyst for the commencement and continuance of an action.

However, a would-be claimant against a professional can have no proprietorial rights in relation to the policy of insurance itself. It is the professional who pays the premium and thus has the relationship with his insurer, which cannot be the subject of any fetter or interference by a claimant. Thus, in *Normid Housing Association Limited* v. *Ralphs & Mansell and Others*,[2] a housing association brought an action against a firm of architects. It sought to argue, *inter alia*, that it should be accorded injunctive relief to prevent a professional from agreeing with his insurers on the extent of the latter's liability to indemnify him under the policy which the claimant maintained was but a fraction of the value of the claimant's own claims. Whereas the claimant argued that to allow the settlement to proceed would mean that the vast majority of the claimant's claims would be uninsurable, the court refused to allow the injunction. The court said that it was not, in this instance, duty-bound to deal with its policies in any particular way. Slade L.J.[3] said:

> "The policies were their own assets and they were are free to deal with their rights under them as with any others of their assets. They owed no professional duty of skill and care to the plaintiffs to deal or not to deal with them in any particular way. Any such dealing would be right outside the course of their professional activities."

The existence or not, as the case may be, of a policy of insurance should have no bearing upon the issue of liability in the first instance. However, in *British Telecommunications Plc* v. *James Thompson & Sons (Engineers) Limited*,[4] the Inner House of the Court of Session in Scotland did not reach that same finding. In a case involving a sub-contractor in a building contract, where there was an awareness that the employer had undertaken to insure against, *inter alia*, the risk of negligence on the part of the sub-contractor, he was entitled to assume not merely that he need not himself insure, but that he was not under a duty of care to the employers with regards to loss or damage caused by his action. This is an

2. (1990) 21 Con L.R. 98.
3. At p. 110.
4. (1996) 82 B.L.R. 1.

altogether surprising finding and undermines the fundamental distinction between insurance and liability. Thus, it has to be the subject of criticism. In that same case, Lord Morison in his dissenting judgment stated that he was not aware of any authority which indicated that, in cases concerning the avoidance of direct physical damage, the existence of a duty of care had ever been determined by concession or otherwise, except by reference to the considerations referred to in *Donoghue* v. *Stevenson*. In *Kelly* v. *Bastible*[5] the Court of Appeal had to consider whether or not to apply the provisions of section 33 of the Limitation Act 1980 to facts involving allegations of medical negligence. The Court of Appeal conceded that it was always right in weighing the prejudice to one side against prejudice to the other for the judge to recognise whether or not the plaintiff had an alternative remedy against his solicitor, who may be culpable in commencing the action late. However, the weight to be given to the mere fact that the defendant (i.e. the medical practitioner) was insured ought to be nil. Thus the defendant and its insurer in this action should be viewed as a composite whole.

2.2. WHAT IS A CLAIM?

Policy wordings which cover professional indemnity risks are underwritten on a "claims made" basis. Thus the insured is covered for any claims which are made within any policy period. In this event, cover will apply irrespective of the dates of the commission of the negligent act or acts that may have given rise to the loss. A "claims made" policy wording is an obvious contrast to policies written on an "events occurring" basis, where it is the occurrence of the event itself and not the claim which is the determining factor as to which policy period the claim relates to. Of course, a "claim" is the claim that is made against the insured. This is not the same thing as the claim under the policy. Thus, the operative time is the date on which the claim is made against the insured for determining which is the relevant policy period. The policy will inevitably provide the timescales for notifying the insurer of the existence of the claim and the requirements and procedures which regulate such action.

5. *The Times*, 15 November 1996.

The significance of underwriting policies on a "claims made" basis may be reflected by the necessity for "run-off" cover where a professional either retires from practice or alternatively moves to a new position. The term "run off" is used to describe specific insurance against future claims, albeit relating to past events. The necessity for such cover is all the more necessary given the rules relating to joint and several liability of partners.

Problems can and often do result from any change of insurer. The difficulty is due to a perceived inability to determine the effective date of the claim, which will thus decide which insurer is liable to indemnify the insured. Inevitably the second insurer will require full disclosure of all material circumstances prior to assuming the risk and may seek to exclude them from cover. Thus, it is possible that the insured will be faced with the prospect of being an uninsured litigant in the event of claims being made, albeit relating to earlier events the existence of which had been disclosed and which had been the subject of specific exclusion by the second insurer. Given this market practice it will clearly be appreciated that it is not in the insured's best interest to change insurer unless considered absolutely necessary, and even in this event care must be taken to ensure if at all possible that there are no excluded risks. Indeed, it should be incumbent upon a broker to advise his client of the inherent risks associated with any change of insurer.

A decision which illustrates the inherent dangers of changing insurers is that of *Thorman and Others* v. *New Hampshire Insurance Company (UK) Limited and Another.*[6] Reference to the facts will also reveal the typical clauses that may be found within a professional indemnity policy for architects. The facts also serve as a very good practical case study of the problems which architects may encounter with their insurers. This was a decision of the Court of Appeal given on 8 October 1987 which was stated by Sir John Donaldson M.R. as being concerned:

> "with the problems which can arise when professional men, in this case a firm of architects, transfer their professional negligence insurance cover from one set of underwriters to another."

Transfer occurred at midnight on 30 September/1 October 1983 and was from the New Hampshire Insurance Company, the first defendant, to the Home Insurance, the second Defendant. The

6. (1987) 39 B.L.R. 45.

plaintiff was a firm of architects against which various allegations of negligence had been made relating to a housing development at premises known as Rose Duryard in Exeter. While liability had been denied the decision was concerned with ascertaining which of the insurers, if any, were liable to indemnify the plaintiff, i.e. the insured, against the risks the subject of the allegations. Each of the two insurers stated that the other was liable, and in addition the Home Insurance advanced a secondary contention based upon the grounds of material non-disclosure. The action brought by the building owners against the plaintiff architects was begun by a generally endorsed writ issued on 3 June 1982 but not served until 30 December 1983. Since then the building owners' claims had been particularised in a Scott Schedule, which showed that they fell into two main categories, although there might be some overlap. These categories were (a) brickwork and (b) other matters and, in particular, roofing. Both companies provided what is known as "scheme" insurances, namely, insurance and terms approved by the RIBA and designed specifically for members of the architects' profession.

Thus in the main the terms in both the Home and the New Hampshire policies were identical, save that the Home policy contained additional terms under the heading of "Special Provisions".

"SPECIAL PROVISIONS

1. INNOCENT MISREPRESENTATION AND NON-DISCLOSURE:

The Company will not exercise its right to avoid this Policy where it is alleged that there has been non-disclosure or misrepresentation of facts or untrue statements in the proposal form, provided always that the Insured shall establish to the Company's satisfaction that such alleged non-disclosure, misrepresentation or untrue statement, was innocent and free of any fraudulent conduct or intent to deceive.

. . .

ALL OTHER TERMS, EXCEPTIONS AND CONDITIONS OF THIS POLICY REMAIN UNALTERED.

EXCEPTIONS

This Policy does not indemnify the Insured against liability:

. . .

7. Arising out of any circumstance disclosed in the proposal for this insurance as likely to result in a claim against the Insured."

The material terms common to both policies were as follows:

"SECTION 1—PROFESSIONAL LIABILITY

The Company will indemnify the Insured against Loss arising from any claim or claims for breach of duty in the professional capacity stated in the Schedule which is made against them during the period set forth in the Schedule by reason of any neglect omission or error whenever or wherever the same was or may have been committed or alleged to have been committed by the Insured or any person now or heretofore employed by the Insured or hereafter to be employed by the Insured during the subsistence of this Policy.

CONDITIONS

4. The Insured shall as a condition precedent to their right to be indemnified under Sections 1 and 2 of this Policy give to the Company immediate notice in writing:
   (a) of any claim made against them
   (b) of the receipt of notice from any person of an intention to make a claim against them.
7. It is hereby agreed by the Insured that in the event of the Company being at any time entitled to void this Policy ab initio by reason of any inaccurate or misleading information given by the Insured to the Company in the proposal form the Company may at their election instead of voiding this Policy ab initio give notice in writing to the Insured that they regard this Policy as of full force and effect save that there shall be excluded from the indemnity afforded hereunder any claim which has arisen or which may arise and which is related to circumstances which ought to have been disclosed in the proposal form but which were not disclosed to the Company. This Policy shall then continue in full force and effect but shall be deemed to exclude as if the same had been specifically endorsed ab initio the particular claim or possible claim referred to in the said notice.
8. If during the currency of this Policy the Insured shall become aware of any occurrence which may be likely to give rise to a claim falling within Section 1 or 2 and shall during the period of this insurance give written notice to the Company of such occurrence any claim which may subsequently be made against the Insured arising out of the occurrence of which notification has been given shall be deemed to be a claim arising during the period of this Policy whenever such claim may actually be made.
12. There shall be no liability hereunder in respect of any claim for which the Insured are entitled to indemnity under any other policy."

It will seen by reference to section 1 that the cover is stated to be on a "claims made" basis and not on an "events occurring" basis. This is subject to two qualifications: the first is in Condition 4 and makes a condition precedent to liability under the policy that not only shall the insured give immediate written notice of any such claim but that he shall also give such notice of any "receipt of notice from any person of an intention to make a claim against them". The second qualification is contained in Condition 8. Section 1 does not apply to claims made at a later time, of which advance notice has been given to the insured under the period of the policy and passed on to underwriters pursuant to Condition 4(b). In the absence of some further provision this would create a situation in which the architects were bound to inform underwriters of claims which were likely to be made during the currency of future policies, but underwriters would, on the issue of those future policies, be able to exclude liability for those claims. This would be an impossible situation, hence the need for Condition 8. Thus, the effect is to back-date any claim made to the date when the insured gave notice to underwriters of any "occurrence" which may be likely to give rise to a claim falling within section 1. Thus, the effective date for the claim would be earlier than the date on which the claim will actually have been made.

The Court of Appeal took the view that a generally endorsed writ constituted a claim covering all matters subsequently particularised in the statement of claim and in the Scott Schedule. In its view the issue of the writ, as distinct from its service, constituted an "occurrence which may be likely to give rise to a claim falling within Section 1" within the meaning of Condition 8, the architects having informed underwriters of that occurrence, any claim against them arising out of that occurrence would be deemed to have been made during the period of the policy. Thus, the court concluded that the whole of the burden fell upon New Hampshire. It was emphasised by the court that it was not possible to set out any clear binding definitions of what would and what would not constitute a single claim.

This decision is of value since it clearly illustrates the distinction between a "claim" and any "circumstances" which may give rise to a claim.

Some policies of insurance seek to avoid the difficulty by including a definition of the term "claim" in the policy itself but with limited effect for the reason as explained above.

The significance of the distinction between "circumstances" or "occurrences" and "claims" may be seen also within the context of complying with the requirements of the insurance policy. Thus, for example, in *Layher Limited* v. *Lowe and Others*,[7] the Court of Appeal had to give consideration to the meaning of the words "immediate ... notice in writing with full particulars of a happening of any occurrence likely to give rise to a claim". The court in this instance interpreted the term "likely" as meaning at least a 50 per cent chance of a claim being made.

In forming the view that the writ constituted a single claim covering all matters subsequently particularised in the statement of claim and in the Scott Schedule, the court in *New Hampshire* considered that there was but a single claim as opposed to a series of separate claims. Thus, Stocker L.J. stated:

"It seems to me, therefore, that the question of whether there is one claim or a series of separate claims depends upon the facts of the case and the contexts in which the question falls to be decided. Furthermore, useful guidelines were given by the Master of the Rolls albeit the emphasis has to be on the circumstances of each particular case."

The guidelines[8] are set out below:

"Let me take some examples. An architect has separate contracts with separate building owners. The architect makes the same negligent mistake in relation to each. The claims have a factor in common, namely the same negligent mistake, and to this extent are related, but clearly they are separate claims. Bringing the claims a little closer together, let us suppose that the architect has a single contract in relation to two separate houses to be built on quite separate sites in different parts of the country. If one claim is in respect of a failure to specify windows of the requisite quality and the other is in respect of failure to supervise the laying of the foundations, I think that once again the claims would be separate. But it would be otherwise if the complaint was the same in relation to both houses. Then take the present example of a single contract for professional services in relation to a number of houses in a single development. A single complaint that they suffered from a wide range of unrelated defects and a demand for compensation would, I think, be regarded as a single claim. But if the defects manifested themselves *seriatim* and each gave rise to a separate complaint, what then? They might be regarded as separate claims. Alternatively, later complaints could be regarded as enlargements of the original claims that the architect had been professionally negligent in his execution of his contract. It would, I think, very much depend upon the facts."

7. 73 P. & C.R. 37.
8. At p. 51.

Insurers are often attracted to the argument that there are a series of claims as opposed to the one single claim, on the ground that the former would give rise to the insured's deductible under the policy being applied in respect to each and every claim, as opposed to only once and for all. This was the issue before the Court of Appeal in *Mitsubishi Electric UK Limited* v. *Royal London Insurance (UK) Limited.*[9] The subject matter of the dispute was a construction contract where the relevant wording prescribed a deductible for "the first £250,000 of each and every loss in respect of any component part which is defective". Thus the Court of Appeal had to consider what was a component part and how many losses had taken place. The contract related to 94 toilet modules, each being a self-contained room including lavatory cubicles and wash hand basins. Each module was tiled and had floor covering, the tiles and floor coverings being fixed by an adhesive to cement particle board. The modules were prefabricated and were lowered in more or less complete form into the building. Problems arose due to the cement particle board being unable to withstand the required changes in temperature and humidity to which it had been exposed. Thus, remedial work had to be undertaken to each of the 94 modules. The Court concluded that there were not in effect 94 separate claims but rather one claim giving rise to 94 damaged items. As there was only one claim, there was only one loss and only one deductible which should be borne by the insured. This finding was clearly consistent with the guideline set out by Stocker L.J. in *New Hampshire*. There was a common mistake giving rise to the damage, the parties were the same, there was a single contract and the separate failures to the modules were not separated by any disproportionate periods of time.

This issue was also the subject of discussion by the Privy Council on appeal from Hong Kong in the case of *Haydon and Others* v. *Lo & Lo and the Worldwide Marine and Fire Insurance Company Limited.*[10] The facts related to a fraudulent clerk employed in a probate department of a firm of solicitors in Hong Kong who performed a series of frauds against two estates, being the Tang estate and the Tso estate. The question before the court was whether the events which had happened gave rise to multiple claims

9. [1994] 2 Lloyd's Rep. 249.
18. *The Times*, 27 June 1997.

against Lo and Lo or to one claim only. The issue was of obvious importance since Lo and Lo had substantial deductibles or excesses under both their primary and secondary layers of cover with their insurers. Whereas there were 43 separate thefts from the Tang estate, the court stated that there could not be 43 separate claims when in reality there was only one demand against the solicitors, being a claim for restitution by their dishonest employee. Similarly, in relation to the Tso estate there were a number of fraudulent share transfers but one plaintiff, that is the Tso estate, and there was only one underlying cause of the plaintiff's loss, namely the clerk's dishonest conduct in forging the Power of Attorney. Thus, in this case also there was but a single claim.

Occasionally, it may be in the insured's interest to argue that there are a number as opposed to a single claim. This will arise where there is a comparatively modest limit of indemnity under the policy. Thus in *Normid Housing Association Limited* v. *Ralphs & Mansell & Others*[11] the policy cover was limited to "£250,000 any one claim". The claims made against the defendant architects amounted to some £5.7 million. The insurers sought to argue that there was effectively but one claim, and thus the limit of any liability was £250,000. The reported decision shows that this issue between the architects and their insurers had to be the subject of reference to an arbitrator for his decision.

Thus, to summarise, the authorities appear to conclude by stating that if the claimant is one and the same and the complaints arise from the same contract there will generally be but one claim for insurance purposes. If the subject matter or cause of the complaint is the same, as in *Haydon*, where it was due to the dishonesty of the clerk, but the claimants are different parties, there will be more than one claim. This was the finding on the basis that there was one claim brought by the Tang estate and one claim brought by the Tso estate. If the claimant is the same person but liabilities arise under separate contracts they may or may not be the subject of more than one claim and much depends upon the proximity of the claims in terms of time and the nature of the complaint itself.

11. (1990) 21 Con. L.R. 98.

2.3. MATERIAL NON-DISCLOSURE AND POLICY COMPLIANCE

All contracts of insurance are based upon the principle of the utmost good faith, and if the utmost good faith is not observed by either party the contract may be avoided by the other. This is the broad general principle which is epitomised in the well-known passage from Lord Mansfield's judgment in *Carter* v. *Boehm*[12]:

"Good faith forbids either party, by concealing what he privately knows, to draw the other into a bargain from his ignorance of that fact, and from his believing the contrary..."

A slightly more recent explanation justifying the requirement of the utmost good faith may be found in the comments by Scrutton L.J. in *Rozanes* v. *Bowen*[13] when he said "as the underwriter knows nothing and the man who comes to him to ask him to insure knows everything, it is the duty of the assured ... to make a full disclosure to the underwriter without being asked of all the material circumstances. This is expressed by saying it is a contract of the utmost good faith." The duty arises when there is negotiation between the insurer and the assured and the obligation continues on each and every occasion where the policy of insurance is renewed. The duty is a positive duty voluntarily to disclose, accurately and fully, all facts material to the risk being proposed. The issue of what facts are and what are not material is often a subject of some considerable debate. In the event that an insurer is able to prove that there has been a failure by the insured to disclose a material fact this will entitle him to regard the policy as being rescinded. Thus, the insurer may be entitled to avoid liability under the policy. In *CTI* v. *Oceanus Mutual Underwriting Association (Bermuda)*[14] it was stated that the law of disclosure for all contracts of general insurance is similar to that in section 18(2) of the Marine Insurance Act 1906, which states:

"Every circumstance is material which would influence the judgment of a prudent insurer in fixing the premium or determining whether he will take the risk."

Influence means affecting the mind of an insurer in weighing up

12. (1776) 3 Burr. 1905.
13. (1928) 32 Ll.L.R. 98.
14. [1982] 2 Lloyd's Rep 178. at 194.

the risk. A circumstance may be material even though full and accurate disclosure of it would not in itself have had a decisive effect on the prudent underwriter's decision whether to accept the risk and, if so, at what premium. However, in addition to needing to prove the issue of materiality, in *Pan Atlantic Insurance Co. Limited and Another* v. *Pine Top Insurance Co. Limited*,[15] the House of Lords was prepared to imply a term into the Marine Insurance Act 1906 that a requirement of a material misrepresentation would only entitle an insurer to avoid the policy if it induced the making of the contract and a similar conclusion was to be reached in the event of non-disclosure. Thus, the requirement of materiality and inducement, being a twofold test, needs to be established, and if the insurer fails in either capacity he will not be entitled to avoid liability. The evidence of the insurer himself will normally be required to satisfy a court of the first question and evidence of an independent broker or underwriter will normally be required to satisfy the court on the second question, i.e. that of inducement.

Most professionals when placing or renewing their cover will need to be more wary of giving incorrect details rather than of failing to give any information altogether. This is due to the practice of requiring the completion of a renewal form (see *post*). It will be seen that examples of matters which would be considered to be material by underwriters are, e.g.:

(a) previous claims record;
(b) previous fee income; and
(c) the precise areas of activity of the professional practice.

A good example of the manner in which the rules for disclosure and, in particular, the Marine Insurance Act 1906 affect insurance of construction risks is *St Paul Fire and Marine Co. (UK) Limited* v. *McConnell Dowell Constructors Limited*.[16] In this case, the true state of affairs was not disclosed to underwriters. The project involved shallow spread foundations rather than piled or other deep foundations on a building project in the Marshall Islands to be designed and built by the contractor. The plans, however, when originally submitted to the underwriters when obtaining the insurance cover showed that the projected buildings had piled foundations. The

15. [1994] 2 Lloyd's Rep. 427 at 430.
16. [1995] 2 Lloyd's Rep. 116.

court, not surprisingly, concluded that the representation was material and that it led to an increased rather than to a diminished risk when, instead, the shallow spread foundation design was adopted. Thus, the insurers were entitled to avoid the policy on the grounds of materiality and inducement. The underwriters were able to convince the court by adducing proof that they were thereby induced to enter into the contract on the terms which they did.

2.3.1 Waiver

Where there is a proposal form there is nonetheless a duty to disclose material facts notwithstanding that these same facts would not have been obtained by consideration of the replies to the questions contained therein. Thus, the overall requirement upon the insured to disclose material facts remains unaffected. However, the defence of waiver may be invoked in the case of a proposal form completed by the insured. A proposal form which asks material questions does away with the duty of disclosure, but only in respect of the subject matter of those same questions.

This was the effect of the decision of the Court of Appeal in *Roberts* v. *Plaisted.*[17] The decision related to insurance cover for a hotel in North Wales. The insurers alleged, following a fire, that there should have been disclosure by the insured of the operation of a discotheque at the hotel. The Court of Appeal concluded that the activity of running a discotheque was a material fact which should have been disclosed. By presenting the proposal form however, the insurers waived any right which they might have had to repudiate. The assured had disclosed in his proposal form that the premises were occupied as a hotel. The court concluded that the discotheque was no more than part and parcel of the whole hotel operation carried on at the premises. In *Economides* v. *Commercial Union*[18] it was confirmed that the duty of disclosure had to be looked at in the context of the proposal form. It is a short step for the courts to take to hold that, where there is a proposal form, there is no duty of disclosure in relation to information which could have been elicited by express questions. However, this is a step which the courts have hitherto refused to take.

17. [1989] 2 Lloyd's Rep. 341.
18. *The Times*, 27 June 1997.

2.3.2 Policy wording

Forms which are for standard use by specific professions inevitably adopt a more benevolent wording toward the professional when considering issues of material non-disclosure. This is reflective of the significant input made by the professional body itself. For example, Special Institution Clause 1 (a) of the Professional Indemnity wording of SURVIS, being the endorsed insurance scheme of the Royal Institution of Chartered Surveyors, states:

"Insurers will not exercise their right to avoid this certificate where there has been non-disclosure or misrepresentation of facts or untrue statements in the proposal form, provided always that the Insured shall establish to Insurers' satisfaction that such non-disclosure, misrepresentation or untrue statement was free of any fraudulent intent..."

Similarly the policy published by RIBA Insurance Agency Limited (reference APIA—RIBA/95) has as its special RIBA Condition 7:

"7.1 Insurers will not exercise their right to avoid the Policy nor will Insurers reject a request for indemnity when it is alleged that there has been:

7.1.1 Non-disclosure of facts; or
7.1.2 Misrepresentation of facts; or
7.1.3 Incorrect particulars or statements; or
7.1.4 Late notification of a claim; or
7.1.5 Late notification of intention to make a claim; or
7.1.6 Late notification of a circumstance or event.

Provided always that the Assured shall establish to Insurers satisfaction that such alleged non-disclosure, misrepresentation or incorrect particulars or statements or late notification was innocent and free of any fraudulent conduct or intent to deceive."

Insurers underwriting these policies will no doubt consider the effects of such generous wording when calculating premiums. However, they at all material times will need to be aware of those risks which they adopt which they would otherwise be entitled to avoid. In addition, where professionals are not insuring on the basis of standard wording as imposed by the professional body, they will obviously need to be made aware of their onerous disclosure responsibilities. Professionals need to be especially aware of the less benevolent attitude of a number of insurers who have faced declining premium income while being beset by an ever-increasing amount of liability by way of claims. Furthermore, while policies of insurance prepared with the assistance of professional bodies may favour the professional this will not obviate entirely the risk of non-compliance with the policy conditions, as is demonstrated by the decision in *Summers* v. *Congreve Horner & Co. (a firm) and Independent Insurance Co. Ltd.*[19]

This decision related to an exclusion clause, being exclusion 11 of the Collective Professional Indemnity Policy formerly issued by the Royal Institution of Chartered Surveyors. The exclusion provided:

> "The Policy shall not indemnify the Assured against any claim or loss arising from survey/inspection and/or valuation report of real property unless such survey/inspection and/or valuation shall have been made:
> (a) by [a person holding prescribed professional qualifications] or
> (b) by anyone who has not less than 5 years experience of such work or such other person nominated by the Assured to execute such work subject always to supervision of such work by a person qualified in accordance with (a) above."

The court had to interpret this clause and whether or not there had been sufficient supervision where surveyors had nominated an employee who had just under $3\frac{1}{2}$ years of practical experience and had carried out the inspection of the property on his own. The draft report prepared by the employee was submitted to his principal, who was a qualified person and who considered it and discussed it in detail with him. He also approved the final report but did not visit the premises surveyed at any material time. The Court of Appeal, reversing the judgment of Judge James Fox-Andrews Q.C. at first instance, considered that the degree of control exercised by the principal was sufficient to justify a finding of supervision, albeit that the principal had not attended the site with the employee. Thus, the surveyors in this instance somewhat fortunately were able to seek indemnity under their policy of insurance. However, this must serve as a salutary lesson and warning.

A policy of insurance provides indemnity to the assured against liability, subject obviously to the terms of the policy itself. The insuring clause defines the scope and extent of the indemnity by reference to the assured's activities. Let us refer to the RIBA Insurance Agency Limited (APIA—RIBA/95) wording and, in particular, section 3.1 thereof, which states:

> "3.1 The Assured is indemnified against any claim made during the Period

19. [1992] 40 E.G. 144.

of Insurance for which the Assured shall become legally liable to pay compensation together with claimant's costs, fees and expenses in accordance with any judgment award or settlement made within the Geographical Limits (or any order made anywhere in the world to enforce such judgment award or settlement in whole or in part) in consequence of:

3.1.1 Any breach of the professional duty of care owed by the Assured to the claimant which term is deemed to include a breach of warranty of authority..."

This wording is fairly wide and generous to the assured. Other policy wordings may not be so generous, and one must look carefully at the exclusions to the policy cover to see what risks do not fall to be the subject of indemnity under the policy. A common limitation or exclusion may be the right of the professional to enter into successive collateral warranties with future prospective purchasers or tenants of a completed property. There may be a limit to the extent to which any such collateral warranties may be given, if at all. Similarly, also, some insurers will not indemnify a professional in the event that a primary risk has been assumed that the design shall be fit for its intended purpose. It is important to note, for example, by reference to the wording as referred to above, that it is the breach of the "professional duty of care" owed by the assured to the claimant which must be the cause of the loss if the indemnity provisions in the policy are to operate.

2.3.3 Warranties and conditions

Whereas lawyers are familiar with the term "warranty", which denotes a term in a contract which is of lesser importance as contrasted with a condition, a warranty in the policy of insurance is fundamentally different. Whereas a breach of a warranty in any other contract means that the injured party has a right to claim damages only, but not in general to consider that the contract has been repudiated, a warranty in an insurance contract if breached entitles the insurer to avoid the policy altogether, irrespective of whether or not the breach of the warranty has been causative of the loss. Thus a warranty is a promise made by the insured to its insurers which, if broken, entitles the insurer to regard the contract as being at an end. Thus it will be readily appreciated that a warranty is an extremely onerous requirement and great care should be taken at all times to ensure that there is no breach thereof. Warranties may arise first on the basis of the policy wording. The use of the term "warranty" or "warranted" thus will put the insured on notice of the effect of any breach. Secondly, it may be implied by statute, for example the Marine Insurance Act 1906. Thirdly, warranties may arise out of answers given to questions on proposal forms if a declaration at the foot of the form states that the answers given form the "basis of the contract". Thus, by virtue of this wording all the answers given to a proposal form become warranties. There are certain limitations upon the introduction of such wordings in non-commercial insurances as a consequence of the publication of the Statement of General Insurance Practice. However, few policies of insurance between construction professionals and insurers could not be classified as "non-commercial insurances", but the principle of the effect of the endorsement that any answers form the "basis of the contract" remains unchallenged.

Certain terms in the policy of insurance are conditions precedent to any liability. Thus, liability will only arise if certain circumstances are fulfilled. Lord Goff in *Bank of Nova Scotia* v. *Hellenic Mutual War Risks Association (Bermuda) Limited*[20] considered the term "condition precedent":

> "In the case of conditions precedent, the word 'condition' is being used in its classical sense in English law, under which the coming into existence of (for example) an obligation, or the duty or further duty to perform an obligation, is dependent upon the fulfilment of the specified condition."

A good example of a condition precedent in a liability policy is the fulfilment of the notification provisions. Thus, in *Hamptons Residential Limited* v. *Field and Others*.[21] The court had to consider, *inter alia*, whether or not a firm of estate agents was entitled to be indemnified under the terms of its policy. The policy stated:

> "The Assured shall as a Condition Precedent to their right to be indemnified under this Policy give to the Underwriters notice as soon as possible during the period of this Policy.
>
> (a) of any circumstances of which the Assured shall first become aware which may give rise to a claim or loss against them or any of them;
>
> (b) or the receipt of notice from any person whether written or oral of any intention to make a claim against them or any of them;

20. [1992] 1 A.C. 233.
21. [1997] 1 Lloyd's Rep. 302.

(c) of the discovery (or reasonable cause for suspicion) of dishonesty or fraud on the part of a past or present . . . employee."

On the ground that the estate agents had not complied with these requirements, the court concluded that the estate agents were not entitled to be indemnified under the terms of the policy.

2.4. INSURABLE INTEREST

In order to be able to effect any policy of insurance there must be an interest which the law recognises as capable of being the subject of insurance. It is in the context of property insurance that the issue arises most frequently, although the principle is of general application. Thus it may be stated that it is not the subject matter itself which the law recognises but the interest in the same subject matter. Thus in *Castellain* v. *Preston*[22] it was stated:

> "What is it that is insured in a fire policy? Not the bricks and material used in building the house but the interest of the insured in the subject matter of insurance."

Thus, for an insurable interest to exist, the law must recognise the existence of a legal interest which the party seeking to insure has in relation to specific property. The legal interest may arise either at common law or by statute or by contract. Within the context of liability insurance one is insuring against the risk of liability being established at law, and of course you cannot fully establish the extent of this liability until and unless the court has determined what it is. However, construction professionals need often to insure against risk of loss to their plans and drawings which they have produced, as in *Glengate-CG Properties Limited* v. *Norwich Union Fire Insurance Society Limited and others*.[23] The question arose whether or not the developer maintained an insurable interest within these drawings. The plaintiff owners maintained that they had an interest and that the property fell within the definition with its insurers on the basis it was "property . . . used by the insured at the premises described". The court concluded that the architects' drawings were owned by the architects and remained in their pos-

22. (1883) 11 Q.B.D. 380.
23. [1996] 1 Lloyd's Rep. 614.

session and thus none of the submissions gave the plaintiffs an interest in the drawings. These formed part of the architects' work in progress which, on the evidence, would normally have been insured by the architects. Thus, following a fire at the building when the plans and drawings were destroyed the plaintiffs were compelled to be responsible for the cost of redrawing by the architects.

2.5. SUBROGATION AND INDEMNITY

In a policy of insurance, the insurer will have to indemnify the insured subject to the terms of the policy itself. If it does this it is entitled to assume all the rights of the insured party it can utilise for the recovery of that same loss from any third party. This right of subrogation, which means no more than the insurer stepping into the shoes of the insured party, arises as a matter of law, but it also will often arise on the basis of the express wording of the policy of insurance itself, e.g. see Clause 5 of the Professional Indemnity wording of SURVIS, being the endorsed insurance scheme of the RICS. However, this clause, in common with other provisions, often stipulates that insurers waive any rights of subrogation against the employees of the insured who may have been responsible for the failures giving rise to the losses unless such failures have been prompted by fraud, dishonesty or any criminal or malicious acts. If no such waiver existed insurers would be able to recover from those parties who themselves cause the losses.

A contribution is often termed as being the corollary of subrogation whereby insurers may seek contributions from other insurers who have insured against those same risks. The portion of loss which insurers may bear *inter se* invariably depends upon the terms of the policies themselves. Liability policies generally include an exclusion clause stating that the indemnification procedures contained therein shall not apply where there is a second policy in being which indemnifies against that same liability. If that second policy however contains a similar exclusion clause the effect will be that the two exclusion clauses will cancel each other out and thus can be ignored. It will be unusual for construction professionals to encounter this problem in practice. The more usual problem encountered is the one already discussed where neither insurer admits that the liability is his. An example of such a clause may be seen by reference to Clause 12 of the policy conditions in *Thorman* (see page 36) and Exclusion Clause 1 of the SURVIS policy conditions.

2.6. RIGHTS OF THIRD PARTIES TO BENEFITS UNDER INSURANCE POLICIES

Many employers, especially those who engage professionals involved in the construction industry, insist upon there being full disclosure of their professional indemnity cover as a condition of appointment. Local authorities in particular have a tendency to insist upon this. If a claim is made against a professional the claimant knows that inevitably his battle is with the insurer of the professional who will be indemnifying the insured, albeit subject to the terms of the policy. It must be appreciated by third parties that the issue of insurance is one which is personal to the insured and the third party cannot in some way assume some beneficial interest in the proceeds of the insurance, nor can it seek to interfere in the relationship between insurer and insured. The issue of insurance is considered sufficiently important to have instigated an Act of Parliament to provide a remedy even in the event of the insolvency of the insured party.

The Third Parties (Rights Against Insurers) Act 1930 is unlikely to provide a claimant with a remedy against the insurer unless liability may be established either by a judgment of a court or an arbitrator's award or by an agreement between the insured and the third party. In addition it is necessary for the insured to be an insolvent person. The purpose of the Act is to remedy the injustice where a creditor had no right to the proceeds as such of any third party insurance effected by an insolvent person when the insurance moneys became payable to meet the claim. In *Nigel Upchurch Associates* v. *The Aldridge Estates Investment Company Limited*[24] a counterclaiming defendant sought an order against a plaintiff firm of architects and the supervisor of his scheme of voluntary arrangement pursuant to section 2 of the Third Parties (Rights against Insurers) Act. The defendant was most anxious to know whether or not the plaintiff had appropriate insurance cover and what the

24. [1993] 1 Lloyd's Rep. 535.

limits of this cover were. However, the request for information was refused on the ground that it was premature, since liability of the plaintiff to the defendant was not yet established. Whereas Counsel for the defendant urged that commercial common sense required early information on insurance cover to be given so that time and money were not wasted on what could turn out to be a fruitless effort, Miss Barbara Dohman Q.C., sitting as an Official Referee, was clearly of the view that the Act was not designed to deal with such mischief. To the contrary, it was designed to remedy the injustice that the creditor had no right to the proceeds. Thus, the application was dismissed.

A similar situation (already referred to above) arose in *Normid Housing Association Limited* v. *Ralphs & Mansell Limited.*[25] It is surprising that no mention was made of it in the *Nigel Upchurch* decision. The issue that came before the Court of Appeal in *Normid Housing* was whether or not the client of a firm of architects had any right to interfere with the proposed settlement of a claim by the architects against their professional indemnity insurers, having regard to the provisions of the Third Parties (Rights Against Insurers) Act 1930. The client of the architects commenced an action in the High Court against them claiming some £5.7 million. The insurers for the defendant architects made them an offer of £250,000.00 in settlement of the claims which the insurers considered as representing the limit of their liability to indemnify. The defendant architects were minded to accept this offer. It was emphasised by the Court of Appeal that at present the plaintiffs had no rights under the 1930 Act, since it applied only in the event of the insured becoming insolvent. This had not taken place. Furthermore there was no liability which had been established which would have allowed the Act to operate. It was emphasised by the court that the issue of insurance was a matter entirely for the judgement of the professionals. Slade L.J. in giving judgment also indicated:

> "Likewise, however in our judgment, after they had in their discretion effected such policies, that duty placed them under no contractual obligation to the Plaintiffs to deal with the policies in any particular way. The policies were their own assets and they were as free to deal with their rights under them as with any others of their assets. They owed no professional duty of skill and care to the Plaintiffs to deal or not to deal with them in

25. (1990) 21 Con. L.R. 98.

any particular way. Any such dealing would be right outside the course of their professional activities. Having rejected the arguments based upon the Third Parties (Rights Against Insurers) Act 1930, the Court indicated that the only basis for the Plaintiff's claim could be on the basis of an application for a Mareva injunction to restrain the Defendants from dealing with or disposing of assets in cases where it appeared likely that the Plaintiff would recover judgment against them for a certain or approximate sum."

Having invited Counsel for the plaintiff to make an application for a Mareva injunction the Court of Appeal, upon further consideration, rejected the application. Any potential claimant must however be aware that the existence of the statute does not confer upon him any preferential rights. The preference operates on the basis that there is a statutory subrogation of the third party to the rights of the insured. The Act thus operates by stating at the relevant date the insured's "rights against the insurer under the contract ... shall ... be transferred to and vest in the third party".[26] Thus the Act operates to provide that the proceeds of the indemnity within the insurance policy are earmarked for the claimant and do not form part of the insolvent party's general estate.

26. S. 1(1) of the Third Parties (Rights Against Insurers) Act 1930.

CHAPTER 3

ARCHITECTS AND ENGINEERS

3.1. INTRODUCTION

Architects have traditionally carried out the design of buildings and the arrangements for, and supervision of, their construction. Engineers have had a similar role in relation to civil engineering projects such as roads, bridges and pipelines or other engineering projects such as the construction of chemical process plants. This chapter concentrates on these two types of professionals. However, it should be borne in mind that the law applicable to architects and engineers may be equally relevant to other professionals who carry out architectural or engineering roles. For example, the task of contract administration and supervision is often undertaken nowadays by project managers of one sort or another, and indeed some contracts adopt the term "project manager" or "supervising officer" even where those roles are normally filled by architects or engineers.

3.1.1 Architects—definition, statutory controls and regulation

The High Court has defined an architect as follows:

"One who possesses, with due regard to aesthetic as well as practical considerations, adequate skill and knowledge to enable him (i) to originate, (ii) to design and plan, (iii) to arrange for and supervise the erection of such buildings or other works calling for skill in design and planning as he might, in the course of his business, reasonably be asked to carry out or in respect of which he offers his services as a specialist . . ."[1]

1. *R* v. *Architects Registration Tribunal, ex parte Jagger* [1945] 2 All E.R. 131.

The word "architect" is a term of art, i.e. one which is known to the law. It is a criminal offence for anyone to practise, or carry on business, under any name, title or style containing the word "architect" unless that person's name appears on the Register of Architects.

The Register is a creation of statute. Following the coming into force on 1 August 1997 of sections 118–124 of the Housing Grants Construction and Regeneration Act 1996[2] the register is now administered by the Architects Registration Board. The Board had published its own "Code for Professional Conduct and Practice". This gives it the power to make certain disciplinary orders against architects—reprimands, fines, suspensions and striking off the register—for "unacceptable professional conduct" (which is defined as conduct which falls short of the standards required of an architect) or "serious professional incompetence". This definition could, it seems, include many cases of negligence, and an appropriate finding by the Board could well assist any client in subsequent litigation. It may be possible to challenge a finding of fact by a professional body if its finding is out of tune with the evidence to the extent that it must have misunderstood that evidence.[3] Previous statutes regulating the profession are now consolidated in the Architects Act 1997.

Architects who are members of their professional bodies are of course also subject to the rules of those bodies. The leading professional body for architects is the Royal Institute of British Architects (RIBA). Consultant architects (i.e. those in private practice) may also belong to the Association of Consultant Architects. The RIBA's Code of Professional Conduct (April 1997) requires a member to apply his knowledge and experience with efficiency and loyalty towards his client or employer, and to have defined "beyond reasonable doubt" (and recorded) the terms of his agreement. An obligation in earlier versions to interpret building contracts "with fairness and impartiality" no longer appears.

The RIBA also runs a conciliation scheme for clients dissatisfied with the behaviour of any of its members.

2. 1996 SI 2892.

3. As in *Hossack* v. *General Dental Council*, *The Times*, 22 April 1997, a decision in relation to a finding of fact by the Professional Conduct Committee of the General Dental Council.

An architect may thus potentially face one or more of the following:

—a complaint to the Architects Registration Board if the allegation is of unacceptable professional conduct or serious professional incompetence;

—a complaint to the RIBA (assuming that the architect in question is a member) for breach of its own professional guidelines;

—legal action for negligence or breach of contract. The standard forms of appointment for architects contain arbitration clauses so that arbitration is usually the appropriate route.

3.1.2 Engineers

By contrast, "engineer" is a wider term than "architect". Engineers are not subject to statutory controls as such. In theory at least there is nothing to stop anyone calling himself an engineer, though a misleading use might give rise to civil liability for misrepresentation; and use of the term "chartered engineer" in any event denotes membership of one of the chartered professional bodies.

There are a number of such bodies. Perhaps the most relevant to the construction industry is the Institution of Civil Engineers which is responsible for publishing one of the major forms of civil engineering contract, the *ICE Conditions* (6th Edition, 1991). The ICE also has professional standards and by-laws that enable it to investigate "improper conduct" on the part of any of its members, and to take appropriate disciplinary action.

3.2. THE STANDARD FORMS OF CONTRACT

The Housing Grants Construction and Regeneration Act 1996 imposes mandatory terms into most terms of engagement of architects and engineers. The relevant parts of the Act have now been brought into force as from 1 May 1998. The implications are discussed in Chapter 9, but the following sections of this chapter need to be read with the proviso that the standard forms discussed do not at the time of writing comply with the requirements of the Act.

3.2.1 SFA/92

This is the *Standard Form of Agreement for the Appointment of an Architect*, published in July 1992 by the RIBA. It is the successor to *The Architect's Appointment* (also known as the "Blue Book"). It comprises:

(a) A memorandum of agreement

(b) Conditions of appointment. These come in four parts, some or all of which may be appropriate for any particular contract. They are:
—conditions applicable to all appointments;
—conditions specific to the design of building projects (work stages A–H of the RIBA document "Plan of Work");
—conditions specific to contract administration supervision (work stages J–L of "Plan of Work");
—conditions where the architect is the lead consultant.

(c) Four schedules which are again alternatives. These cover information to be supplied by the client; services that will be performed by the architect; payment; and matters relating to the appointment of other consultants where the architect is the "lead" consultant.

Any professional negligence action will generally be based on allegations of breaches of specific terms within this standard form, or of the overriding general obligation which states:

> "The Architect shall in providing the services exercise reasonable skill and care in conformity with the normal standards of the Architect's profession."[4]

Clients need to be aware of the following points that may operate to restrict the architect's liability:

—Responsibility for loss or damage is limited to a stated figure (article 6.6.2);
—There is a limitation against taking action against the architect after the expiry of a stated number of years from practical completion (article 5)—the number of years is to be inserted by the parties;

4. Cl. 1.2.1.

—There is a "fair contribution" clause, which applies where the architect and at least one other party are jointly liable. Under this, the liability of the architect is limited to "such sums as the architect ought reasonably to pay having regard to the responsibility for the same", irrespective of whether the other parties to blame are also sued or can pay (article 6.1);

—The architect does not warrant that services can be completed within the timescale agreed with the client (clause 1.3.7);

—The architect is not responsible for work on site (clauses 3.2.2 and 3.2.3). This is so despite the architect's duty to inspect;

—The architect is not responsible for design or work carried out by other specialists or consultants (clauses 4.1.7 and 4.2.5);

—The client may not withhold or reduce any sum payable to the architects by reason of claims or alleged claims against the architect and all rights of set off are excluded (clause 1.5.15). On the face of it, this is an onerous clause for the client, but he might circumvent it in two ways. The first is to argue that no sum is payable under the clause in the first place, because of defective performance. The second is to invoke the Unfair Contract Terms Act 1977 (UCTA 1997) and to argue that the clause is an unreasonable exclusion or restriction of the architect's liability;[5]

—Extra payment must be made for "delay for any [other] reason beyond the architect's control" (clause 1.5.7).

3.2.2 The ACE Conditions 1995

These are the Association of Consultant Engineers' Conditions of Engagement 1995. They come in the following forms:

Agreement A(1)—where the engineer is lead consultant (comments on the form in the following paragraphs will generally be on this form of the agreement);

5. See *Stewart Gill* v. *Horatio Myer & Co.* [1992] Q.B. 600 (C.A.), which confirms that UCTA 1997 may be applied to set-off clauses in principle.

Agreement B(1)—where the engineer is not lead consultant, but engaged directly by the client;

Agreement C(1)—where the engineer provides design services of a "design and construct" contractor;

Agreement D—where the engineer is to provide reporting and advisory services;

Agreement E—where the engineer is engaged as project manager;

Agreement F—where the engineer is planning supervisor in accordance with the Construction (Design and Management) Regulations 1994.

In addition, agreements A, B and C are published in two variants, the first for civil and structural engineering, the second for electrical and mechanical services engineering. There are also agreements for minor works (agreement G); for situations where the engineer is the client's representative for design and construct work (agreement H); and for sub-consultancy cases (agreement I).

The forms comprise a Memorandum of Agreement, conditions and appendices covering the engineer's services and remuneration. There are limitations similar to some of those under SFA/92. In particular, liability is limited to a period of a certain number of years from practical completion; there is an overall financial limit; and a "fair contribution" clause also appears. The engineer is only obliged to use reasonable endeavours to keep to the agreed programme, and even this is subject to conditions beyond his reasonable control. The British Property Federation has issued a warning advising its members to treat the form with "utmost care".[6]

The skill and care obligation is contained in clause 2.4 as follows:

"The Consulting Engineer shall exercise reasonable skill, care and diligence in the performance of the Services."

3.2.3 The Professional Services Contract

That is part of the Engineering and Construction Contract ("ECC") (formally the New Engineering Contract) "family" of forms published by the Institution of Civil Engineers, which received an enthusiastic recommendation from Sir Michael Latham in his report "Constructing the Team".[7] The language, like that of

6. "Building", 2 June 1995.
7. HMSO, July 1994.

the ECC itself is unusual and untested by the courts. The brief is a particularly important document that needs to be carefully drafted if the contract is to work. The contract can be used for various fee options that the client may agree with his professional, varying from "cost-reimbursable" (where the professional is, in principle, paid for the costs of the work that he actually carries out) through to lump sum and target contracts.

The notes with the form suggest that the client may wish to put the professional under an obligation of fitness for purpose, rather than merely of reasonable skill and care, but a professional would be advised not to take on such an obligation. The effect would be a warranty as to the result of his work. Otherwise the reasonable skill and care obligation is similar to that at common law and contained in clause 21.2.

The contract contains "fair contribution" arrangements where the professional is jointly liable with others. There is provision for a timetable within which the client must provide information, and the professional carry out his work. There are elaborate provisions for early warnings by one side to the other if it appears likely that the timetable will be affected, and the professional's fees may be adjusted by "compensation events" affecting the works. These mirror the provisions in the Engineering and Construction Contract/NEC itself. A facet of the contract is that where problems or faults appear, the professional generally corrects them, and only later do the parties argue about who is to blame.

3.3. LIABILITY IN GENERAL

Architects and engineers are subject to what has come to be known as the "Bolam" test after the medical negligence of *Bolam* v. *Friern Hospital Management Committee.*[8] The test is whether the professional has exercised the reasonable skill and care to be expected of a member of his profession. Since the standard forms of engagement discussed above contain broadly similar terms to this, the test is almost a universal one for actions against architects and engineers involving professional negligence (but remember that actions

8. [1957] 1 W.L.R. 582.

against professionals will often involve allegations of breaches of specific clauses of the contract as well).

3.3.1 Standards of care that are higher or lower than usual

Can an architect argue that in a low budget case his standard of care is lower than the normal standard? In *Cotton* v. *Wallis*[9] the Court of Appeal refused to alter a trial judge's finding that there must be some tolerance in assessing the standard of care where a house had been "built down to a price". Similarly in *Brown and Brown* v. *Gilbert-Scott and Another*[10] the court in assessing an architect's design liability took into account the fact that the plaintiff client had instructed the architect to try to reduce the price of a conservatory that he was to design, and had also accepted a particularly low quotation. However, it seems unlikely that there is, in effect, a two-tier standard of care. This would be contrary to principle.[11]

In *Gloucestershire Health Authority and Others* v. *M. A. Torpy & Partners Ltd*[12] it was submitted that the client's own special skills were capable of reducing the duty owed to him by his architect. The judge firmly dismissed this submission, noting that, if correct, it would mean that a solicitor engaged to carry out conveyancing for (for example) a barrister client would owe a lower duty of care than normal where the barrister happened to be a specialist in property or conveyancing matters. The judge also noted that claiming experience at something did not necessarily mean that one claimed to have a specialist ability at it.

Are there cases where the professional's obligation is *higher* than usual? In *Duchess of Argyle* v. *Beuselinck*,[13] Megarry J. said:

> "If the client engages an expert, and doubtless expects to pay commensurate fees, is he not entitled to expect something more than the standard of the reasonably competent?"

9. [1955] 1 W.L.R. 1168.
10. (1995) 35 Con. L.R. 120.
11. *Hudson's Building and Civil Engineering Contracts* (11th ed.) describes the *Cotton* v. *Wallis* decision as "otherwise difficult" and argues that the reason the architect was not liable was because he honestly adopted one of two possible interpretations of the contract: paras. 2–198 at p. 353.
12. (1997) 55 Con. L.R. 124.
13. [1972] 2 Lloyd's Rep. 172.

It does not appear to be the law, however, that a professional of higher than ordinary expertise is under a higher standard of care than his fellow professionals, although in *George Wimpey & Co.* v. *D. V. Poole*[14] Webster J. accepted that a professional man who *in fact* possessed a high level of knowledge should not be judged by reference to the lesser degree of knowledge possessed by the ordinary practitioner.

3.4. DESIGN LIABILITIES IN GENERAL

3.4.1 The scope of the duty

It is of great importance that the designer clarifies with the client at the outset precisely what he is to do. The RIBA Code of Professional Conduct, for example, requires a member to have defined "beyond reasonable doubt" and recorded the terms of engagement, including the allocation of responsibilities and scope of service. *Richard Roberts Holdings Ltd* v. *Douglas Smith Stimson Partnership*[15] shows what can go wrong if this is not done.

The Plaintiff retained the defendant architect to design an effluent tank for use in a dye works, which was being rebuilt after a fire. It was accepted by both parties that the tank would need to be lined, and the architect's design assumed that this would be with stainless steel. There then followed discussions between the plaintiff and the defendant's representatives regarding the choice of lining. The parties investigated a number of possible firms to supply the lining including ECC, who were defendants in the action. At the plaintiff's suggestion, the architects asked ECC to quote. Their quotation was accepted after the architect had confirmed to the plaintiff that he felt that the plaintiff's outstanding queries had now been answered. The plaintiff then entered into a direct contract with ECC.

Subsequently, large areas of the lining became detached, causing erosion of the concrete walls. The architect argued that he had no legal responsibility for the lining since:

14. (1984) 27 B.L.R. 58.
15. (1988) 46 B.L.R. 50.

(a) The plaintiff was aware that they had no knowledge of linings;
(b) The plaintiff had taken independent advice from a trade association about the linings;
(c) The architect had not charged a fee for his work in relation to the choice of linings;
(d) The architect's input had been mainly directly to helping the plaintiff to perform its part of the project.

The court held, however, that the architect was employed for the creation of the *whole* dye works. Judge Newey Q.C. said:

"The lining was I think an integral part of the tank. The architects did not know about linings, but part of their expertise as architects was to be able to collect information about materials of which they lacked knowledge and/or experience and to form a view about them. If the architects felt that they could not form a reliable judgment about a lining for the tank, they should have informed [the plaintiff] of that fact and advised them to take other advice, possibly from a chemist".

Despite certain "alarm bells", such as suspiciously cheap quotation from ECC, the architect did not warn the plaintiff in any way. As between ECC and the architect, the court held both parties equally to blame.

3.4.2 Liability for areas outside the professional's usual sphere

Holland Hannen and Cubitts (North) Ltd v. *Welsh Health Technical Services Organisation*[16] was a complex multi-party action.

WHTSO engaged Cubitts to construct a new hospital at Rhyl in Wales. CED were nominated as sub-contractors to design the floor. They in turn instructed Alan Marshall & Partners (AMP), structural engineers, to assist them. The floors suffered from some deflection, and the employer's architects, Percy Thomas Partnership (PTP), therefore amended the specification half way through the design stage. The floors then failed to comply with the amended specification and were condemned by PTP.

Cubitts, the contractor, had its work delayed and sued WHTSO for its losses. On the 85th day of the trial, CED, PTP and the

16. (1985) 35 B.L.R. 1 (C.A).

structural engineering consultants acting for WHTSO agreed to pay Cubitts £396,681 for their delay-related losses. The trial judge, and subsequently the Court of Appeal, then went on to consider the apportionment of blame as between the other parties.

The Court of Appeal held that CED should pay one-third of Cubitts' losses (the trial judge had ordered two thirds), and PTP and the engineering consultants the other two-thirds. The Court of Appeal held that the judge had not sufficiently taken into account PTP's failure to grapple with the floor problem earlier. CED were held one-third liable because (*per* Lawton L.J.) they produced floors which "visually looked wrong" and (*per* Robert Goff L.J.) the floors were unserviceable and CED should have probably considered their profile.

The court also held by a majority that AMP were not negligent at all. The majority held that, as structural engineers, it was a matter for the architect, and not them, to consider matters of visual appearance or aesthetic effect. Dillon L.J. noted:

> "It is for the structural engineer to work out what the deflections of a floor will be; it is for the architect to decide whether a floor with those deflections will be visually or aesthetically satisfactory when the finishes chosen by the architect have been applied."

The other member of the majority, Lawton L.J., was influenced by AMP's previous engagement with CED on a different floor, and held that AMP's responsibility as advisers ended with the putting down of the screed finish. Robert Goff L.J. dissented, saying that a structural engineer could not be unconcerned with matters of visual appearance.

Despite the powerful minority opinion, the case is nevertheless authority at Court of Appeal level for the proposition that in certain circumstances a structural engineer need not be concerned with visual appearance or aesthetics; and that, more generally, a professional is not liable for matters outside his own sphere of expertise, especially where the client has retained another professional to deal with that area.

3.4.3 Duty to warn or advise regarding the work of other professionals

To what extent is the professional liable for failing to warn or advise in relation to other members of the professional team? In certain circumstances it will be possible to imply the appropriate term. In *Investors in Industry* v. *South Bedfordshire District Council*[17] the court had to consider a term in an architect's engagement which read:

"The architect will advise on the need for independent consultants and will be responsible for the direction and integration of their work but not for their detailed design, inspection and performance of the work entrusted to them" (the broad thrust of the clause is maintained in clauses 4.2.4 and 4.2.5 of SFA/92).

The Court of Appeal noted that the conditions contemplated the possibility that an architect might recommend a specialist in certain areas and added:

"If following such a recommendation a consultant with these qualifications is appointed, the architect will normally carry no legal responsibility for the work to be done by the expert which is beyond the capability of an architect of ordinary competence; in relation to the work allotted to the expert, the architect's legal responsibility will normally be confined to directing and coordinating the expert's work in the whole. However, this is subject to one important qualification. If any danger or problem arises in connection with the work allotted to the expert, of which an architect of ordinary competence reasonably ought to be aware and reasonably could be expected to warn the client . . . the duty of the architect [is] to warn the client. In such a contingency he is not entitled to rely blindly on the expert . . ."

In this case, the architect was the "lead" designer. In such a case it is easier to imply an "obligation to warn".

In the somewhat complex case of *Chesham Properties Ltd* v. *Bucknall Austin Project Management Services Ltd*,[18] the court considered the interrelationship of a number of professionals.

The plaintiff was a property developer involved in a scheme to develop a site at Cadogan Place, London, S.W.1. The defendants to the action were the plaintiff's structural engineer, architect, quantity surveyor and project manager. Allegations of professional negligence were made against all of these. Specifically, the plaintiff blamed the architect and project manager for granting excessive extensions of time and awarding loss and expense to the contractor, John Lelliott Ltd.

The plaintiff sought to make certain amendments to its pleadings,

17. (1985) 32 B.L.R. 1.
18. (1996) 82 B.L.R. 92.

which the defendants resisted. The judge therefore tried certain matters as preliminary issues, assuming the plaintiff's factual allegations to be correct. He had to consider first whether the plaintiff could show an arguable cause of action, and, secondly, whether the term alleged could in fact be found, expressly or impliedly (he did not consider the third question, namely whether it was breached).

The judge held, in relation to the various professionals, as follows:

(a) *The project manager*

The judge held that the project manager had a duty to advise and/or inform—here the plaintiff had at least an arguable case that the project manager had a duty to advise and/or inform the plaintiff of actual or potential deficiencies in the performance of the other defendants. The term was express, alternatively implied. It was of significance that the project manager's contract contained the obligation to "implement . . . *all monitoring procedures* including the performance of ... all consultants" (emphasis supplied). The judge noted that:

> "monitoring, in such a context, cannot sensibly be confined to passive observation. It must include reporting to the principal on the performance being monitored by reference to the standards which should be achieved."

(b) *The architect*

The judge held that, although the position was not clear-cut, the architect had a contractual duty (express or implied) to warn and/or advise of actual or potential deficiencies in the work of the *structural engineers and quantity surveyors*. There was again an express obligation to "monitor" as part of the architect's general managerial responsibilities.

However, there was no arguable case that the architect had to warn in relation to the *project manager*, because at the time of the architect's appointment no project manager was contemplated.

(c) *The structural engineers*

The structural engineer's terms of engagement included the express term "checking and advising upon any part of the project not designed by [the structural engineer]", which was obviously of significance. However, although the plaintiff had shown an arguable cause of action that the structural engineer had a duty to warn or advise of deficiencies in the work of the *architect or quantity surveyor* (i.e. the argument was not "obviously unsustainable"), on the balance of probabilities no duty existed in contract or tort (so that the plaintiff's claim in effect was doomed to failure on this point).

The structural engineer, like the architect, had no liability for the *project manager's* defaults.

(d) *The quantity surveyor*
Here the plaintiff could not show any arguable cause of action to warn or advise in respect of any of the other professionals. The quantity surveyor had no written contract, so that there were no express terms; and no terms could be implied.

3.4.4 Duty to reconsider or revise design—or to warn of one's own shortcomings

The *Chesham Properties* case also dealt with the issue of whether any of the professionals had duties to warn or advise the employer in relation to their *own* failings. (An initial reaction to this may be: why is this important, since if the professional is in breach, he can presumably be sued anyway? The answer lies in the issue of limitation. If a plaintiff is out of time in suing on the original breach, but can nevertheless prove a continuing duty of a professional to advise in relation to one's own shortcomings, limitation problems may be avoided.)

Judge Hicks Q.C. noted:

"the authorities display a reluctance to import a duty of self-accusation except in very clear cases."

Except in relation to the architects, the court held that no cause of action was even disclosed against any of the professionals—and even in relation to the architects, the court did not find such a duty actually established (while not going so far as to say that the pleading should be struck out altogether on this point). In another case[19]

19. *University Court of Glasgow* v. *William Whitfield* (1988) 42 B.L.R. 66.

Judge Bowsher Q.C. had said, in relation to an architect who had designed an art gallery:

> "where, as here, an architect has had drawn to his attention that damage has resulted from a design which he knew or ought to have known was bad from the start, he has a particular duty to his client to disclose what he has been under a continuing duty to reveal, namely what he knows of the design defects as possible causes of the problem."

Judge Hicks Q.C. commented that the duty pleaded against the architect in *Chesham* (which was to advise, warn or inform of their own actual or potential deficiencies in performance) was more specific and directly contrary to the architects' own interests than that duty considered by Judge Bowsher, and was therefore less likely to arise either by construction or implication.

There is authority for the view that a duty to reconsider or revise a design exists, even though a duty of self-accusation may less easily be implied. In *Hubert Leach and Another* v. *Norman Crossley & Partners*[20] a structural engineer was held to be negligent in failing to reappraise loading figures in relation to his design for a car deck on a warehouse roof. This was after he had become aware of facts that, in turn, should have alerted him to realise that his client was intending to use a heavier material on the roof than that for which the design had originally been made. Certainly where an architect has supervisory or other duties, continuing into the construction phase, it appears to be reasonably well-established that a duty to reconsider his design continues. The following words of Sachs L.J. in *Brickfield Properties Ltd* v. *Newton*[21] are often quoted:

> "The architect is under a continuing duty to check that this design will work in practice and to correct any errors which may emerge. It savours of the ridiculous for the architect to be able to say, as it was here suggested that he could say: 'true my design was faulty, but of course I saw to it that the contractors followed it faithfully'."

For how long might such a duty last? In *Chelmsford District Council* v. *Evers*[22] His Honour Judge Smout Q.C. saw it as lasting "until the works are completed". It has been held to last until practical

20. (1984) 8 Con L.R. 7 (C.A.).
21. [1971] 1 W.L.R. 862 at 873.
22. (1985) 25 B.L.R. 99 at 106.

completion.[23] In the *University Court of Glasgow* case, Judge Bowsher saw no reason why the duty to disclose design defects as possible causes of known damage should extend only to the date of practical completion, and held that the duty continued until the building was complete.[24]

It seems unlikely that the duties of a designer who is also carrying out supervisory functions could continue even after his contractual obligation have otherwise ceased. In *Eckersley* v. *Binnie*[25] Bingham L.J. said:

> "It has never, to my knowledge, been held that a professional man who advises on a tax scheme, or on draft trading conditions, is thereafter bound to advise his client if, within a period of years, the statutory provisions or the relevant authorities change."

However, Bingham L.J. referred to "persuasive examples" involving dangers to life and health where "some response by a professional man might well be called for". It is possible that in such exceptional cases a duty to warn or advise in relation to a design could yet be found. Such cases would however be highly unusual.

There is authority that the obligation to review a design does not in general extend to third parties in tort.[26]

3.4.5 Duties in relation to recommending others

An architect may be liable for recommending a builder who subsequently carries out defective work.[27] Depending on the facts, it may be part of an architect's duty to his client to check the financial status of the contractor, e.g. by obtaining a bank or trade credit

23. H.H. Judge Newey Q.C. in *Equitable Debenture Assets Corporation Limited* v. *William Moss and Others* (1984) 2 Con. L.R. 1 at 24; *Victoria University of Manchester* v. *Hugh Wilson* (1984) 2 Con. L.R. 43 at 73; *Tesco Stores Ltd* v. *The Norman Hitchcox Partnership Ltd and Others* [1997] C.I.L.L. 1301 at 1303.

24. See article by A. Nissen in (1997) 13(4) Construction Law Journal 221, "The Duty to Review a Design—is it Real or Artificial?" where the view is expressed that the duty on an architectural engineer to review his design *should* arise when he has been asked to supervise the implementation of his design and some event occurs during construction which would put a reasonably competent architect or engineer on notice that his design ought to be reviewed.

25. (1988) 18 Con. L.R. 1.

26. *Tesco Store Ltd* v. *The Norman Hitchcox Partnership Ltd and Others* [1997] C.I.L.L. 1301 at 1303.

27. *Pratt* v. *George J. Hill Associates (a firm)* (1987) 38 B.L.R. 25 (C.A.).

reference or carrying out a company search.[28] An architect has been held liable for failing to make sufficient enquiries at tender stage of a nominated sub-contractor, where further enquiries in respect of a "somewhat superficial tender" would have revealed that the sub-contractor had been in business for a short time only, and that the claim to have experience of similar projects was misleading.[29]. In the *Richard Robert Holdings* case discussed above, the failure of the architect to pay proper regard to a quotation which was "not only suspiciously cheap but obviously not properly considered" was a factor in the finding of negligence.

3.4.6 Fitness for purpose

A supplier of goods is generally held as a matter of law impliedly to promise that his goods are of satisfactory quality, and are reasonably fit for any intended purpose expressly or impliedly made known to him by the buyer.[30] Can a designer be held to promise that his design is fit for the client's purpose? The question is an important one. If such an application exists, the client would generally only have to show that (for example) a building does not function properly or a bridge does not carry the loads that were intended for it—instead of having to discharge the further onus of showing a lack of reasonable care and skill on the part of the designer.

However cases where such obligations will be implied are relatively few and far between. Three possible cases are as follows:

(a) Where the designer also supplies an item. In *Samuels* v. *Davis*[31] the court held that where a professional undertook to make a denture for a patient, he impliedly promised that the denture would be fit for its intended purpose, even though his professional work generally was subject only to the usual obligation of reasonable care and skill. Lord Scarman (obiter) took up dicta from this case in *Independent Broadcasting Authority* v. *EMI Electronics Ltd and BICC Construction Limited*[32] which involved the collapse of

28. *Partridge* v. *Morris* [1995] C.I.L.L. 1095.
29. *EDAC* v. *Moss* (1989) 2 Con. L.R. 1.
30. Sale of Goods Act 1979, s. 14(2) and (3), as amended by the Sale and Supply of Goods Act 1994.
31. [1943] K.B. 526.
32. (1980) 14 B.L.R. 1.

a television aerial mast in Yorkshire. Lord Scarman said:

> "I see no reason why one who in the course of his business contracts to design, supply and erect a television aerial mast is not under an obligation to ensure that it is reasonably fit for the purpose for which he knows it is intended to be used . . . However I do not accept that the design and obligation of the supplier of an article is to equated with the obligation of a professional man in the practice of his profession."

(b) In certain "design and build" joint venture projects. An example is *Consultants Group International* v. *John Worman Ltd.*[33] In this case, Worman were engaged as building contractors to renovate an abattoir. They engaged architects to provide design services. The court assumed, for the purposes of deciding what duties were owed, that the work as designed failed to comply with the relevant EC standards, thus depriving the employer of the benefit of certain EC grants. The judge held that the building contract put Worman under an obligation to ensure that the works achieved the necessary EC standard, and held, further, that the architects were under a similar obligation to Worman. This was because they were the "prime movers" in the project from start to finish and were not retained by the contractor to provide architectural services in the usual way. The relationship was akin to a "joint venture" and the particular circumstances therefore justified imposing the higher "fitness for purpose" obligation.

(c) Where the evidence indicates that, unusually, the professional has agreed to achieve a result. In *Greaves (Contractors) Ltd* v. *Baynham Meikle & Partners*,[34] structural engineers were employed to design a warehouse floor. However, the design failed to provide floors with sufficient strength to withstand vibrations produced by forklift trucks carrying oil drums, as had been intended. The Court of Appeal noted that although a surgeon does not promise to cure his patient, or a solicitor to win his client's case, there were two reasons for imposing an obligation on the engineer to ensure that the design allowed for the load in question:

33. (1985) 9 Con. L.R. 46.
34. (1975) 4 B.L.R. 56 (C.A.).

(i) In cross-examination the engineer had admitted that it was his job to produce a building that would be fit to be used to store oil drums and for use by stacker trucks;
(ii) In its pleading, the engineer had originally admitted the existence of a fitness for purpose criterion but had been given leave on the second day of the trial to amend so as to withdraw the concession. The fact that the term had been initially accepted was held to be evidence of the fact that it was indeed a term of the contract.

Such terms will not be present in most cases, and Geoffrey Lane L.J. in the Court of Appeal saw the case as deciding "no great issue of principle".

3.4.7 Delegation or transfer of design duties

Duties can be transferred from a professional to someone else by assignment (of the benefit of the contract); by novation (an arrangement whereby a contract between A and B is transformed, by way of a three-party agreement, into a contract between A and C. Effectively C steps into B's shoes with the consent of all parties and assumes the rights and obligations that B originally had); or by sub-contracting.

The first two of these will always require the employer's consent. However in relation to sub-contracting, two questions arise:

(i) In what circumstances may a professional sub-contract some or all of his work?
(ii) If he does, to what extent does he remain liable for the sub-contractor's performance?

3.4.7.1 The standard forms

Under SFA/92 the architect may sub-contract work if the client consents in writing, but the client cannot unreasonably withhold such consent.[35] The architect is not responsible for the work of other "specialists"[36] who are defined as designer-suppliers of goods

35. Cl. 1.4.2.
36. Cl. 4.2.5.

or components, nor for the work of "consultants".[37] It seems that liability for services sub-contractors is also excluded by clause 1.3.7, which states that the architect does not warrant the work or products of "others".

The ACE conditions allow the engineer to recommend that the client sub-lets any services (again the client must not unreasonably withhold consent). Here, however, the engineer remains responsible for the performance of any sub-contractor.[38] The engineer may also recommend that the *detailed design* be carried out by a specialist, and again the client cannot unreasonably withhold consent, but here the engineer is *not* responsible for the designer's performance.[39]

The Professional Services Contract treats assignment and sub-contracting together as "sub-consulting" under clause 24.1. The professional needs the employer's consent to sub-contract, but consent can only be refused on three grounds (all of which are to the effect that the proposed sub-contractor will not be able to perform as well as the professional). The professional is entirely responsible for the sub-consultant's performance.

To summarise: all three forms allow sub-contracting with consent, which cannot be unreasonably refused. SFA/92 excludes the architect's liability for the sub-contractor; the ACE conditions exclude it for "detailed design" only; and the PSC does not exclude it at all.

3.4.7.2 The common law position

Whether performance of an obligation can lawfully be sub-contracted at common law depends upon the terms of the contract and the subject matter. In *Southway Group Ltd* v. *Wolff and Wolff*[40] Bingham L.J. said:

> "In some classes of contract, as where B commissions A to write a book or paint a picture or teach him to play the violin, it would usually be clear that personal performance by A was required. In other cases, as where A undertakes to repair B's shoes, or mend B's watch or drive B to the airport, it may be open to A to perform the contract vicariously by employing the services of C."

37. Cl. 4.1.7.
38. Cl. 2.7.
39. Cl. 2.8.
40. (1991) 57 B.L.R. 33 at 52.

Since "personal" performance (whether by a firm or an individual) is generally required in architects' and engineers' engagements, it will rarely be that a designer can unilaterally delegate all or most of his obligations. However where an architect or engineer argues for the right to delegate a small *part* of his obligations—perhaps a specialised area—the position is less clear cut.

In *Moresk Cleaners Ltd* v. *Thomas Henwood Hicks*,[41], the plaintiff employed the defendant architect to design an extension for a laundry. Unknown to the plaintiff, the architect invited the main contractor, with whom he was acquainted, to design the structure. The purlins were too weak to support the roof, and the portal frames, which should have been tied together, had spread, causing them to come apart from the cladding. The design was therefore defective. The judge held that there was no implied term in the contract giving the architect the power to delegate the design duty at all, certainly not to the contractor whose interests were entirely opposed to those of the plaintiff.

Conversely, in *London Borough Council of Merton* v. *Lowe*[42] the defendant architects were retained to design a swimming pool and to supervise its erection. Their design incorporated the use of Pyrok, a material used in suspended ceilings, being a proprietary product produced by Pyrok Ltd who became nominated sub-contractors. The ceilings later developed cracks because the mix used in the Pyrok coat was stronger than that used in the underlying coat; and also because of poor workmanship.

The architects were held not to be liable for the design error, even though it had undoubtedly been their obligation to design the pool (they were in fact held liable on other grounds relating to supervision). Waller L.J. saw the *Moresk* case as being distinguishable because:

> "There architect had virtually handed over to another the whole task of design ... This was different. Pyrok were nominated sub-contractors employed for a specialised task of making a ceiling with their own proprietary materials. It was the defendants' duty to use reasonable care as architects. In view of successful work done elsewhere [it was reasonable to employ Pyrok]."

The above cases read together appear to suggest that the position is as follows:

41. (1966) 4 B.L.R. 50.
42. (1981) 18 B.L.R. 130 (C.A.).

(i) An architect or engineer cannot delegate a major area of the design, where that area is one that the employer reasonably expects him to perform personally.

(ii) However, in certain circumstances the contract of engagement may be construed so as to allow him to discharge his design obligations relating to a particular specialised area by reasonably choosing a skilled specialist to carry out that work. (This approach is less likely to be adopted where it would leave the employer without a remedy against a specialist designer—such a remedy was available in *Merton*.)

3.4.8 The impact of the Construction (Design and Management) Regulations 1994

These Regulations, often referred to as the "CDM" Regulations, came into force on 31 March 1995 (there are transitional provisions for projects begun after that date). The Regulations as a whole apply only to "construction work".[43] They do not apply to small projects.[44]

A designer is defined in Regulation 2(1) as any person who carried on a trade, business or other undertaking, in connection with which he prepares a design relating to a "structure" (which includes roads, railways, tunnels, pipes, cables and temporary items such as scaffold, formwork and falsework) or arranges for an employee or other person under his control to do so. The obligations imposed under Regulation 13 are broadly threefold:

(a) To ensure that the design has positive regard for the health and safety of persons carrying out the construction work;

(b) To ensure that the design contains information regarding any aspect of the project, including materials, that might affect such health and safety;

43. Reg. 3.

44. I.e. if the largest number of persons carrying out the work at any one time is fewer than 5 and the construction phase will not last longer than 30 days or involve 500 person-days of construction work and does not involve dismantling or demolition of a structure (which is defined to include scaffolding, thus potentially catching within the legislation many small projects). However Reg. 13 (designer's obligations) applies to all projects of construction work, and architects and engineers therefore need to consider health and safety aspects of their design.

(c) To co-operate with the client's "planning supervisor" (who will often be the architect or engineer himself) and any other designer involved.

The sanctions are criminal, but architects and engineers need to consider the possibility of professional negligence actions from the following persons where the design fails to take into account health and safety matters:

(a) From persons injured on site because of the defective design (there would often be a duty of care in tort to such persons);
(b) From the client (who might be facing a personal injury claim from a construction site worker himself);
(c) From the planning supervisor, principal contractor, or others.

There must also be possibilities of contribution actions under the Civil Liability (Contribution) Act 1978 by any person faced with a personal injury claim. That person would argue against the designer that he was negligent in respect of the same damage as that for which he was himself being sued, and should therefore contribute to it.

3.4.9 *Practicality of design*

Designers must consider the practicality of their design in the context of the work that will be carried out on site. In *EDAC* v. *Moss*[45] His Honour Judge Newey Q.C. held that the designer should take into account foreseeable conditions in relation to his design, such as windiness, the fact that scaffolding would be needed, the fact that exceptional skill was required on site etc., and said that if these were not considered properly the design would lack "buildability". He continued:

> "Similarly, I think that if a design requires work to be carried out on site in such a way that those whose duty it is to supervise it and/or check that it has been done well will encounter great difficulty in doing so, then the design will again be defective. It may perhaps be described as lacking 'supervisability'."

45. (1989) 2 Con. L.R. 1.

3.4.10 *Innovative design*

Although it may be said that the frontiers of design cannot be extended without experimentation, it seems that the innovative designer must ensure that his client is well aware of potential risks in the design. In *Victoria University of Manchester* v. *Hugh Wilson*[46] the architect adopted what in the 1960s was an innovative cladding design for a university building involving the use of brick and ceramic tiles. The judge noted that although it was not wrong in itself to use untried materials or techniques, the architect who was venturing into the "untried or little tried" should first warn his client of what he was doing, and then obtain their express approval.

3.4.11 *Provision of estimates*

3.4.11.1 Cost estimates

Costs overruns are a frequent source of friction between client and professional advisor. An overrun on the original contract sum will not in itself be evidence of negligence on the part of the designer, unless the designer or advisor can be held to have *warranted* that the work could be carried out for a particular sum (which would hardly ever be the case). However, since the contract sum will usually fall to be adjusted during the contract for such matters as variations and other items, the architect or engineer who does not make his client aware of this at the outset, particular if the client is inexperienced, may well be negligent.

Cases involving negligent advice regarding costs tend to depend on their facts. Matters to take into consideration will be the amount by which the final cost exceeds the estimated cost, the context in which any estimate was given (including any qualifications made) and the extent to which the architect or engineer should have indicated, and did indicate, that the estimate might be exceeded in practice.

Nye Saunders & Partners v. *Bristow*[47] illustrates the liability for an architect in failing to warn his client of the possible effect of inflation on building prices. The architects were retained by the defendant to prepare a planning application and provide services in connection

46. (1984) 2 Con. L.R. 43.
47. (1987) 37 B.L.R. 92 (C.A.).

with the renovation of the defendant's mansion and installation of a swimming pool. The defendant made clear that he had approximately £250,000 to spend. The architects provided a written estimate of £238,000 (in fact obtained from an independent quantity surveyor). However, some seven months later, the project costs had risen to some £440,000, and the client aborted the project and terminated the architects' retainer. The architects then sued for their fees.

The architects were held to be negligent in failing to warn the client (an experienced businessman) about the possible effects of inflation. The trial judge had been impressed by expert evidence that it was not proper practice for architects to omit such a warning. Further, the client had consistently sought and obtained the architects' confirmation over several months that the estimate still stood.

The case of *Copthorne Hotel (Newcastle) Ltd* v. *Arup Associates & Another*[48] contains useful points on evidence required in these types of cases. The plaintiff alleged that consultants had confirmed that a hotel designed by them could be completed for a certain sum within a margin of plus or minus 5 per cent. One of the issues was in relation to the consultant engineer's estimate for piling works as part of the overall construction costs estimate. Structural engineers had allowed £425,000 for the piling works, whereas tenders were in fact received at sums between £711,000 and £1,058,000. The successful tender was in the figure of £897,500. The plaintiffs alleged that the consultant engineers should have allowed £930,000, not £425,000.

It might be thought that the plaintiff could simply point to the difference between the consultant's estimates and the actual tender figures as evidence of negligence. However, the judge held that this was not enough. After noting that everyone involved in the project had been "thunderstruck" by the amount of the tender prices, he added:

"The plaintiff's main hope was that I would be persuaded to find in their favour simply by the size of the gap, absolutely and proportionately, between the cost estimate and the successful tender . . . the gap was indeed enormous. It astonished and appalled the parties at the time and it astonishes me. I do not see however that that alone can carry the plaintiff home. There is no plea or argument that the maxim *res ipsa loquitur* applies. Culpable underestimation is of course one of the explanations of such a

48. [1996] C.I.L.L. 1193.

discrepancy, but far from the only one. The successful tender was not the lowest, the contractor may have over-specified from excessive caution, or to obtain a greater profit, or to suit the drilling equipment available, or for some other reason. . . ."

It may be noted that the Judge did not *rule out* a plea of *res ipsa loquitur* in principle for this type of case. Clearly, however, to bring an action against a professional upon that ground alone, and without calling other evidence of negligence, would be risky.

3.4.11.2 Estimates generally

Gable House Estates Ltd v. *The Halpern Partnership and Bovis Construction Ltd*[49] illustrates an architect's obligation to qualify estimates appropriately.

The plaintiffs were owners of a building in Leadenhall Street in the City of London. Their options were to sell the building (with or without refurbishment) or to re-develop and let it. They engaged the defendant architects to design the proposed redevelopment. The clients' quantity surveyor prepared three cost plans and various schedules of areas which were provided to the clients, sometimes direct by the quantity surveyor, but with the architect's knowledge (as lead consultant). The architect was aware that an important factor in the clients' decision to redevelop was the space that could be let. One of the schedules of areas indicated that the lettable space was some 34,000 sq.ft (in fact only some 32,000 sq.ft could be let). The schedules bore the phrase "all areas approximate". A later schedule referred to "usable office space" instead of "lettable areas" although the difference was not explained to the client. The client sued for damages of £32.5 million, over five times the project value, based on its getting a lower letting space than it had been led to be believe would be achievable.

The judge found:

(a) The use of the phrase "all areas approximate" was not a sufficient warning to the clients;
(b) The architect should have warned the clients of the uncertainties that could affect the lettable area;
(c) The architect should have explained to the clients that

49. (1995) 48 Con. L.R. 1.

"lettable area" and "usable office space" did not mean the same thing;

(d) The fact that some of the schedules of area were prepared by the quantity surveyor, who sent them direct to the clients, did not help the architect who was a co-ordinator of the professional team and knew of the importance of these schedules to the clients.

Since the clients relied on the information about lettable area, and would not have redeveloped had they known of the true area, their losses were potentially very high. The case is thus a stark warning to architects and engineers of the need to qualify estimates appropriately.

3.5. LIABILITY DURING THE CONSTRUCTION PERIOD

Architects and engineers are often appointed by the employer to supervise the construction phase. This section deals with their potential liability to the employer during that period. Their liability to the contractor is considered in section 6.4 below.

It may be noted that if suggestions in the Latham Report are followed, there may be a decline in the use of independent external (as opposed to in-house) project managers to supervise projects, and indeed that report recommends reconsidering the role of the adviser once the decision has been made whether to proceed with the project.[50]

3.5.1 Inspection and supervision duties

The supervising officer's general obligations are summarised in a much cited passage of Lord Upjohn in *East Ham Corporation* v. *Bernard Sunley & Sons Ltd*[51]:

"As is well known the architect is not permanently on the site but appears at intervals, it may be of a week or a fortnight, and he has, of course, to inspect the progress of the work. When he arrives on the site there may be very many important matters with which he has to deal: the work may be getting behind-hand through labour trouble; some of the suppliers of

50. *Constructing the Team* (HMSO, July 1994), paras. 6.18 and 3.6.
51. [1966] A.C. 406 at 433.

materials or the sub-contractors may be lagging; there may be physical trouble on the site itself, such as finding an unexpected amount of underground water. All these are matters which may call for important decisions by the architect. He may in such circumstances think that he knows the builder sufficiently well and can rely upon him to carry out a good job; that it is more important that he should deal with urgent matters on the site than that he should make a minute inspection on the site to see that the builder is complying with the specifications laid down ... It by no means follows that, in failing to discover a defect which a reasonable examination would have disclosed, in fact the architect was necessarily thereby in breach of his duty to the building owner so as to be liable in an action for negligence. It may well be that the omission of the architect to find a defect was due to no more than an error of judgment, or was a deliberately calculated risk which, in all the circumstances of the case, was reasonable and proper."

As with other aspects of professional negligence, the mere fact that a building defect has gone unnoticed does not necessarily imply negligence—the supervising officer has a number of tasks to which he has to direct his attention.

The frequency of visits required is often a source of complaint. Under SFA/92 the architect must make such a visit as, at the date of his appointment, he reasonably expects to be necessary.[52] These conditions allow him to recommend later to the client that the frequency of visits should be increased, subject to the architect being paid increased fees—it is then up to the client to decide whether to take up the recommendations. Under the ACE Conditions, the frequency of the engineers' attendance at site meetings and his site visits are specified in the memorandum. The Professional Services Contract does not refer to visits, but the brief should contain the details.

The obligations at common law are generally dependent on the factual circumstances of the case, bearing in mind Lord Upjohn's guidelines as above. In *London Borough of Merton* v. *Lowe*[53] it was held not sufficient for the architect to ask the manager of a swimming pool, who was not an expert, to oversee the contractor's day-to-day work, rather than for the architect to visit himself. It has also been held that an architect's duty to visit is not reduced merely by the fact that his office is some distance from site.[54]

52. Cl. 3.1.
53. (1981) 18 B.L.R. 135.
54. *Brown & Brown* v. *Gilbert-Scott and Another* (1992) 35 Con. L.R. 120 at 123.

An architect will be required to devote more supervision where the contractor is inexperienced than where he is tried and trusted. This was a factor in one case where, although it was not right to say that the architect should have watched a young and inexperienced builder "like a hawk", nonetheless his age and experience were a factor that the architect should have borne in mind when discharging his obligation to inspect and supervise.[55] Conversely in *Corfield* v. *Grant*[56] the builder did not need a great deal of supervision, the judge held, so long as he was given enough information about what he had to do, and so long as the architect kept a firm watch on his pricing, which was based on the limit of what the market would bear. In *Sutcliffe* v. *Chippendale and Edmondson*[57] Judge Stabb Q.C. said:

> "I think that the degree of supervision required of an architect must be governed to some extent by his confidence in the contractor, if and when something occurs which indicates to him a lack of competence in a contractor, then, in the interest of his employer, the standard of his supervision should be higher" (the case was subsequently appealed up to the House of Lords but these observations were unaffected).

Criticisms of supervising officers who fail to get a firm grip on the construction phase have often appeared in reported cases. In *EDAC* v. *Moss*[58] the architect was described as a " 'poor organiser' [lacking] the firmness of purpose and assertiveness required for effective supervision of a large project" and having "simply hoped for the best". The architect in *Corfield* v. *Grant*[59] presided over the project, a hotel conversion, in a way that left it as an "inadequately controlled muddle". The architect also failed to appoint an experienced assistant, where clearly one was needed.

3.5.1.1 Deliberately concealed bad work

Where the contractor carries out grossly incompetent work, and then deliberately conceals it from the architect, there are two possible approaches. The first is that an architect faced with a calculated course of action of this nature would have to have a particularly

55. *Ibid.* at p. 122.
56. (1992) 59 B.L.R. 102.
57. (1971) 18 B.L.R. 149.
58. (1989) 2 Con. L.R. 1.
59. (1992) 59 B.L.R. 102.

eagle eye to spot what is going on. In *Gray* v. *T. P. Bennett*[60] a 10-storey reinforced concrete building was designed so that concrete projections or nibs provided support for the brick cladding. Concrete panels were opened up some 17 years after construction after bulges had appeared in the brickwork. It was discovered that about 90 per cent of the nibs had been "hacked back or butchered", to which the experts supplied epithets such as "appalling", "destructive" and "mindless vandalism". The judge decided that the operatives must have been engaged in a deliberate policy of concealing from the supervising officer "destruction on a massive scale" and held the architect not negligent in failing to discover what was going on on his routine visits. The judge also held that the true *cause* of the damage was the deliberate action of the fixers.

The second approach is to argue that the more serious the contractor's breach is, the more culpable is the architect who fails to notice them. Although this was not specifically the approach in *Kensington and Chelsea and Westminster Area Health Authority* v. *Wettern Composites*,[61] that case provides an example of an architect who was negligent in failing to notice "startling" defects in fixing of pre-cast concrete mullions for a hospital conversion (the vertical supports of some 85 per cent of the mullions examined, and the horizontal supports of some 25 per cent, were unsatisfactory). It was held that the architects had been alerted relatively early on to the poor workmanship and lack of honesty of the sub-contractor, and also that the burden of supervision was greater where, as here, poor workmanship could result in physical danger. Most significantly, the judge noted that the fixing of the mullions was work that, by its nature, could be speedily covered up in the course of erection, which made closer supervision all the more essential.

3.5.2 The supervising officer's obligation to issue instructions or provide information

Under many of the standard forms of building contract, the contractor may make claims for direct loss and/or expense caused by failure to provide information, or by the issue of variation instructions by the supervising officer—see for example JCT 80 clauses

60. (1987) 43 B.L.R. 63.
61. (1984) 31 B.L.R. 57.

26.2.1 and 26.2.7. Under JCT 80 clause 5.4 the architect must also provide such further drawings or details as are reasonably necessary to explain or exemplify the contract drawings or to enable the contractor to carry out the work and, under Amendment 18 of April 1998, must provide information in accordance with his "Information Release Schedule". Further, terms are often implied into building contracts to the effect that the employer will not hinder or prevent the contractor from carrying out the work (which in turn obliges the architect to provide a contractor with full correct and co-ordinated information) and will do all things reasonably necessary to enable the contractor to carry out the work.[62]

The ICE conditions contain comparable obligations. There, the contractor can claim additional payment for delay, drawings or instructions, variation instructions and other matters.[63] Clause 7 of the ICE Conditions (6th Edition) contains an obligation to provide such drawings, specification and information as the engineer considers necessary.

Once more, it is important to reiterate that the mere fact of payment of loss and/or expense or additional payment does not necessarily imply any fault on the supervising officer's part, and even a failure to provide information in time (for example) does not necessarily amount to negligence. In particular, on a large project, it will be unlikely that all information will be provided precisely at the time the contractor needed it. Nevertheless, supervising officers are open to attack from their clients when the contractors make claims under this sort of head.

An architect may be liable to his employer for failing to issue an instruction which is needed to overcome a problem on site. In *Holland Hannen & Cubitts* v. *WHTSO*[64] a nominated sub-contractor put forward a proposed solution to the problem of water ingress in windows to the main contractor and to the architect. The architect prepared a draft variation instruction to cover this work, but never formally issued it (partly because of the dispute that was then extant between it and the contractor about who was in the right). The works were subsequently delayed. The judge, however, held that the architect, in failing to issue the variation instruction, had made it impossible for the contractor and nominated sub-contractor to

62. *London Borough of Merton* v. *Stanley Hugh Leach Ltd* (1985) 32 B.L.R. 51.
63. ICE, 6th ed., Conditions clauses 7(4)(a) and 5(2).
64. (1981) 18 B.L.R. 80.

carry on with their work, and the architect was held liable to the employer for breach of contract, because the building contract required him to issue an instruction whenever it was "necessary" for completion of the works. The judge held that, alternatively, there was an implied term that the architect would do all things necessary to enable the contractor to complete the work, and went on to criticise the architect's "passive attitude".

Architects should also beware of provisions typically to be found in building and engineering contracts where instructions are required to be in writing, but where provision is made for the contractor to confirm any oral instructions of the architect. If the contractor does so confirm and the architect does not dissent, the verbal instruction then becomes effective.[65]

3.5.3 Obligations to issue certificates

The House of Lords has definitively rejected the argument that architects acting as certifiers enjoy an immunity from actions in negligence akin to those of an arbitrator or judge.[66] Therefore a supervising officer may in principle be negligent in respect of his certification as for any other part of his functions under a building or engineering contract.

Three sorts of certificate are now considered.

3.5.3.1 Interim valuation certificates

The ICE Conditions, clause 60(7), allow the contractor compound interest where the engineer has failed to certify in accordance with sub-clauses (2), (4) and (6) of that clause. However, interim certificates are necessarily approximate, and can be corrected at the next monthly (or other) stage. It therefore appears that architects may have some latitude in making approximations as to the correct value to be certified—see *Secretary of State for Transport* v. *Birse Farr Joint Venture:*[67]

"Certification may be a complex exercise involving an exercise of judgment and an investigation and assessment of potentially complex and voluminous material. An assessment by an engineer of the appropriate interim payment may have a margin of error either way ... At the interim stage it cannot always be a wholly exact exercise".

65. See, e.g., JCT 80, cl. 4.3.2; and ICE Conditions (6th ed.), cl. 2(6).
66. *Sutcliffe* v. *Thackrah* [1974] A.C. 727.
67. (1993) 62 B.L.R. 36 at 53.

Thus, *merely* failing to certify the correct amount on an interim certificate, or certifying the correct sum but late, does not of itself allow a claim.

In *Sutcliffe* v. *Chippendale and Edmondson*[68] Judge Stabb Q.C. accepted that, while a prolonged or detailed inspection or measurement at the interim stage was impractical, "more than a glance round" was required. It was noted that the architect should not disregard defective work on the assumption that the contractor would rectify it at a later stage, since the contract might be terminated by reason of the contractor's insolvency or otherwise before such work was corrected. The architect was also obliged to keep the quantity surveyor continually informed of any defective work that he saw.

In *Townsend* v. *Stone Toms & Partners*[69] the architect argued that he was entitled to include defective work in the valuation certificates because this would in any event be covered by the retention. The argument was rejected—again there could be consequences to the employer if the contractor had become insolvent before the defects had been made good.

3.5.3.2 Extension of time awards

Contractors may litigate or arbitrate against an employer to have an architect's extension of time reversed, so as to obtain a return of liquidated damages deducted and also, indirectly, to prepare the basis for a claim for loss and/or expense or damages. It might be thought that an employer who wished to sue his architect would first have to have established, by way of proceedings involving the contractor, what the contractor's rights to extensions of time and loss and/or expense in fact were, so that the employer's loss could be definitively stated. However, *Wessex Regional Health Authority* v. *HLM Design Limited,*[70] a decision on assumed facts, suggests otherwise. In that case an employer settled an arbitration brought by its contractor on relatively unfavourable terms, mainly because of evidential difficulties and then commenced High Court proceedings against its architect to recover the settlement sums and arbitration

68. (1971) 18 B.L.R. 149.
69. (1984) 27 B.L.R. 26 (C.A.).
70. (1995) 71 B.L.R. 32.

costs. The architect objected to this course of action, but the Judge "reluctantly" held that an employer has independent causes of action against his contractor and architect and can sue them in whichever order he chooses.

The pressure from contractors on architects and engineers to increase extensions of time can be immense, particularly where the contractor is armed with computer-based retrospective analyses of delay and criticality. In *John Barker Construction Limited* v. *London Portman Hotel Ltd*[71] the judge was impressed by the analysis carried out by the contractor's expert. Conversely, the judge held that the architect's assessment was "fundamentally flawed" because he:

> "did not carry out a logical analysis in a methodical way of the impact which the relevant matters had" and "impressionistic, rather than a calculated, assessment of the time which he thought was reasonable for the various items individually and overall."

There was no suggestion of negligence in this case, but the tenor of the judgment is clear and serves as a warning to architects and engineers to adopt rigorous and logical approaches when exercising their functions in relation to assessments of delay.

3.5.3.3 The Final Certificate

This is an important certificate found in many building and engineering contracts. JCT 80, for example, provides that unless arbitration proceedings have been instituted within 28 days of its issue, it is conclusive evidence, against the employer, that where and to the extent that the quality of materials or the standard of workmanship is required by the contract to be to the satisfaction of the architect, the work is in fact to his satisfaction. It had been assumed prior to *Colbart* v. *Kumar*[72] that this evidential bar applied only to standards of workmanship and materials that the contract made *expressly* to be subject to the architect's satisfaction. However, the Official Referee in that case held (in relation to the Intermediate Form of Contract IFC 84) that the bar applied to *all* matters that were "inherently" a matter for the architect's discretion, effectively including all types of defective workmanship and materials. The decision was endorsed in respect of the JCT 80 contract by the

71. (1996) 83 B.L.R. 31.
72. (1992) 59 B.L.R. 89.

Court of Appeal in *Crown Estate Commissioners* v. *Mowlem*.[73]

The *Crown Estates* reasoning may well apply to latent defects as well as patent ones, thus giving the employer a 28-day limitation period instead of the usual six or 12 years, and also removing his rights under the Latent Damage Act 1986 to "start the clock" in respect of latent defects as soon as the defect is reasonably discoverable. Although the JCT have issued an amendment[74] to JCT 80 "correcting" the effect of the *Crown Estates* case, contracts that are affected by the original wording may still attract actions from disgruntled employers who are unable to claim against their contractors for defective work.

3.5.4 Other obligations

Architects and engineers cannot be expected to have the experience of lawyers, but neither can they afford to ignore the law. In *B.L. Holdings* v. *Robert J. Wood & Partners*[75] Ralph Gibson J. said:

> "A professional man such as an architect who agrees to act in some field of activity commonly carried out by architects, in which a knowledge and understanding of certain principles of law is required ... must have a sufficient knowledge of those principles of law in order reasonably to protect his client from damage and loss."

West Faulkner v. *London Borough of Newham*[76] provides a striking illustration of architect's liability. JCT 80 clause 25 gives the architect the power to determine the contractor's employment if he fails to proceed "regularly and diligently". The architect in this case incorrectly maintained to his employers that he was unable in law to issue a determination notice to a tardy contractor, because (the Court of Appeal found) he was under the mistaken impression that such a notice could only be served if the contractor was failing to proceed both regularly *and* diligently (whereas the contractor was in fact proceeding regularly, albeit slowly). The question was whether the architect's interpretation, though incorrect, was negligent.

73. (1994) 70 B.L.R. 1 (C.A.)—see the criticism of this decision by I. N. Duncan Wallace Q.C. in "Not What the RIBA/JCT Meant: Loose Cannon in the Court of Appeal" (1995) Const. L.J. 184.
74. Amendment 15 (July 1995).
75. (1979) 10 B.L.R. 48.
76. (1994) 71 B.L.R. 1 (C.A.).

Perhaps surprisingly, it was held that the construction of the clause was one that no reasonably competent architect could have arrived at. This was so despite the fact that another professional man (the quantity surveyor in question) had construed the clause in the same way as the architect—and despite the fact that independent advice contained in a letter to the council from a firm of specialist solicitors appeared to indicate that the issue whether the contractor's employment could be determined was "borderline" (the court held that the letter was not in fact directed to the construction of the clause). However, in cases where the construction of the clause is difficult, it would be rare that an architect will fail to discharge his onus to advise if he goes so far as recommending independent legal advice.

The supervising officer's obligations in respect of other professionals is discussed at sections 4.2 and 4.3 above.

Finally, engineers acting under the ICE Conditions (5th or 6th Edition) need to bear in mind the possibility of aggrieved employers claiming against them for sums that they may have to pay as interest to the contractor under clause 60(7) (formerly clause 60(6) of the 5th Edition Conditions). Such interest, which is compounded under the 6th Edition Conditions, is due where the engineer has failed to certify in accordance with the certification provisions in the contract. In *Secretary of State for Transport* v. *Birse Farr Joint Venture*[77] Hobhouse J. held that the mere delay by an engineer would not bring a case within this clause, and that there had to be "some misapplication or misunderstanding of the contract by the engineer". Even that will not necessarily amount to negligence, but clearly employers will be alert to consider whether negligence has in fact occurred so as to enable them to recover from their engineer interest that they have paid out.

3.6. LIABILITY TO THIRD PARTIES (INCLUDING LIABILITY IN TORT)

3.6.1 Tort and contract

The words "professional negligence" are often used to refer to a

77. (1993) 62 B.L.R. 36.

breach of the *contractual* obligation to perform with reasonable care and skill, rather than the tortious situation of owing a duty of care to some other person. However, even in contract cases, a concurrent claim in tort is often alleged alongside the breach of contract. It has now been authoritatively established at House of Lords level (*Henderson* v. *Merrett Syndicates Ltd*,[78]) that the duty in tort may exist side by side with a contractual obligation—i.e. the principle of concurrent liability has been established.

Why should a plaintiff wish to plead a case in tort as well as in contract? There may be at least three reasons:

(a) To take advantage of the longer limitation period available to parties in tort as compared with contract. In both cases, the limitation period runs from when the cause of action accrues,[79] but in contract this is when the breach takes place,[80] whereas in tort it is from the time when the Plaintiff suffers damage, which may be later.[81]

(b) There may be clauses in the contract which, subject to arguments about unreasonableness under the Unfair Contract Terms Act 1977, exclude or limit the liability of the architect or engineer, but which would not affect the position in tort.

(c) There is often perceived need to "plug any gaps", so that any actions by the architect or engineer that are complained of are capable of being fitted into the tortious or contractual framework, one way or the other. That said, it is not easy to picture cases where an architect or engineer is in breach of his tortious duties without also being in breach of the contractual obligation of reasonable care and skill.[82]

However it does appear that it is open to a defendant to plead contributory negligence, even if the action is brought against him only in *contract*, in certain cases.[83]

78. [1995] 2 A.C. 145.

79. Limitation Act 1980, ss. 2 and 5.

80. See, e.g., *East India Co.* v. *Oditchurn and Paul* (1850) 7 Moo. PCC 85; Gibbs v. *Guild* (1881) 8 Q.B.D. 296 at 302.

81. E.g. *Cartlege* v. *E. Jopling & Sons Ltd* [1983] A.C. 758.

82. Although for an alternative view see the difficult decision in *Holt* v. *Payne Skillington and de Groot Collis* (1995) 79 B.L.R. 51 (C.A.) discussed at 6.2.4 below.

83. See para. 7.9 below.

Although, therefore, concurrent actions in tort and contract are possible, and indeed commonplace, this chapter focuses on a situation where a claim is made by a third party against an architect or engineer, aside from the contractual relationship.

3.6.2 Liability for negligent acts and for negligent misstatements

Until 1964 it appeared to be the law that a plaintiff was not entitled to sue in tort for what was termed "pure economic loss", i.e. purely financial loss without suffering any physical damage. The reasons for this policy decision, and the relevant cases, are not discussed here. In addition, it had been thought that damage to a building did not qualify as "physical damage" for these purposes, since what the plaintiff was generally claiming was the financial cost of repairing the building. However, in the cases of *Dutton* v. *Bognor Regis Urban District Council*[84] and *Anns* v. *London Borough Council of Merton*[85] local authorities were held liable to plaintiffs for negligent inspection by the building inspector of foundations (*Dutton*) and negligent passing of the contractor's plans which breached by law requirements as to foundations (*Anns*).

However, both of these cases were formally overruled by the House of Lords in *Murphy* v. *Brentwood District Council*,[86] a landmark decision by a seven-man House of Lords, in which the previous orthodoxy was restated. Any duty of care in tort owed to occupiers of property is limited. The owner or occupier will only be able to claim for physical injury or damage to himself or *other* property (i.e. property other than that which is the subject of the alleged negligence). The House of Lords reiterated that damage to the building in question—e.g. following a negligent survey or advice—is pure economic loss for these purposes, and therefore irrecoverable.[87]

84. [1972] 1 Q.B. 373.
85. [1977] 2 W.L.R. 1024.
86. [1991] 1 A.C. 398.
87. Three commonwealth jurisdictions have not followed Murphy, so that the Anns doctrine is, in broad terms, still good law there—the relevant decisions for New Zealand, Australia and Canada are, respectively, *Invercargill City Council* v. *Hamlyn* (1996) 78 B.L.R. 78 (P.C.); *Bryan* v. *Maloney*, High Court of Australia (1995) 11(4) Const. L.J. and *Winnipeg Condominium Corporation No. 36* v. *Bird Construction Company Limited* (1995) 11(4) Const. L.J. 306—see also article sum-

Since 1964, there has been a parallel action in tort based not on negligent *acts*, but on negligent *statements*. This action was founded on the House of Lords decision in *Hedley Byrne* v. *Heller & Partners*.[88] In that case a bank customer sought a reference from the bank regarding a company with which he was doing business and was told that it was financially sound, which was not in fact the position. The House of Lords held that the bank was liable. It restricted such liability to cases where there was a "special relationship" between the plaintiff and defendant, and where the defendant should foresee that the plaintiff might rely on the statement; or where the defendant had "assumed a responsibility" towards the plaintiff in making the statement.

The interrelationship between the above criteria had not been completely clarified even in the *Hedley Byrne* case itself and judges have sought to explore the position further.[89] However, in various decisions, in particular *Henderson* v. *Merrett Syndicates Limited* (see above) the test whether the defendant could be said to have assumed a responsibility to the plaintiff (which in effect is dependent on whether he could be said to have foreseen that the Plaintiff might rely) has become paramount. Lord Goff stated:

"It follows that, once the case is identified as falling within the Hedley Byrne principle, there should be no need to embark upon any further enquiry whether it is 'fair, just and reasonable' to impose liability for economic loss—a point which is, I consider, of some importance in the present case."

Since the closing off of liability for negligent acts (where economic loss is caused) following the *Murphy* decision of 1990, it appears that the possibility of suing under the separate *Hedley Byrne* doctrine for negligent *statements* has widened. The following cases are instructive.

3.6.2.1 Liability for omissions?

In *Henderson* v. *Merrett Syndicates*[90] Lord Goff said:

marising these decisions by I. Duncan Wallace Q.C. (the *Invercargill* decision had not at that point been endorsed by the Privy Council, as it subsequently was) at (1995) 11(4) Const. L.J. 249.

88. [1964] A.C. 465.
89. For a recent example see Neill L.J. in *Machin* v. *Adams* [1997] C.I.L.L. 1273.
90. [1995] 2 A.C. 145.

"An assumption of responsibility by, for example, a professional man, may give rise to liability in respect of negligent omissions as much as negligent acts of commission, as for example when a solicitor assumes responsibility for business on behalf of his client and omits to take a certain step, such as the service of a document, which falls within the responsibility so assumed by him."

In order words, professionals, and not just solicitors, can be liable for omissions as well as statements—although it may be noted that the above paragraph was concerned with solicitors.

3.6.2.2 Liability without reliance?

In *White* v. *Jones*[91] a negligent solicitor failed to carry out the testator's wish to alter a will, and was successfully sued by the disappointed beneficiaries. It was held that *Hedley Byrne* liability lay even though there was no reliance by the beneficiaries (they did not know of the instructions to alter the will) and the negligence consisted of an omission—nor was there any relationship between them and the solicitor, and certainly no special relationship. The House of Lords decision was three to two, and it may be relevant that the case involved solicitors again, but once more the possibility of *Hedley Byrne* liability being widened is clearly there.

3.6.2.3 Liability for acts as well as statements?

In *Conway* v. *Crowe Kelsey & Partners*,[92] Judge Newman Q.C. held that so long as there was an "assumption of responsibility" the distinction between negligent acts and statements was "unsustainable" and not relevant. He held that consulting engineers could be liable in tort under *Hedley Byrne* to their clients (the contractual limitation period had expired) because of negligent design and supervision consisting of actions.

In *Lancashire and Cheshire Association of Baptist Church Inc* v. *Seddon*[93] it had been held that where an architect submitted drawings to his employer, so that the employer had considered the design, it would be artificial to say that the architect was making a *statement* for the purposes of *Hedley Byrne* liability, as opposed to

91. [1995] 2 A.C. 207.
92. (1994) 39 Con. L.R. 1.
93. (1994) 65 B.L.R. 21.

carrying out an *act*. This may be correct in terms of language, but clearly it would mean that an architect who submits a drawing accompanied by some form of assurance that the drawing represents a workable design (or who approved as satisfactory an installation drawing of the sub-contractor, for example) would be in a less favourable position than the architect who merely submitted a drawing unaccompanied by any form of statement. This "debilitating distinction" was criticised by the editors of the Building Law Reports in their commentary on *Henderson*,[94] and, in the light of *Conway* (and *Henderson*) it must be doubted whether it is good law. There is therefore now no longer a distinction between an architect or engineer providing a drawing or design (act) and advising in relation to a drawing or design or approving the drawing of another person (statement).

3.6.2.4 Liability in tort wider than in contract?

In *Holt* v. *Payne Skillington and de Groot Collis*[95] the plaintiffs wanted to buy a property in Mayfair. They made clear to their professional team that having planning permission was vital. However, it was not a term of the contract with their advisers that the advisers would investigate planning permission. Nevertheless, the advisers went forward and took steps to ascertain the position, and then appeared to pass on incorrect information to the client.

Hirst L.J. said:

> "In our opinion there is no reason in principle why a *Hedley Byrne* type duty of care cannot arise in an overall set of circumstances where, by reference to certain limited aspects of those circumstances, the same parties enter into a contractual relationship involving more limited obligations than those imposed by the duty of care in tort. In such circumstances, the duty of care in tort and the duties imposed by the contract will be concurrent but not coextensive. The difference in scope between the two will reflect the more limited factual basis which gave rise to the contract and the absence of any term in that contract which precludes or restricts the wide duty of care in tort."

It therefore now appears that the architect who proffers advice on a certain matter (e.g. M&E services outside his contract) may

94. At (1994) 69 B.L.R. 31.
95. (1995) 77 B.L.R. 51 (C.A.).

still be liable, even though the advice was outside the retainer—so long as it was reasonable for the client to rely, etc. The remedies for architects and engineers must be first to check their contractual obligations, and to restrict their advice to what they are obliged to give; and secondly to insert in their contract conditions that they have no liability in tort to their client (and further, to protect themselves against any other third parties, that no party should rely upon their report which is intended for the client only).

The case may, however, need to be treated with some care, bearing in mind the often-cited words of Lord Scarman in *Tai Hing Cotton Mill Ltd* v. *Liu Chong Hing Bank Ltd*:[96]

> "Their Lordships do not, however, accept that the parties' mutual obligations in tort can be any greater than those to be found expressly or by necessary implication in their contract"

In summary:

- —Assumption of responsibility is now the dominant test. Note however that the disclaimers will still work in principle, e.g. *McCullagh* v. *Lane Fox & Partners*[97] and *Hedley Byrne* itself.
- —There may be liability for omissions.
- —There may be liability for negligent acts as well as statements.
- —The "special relationship" criterion seems to have been slightly relaxed.
- —Reliance is no longer strictly necessary.
- —Duties in tort can co-exist with contractual duties and *may* even be wider.

3.6.3 The Defective Premises Act 1972

Under this Act, architects and engineers may have statutory liabilities in respect of their design, supervision or other work in relation to *dwelling houses*. That liability may be to persons with whom they have no contractual relationship, e.g. future owners or tenants of the dwelling house. Section 1 of the Act provides as follows:

> "A person taking on work for or in connection with the provision of a dwelling (whether the dwelling is provided by the erection or by the conversion or enlargement of a building) owes a duty—

96. [1986] A.C. 80 at 107.
97. [1996] 1 E.G.L.R. 35.

(a) if the dwelling is provided to the order of any person, to that person; and
(b) without prejudice to paragraph (a) above, to every person who acquired an interest (whether legal or equitable) in the dwelling;

to see that the work which he takes on is done in a workmanlike, or as the case may be, professional manner, with proper materials and so that as regards that work the dwelling will be fit for habitation when completed."

New homes covered by the National House Builders' Registration Council (NHBC) scheme are also subject to the provisions of the Act, despite the apparent exemption in section 2, 4 and "approved scheme".[98]

However, the applicability of the Act may be restricted for architects and engineers by reason of the following:

(a) The limitation period runs from completion of the dwelling (section 1(5)). Therefore, later purchasers and tenants may have little time in which to commence actions.
(b) The Official Referee's Court has held that the Act applies only to cases involving the *creation* of the dwelling house, not to repair or rectification works on *existing* dwellings.[99]
(c) It appears that even if the work is carried out in an unprofessional or non-workmanlike way, with inadequate materials, no liability will arise unless the dwelling house is unfit for human habitation by reason of the work in question. In other words, it seems that section 1 imposes one obligation, reading the words of the section conjunctively, rather than several separate obligations. Authority for this view is contained in the Court of Appeal decision in *Alexander* v. *Mercouris*.[100] The Court of Appeal's views were obiter, but its reasoning was followed by His Honour Judge Lewis Q.C. in *Miles Charles Thompson and Others* v. *Clive Alexander & Partners*,[101] who felt that the "plain intention" of the Act was to ensure fitness for habitation, rather than to impose liability for "trivial" defects in design or construction.

98. See I. N. Duncan-Wallace Q.C. "Anns Beyond Repair" (1991) 107 L.Q.R. 228 at 243; and *Hudson's Building and Engineering Contracts* (11th ed., para. 1–361).
99. *Jacobs* v. *Morton & Partners* (1994) 72 B.L.R. 92.
100. [1979] 1 W.L.R. 1270 (C.A.).
101. (1992) 59 B.L.R. 81.

3.6.4 Liability to contractors and sub-contractors

3.6.4.1 Health and safety

In cases where an architect or engineer is alleged to have failed in his duties relating to health and safety on site, it will often be necessary to consider the impact of the Construction (Design and Management) Regulations 1994. These may impose liability on an architect or engineer where that person is appointed as "planning supervisor" under them. Although liability is criminal, not civil, there are potential implications for civil actions (see paragraph 3.4.8 above).

In general, the primary duty of a supervising officer, owed to his employer-client, is to do his best to ensure that a building is built as the contract documents provide. *How* the building is to be built ("buildability") and related safety matters are matters that fall within the responsibility of the contractor. Two cases are illustrative of this. In *Oldschool* v. *Gleeson (Contractors) Ltd*[102] Judge Stabb Q.C. said:

> "It seems abundantly plain that the duty of care of an architect or of a consulting engineer in no way extends into the area of how the work is carried out. Not only has he no duty to instruct the builder how to do the work, or what safety precautions to take, but he has no right to do so."

In *Clayton* v. *Woodman & Son (Builders)*[103] an experienced bricklayer employed by the contractor on a project suggested to the architect on site that there would be difficulties in cutting a chase in an existing gable wall, and suggested that a completely new wall should be built instead. The architect rejected this criticism. The chase was later cut in the wall without it being sufficiently shored up, and it collapsed, injuring the bricklayer. The Court of Appeal dismissed his action against the architect. Pearson L.J. said:

> "It is quite plain, in my view, both as a general proposition and under the particular contract in this case, that the builder, as the employer of the workman, has the responsibility at common law to provide a safe system of work. . . . The architect on the other hand is engaged as the agent of the owner of the building for whom the building is being erected, and his function is to make sure that in the end, when the work has been completed, the owner will have a building properly constructed in accordance with the contract and plans and specification and drawings. . . . The architect does

102. (1976) 4 B.L.R. 105.
103. [1962] 2 Q.B. 533.

not undertake (as I understand the position) to advise the builder as to what safety precautions should be taken or, in particular, as to how he should carry out his building operations. It is the function and the right of the builder to carry out his own building operations as he thinks fit and, of course, in doing so, to comply with the obligations to the workmen."

3.6.4.2 Certification etc

The architect or engineer supervising a construction contract is the agent of the client, the employer. Nevertheless, it is implicit in his position that he will act fairly "holding the balance between his client and the contractor".[104] It might be thought that where an architect or engineer administers the contract negligently, e.g. by undercertifying or by misapplying the contractual provisions in some way, a contractor who suffers a loss should have a remedy against him. However, despite an obiter dictum of the House of Lords,[105] which was subsequently taken up in two first instance decisions,[106] this is not the position. The leading case is now *Pacific Associates* v. *Baxter.*[107]

In that case, Pacific were contractors under a FIDIC engineering contract for the dredging of a lagoon in the Persian Gulf. Halcrow were the engineers appointed to administer the contract. Pacific claimed extensions of time and additional expense. Their application was rejected by Halcrow. Pacific then commenced arbitration proceedings against the employer, and settled an action at a figure of some £10 million. They then pursued Halcrow for the balance of the claim of some £45 million. The Court of Appeal struck the claim out as disclosing no cause of action.

The principles emanating from the decision are not entirely clear, partly because the case was affected by a clause in the engineer's contract with his employer excluding his liability *against the employer* for his defaults or omissions. However, two of the three Lords Justice would have come to the same decision in any event.[108] The crucial factor for the court was that the contractual mechanism

104. Lord Reid in *Sutcliffe* v. *Thackrah* [1974] A.C. 727.

105. *Arenson* v. *Arenson* [1977] A.C. 405.

106. *Shui On Construction Ltd* v. *Shui Kay Co. Ltd* (1985) 1 Const. L.J. 305, a decision of the Hong Kong Supreme Court; and *Michael Sallis & Co. Ltd* v. *Calil* (1988) 4 Const. L.J. 125.

107. (1988) 44 B.L.R. 33 (C.A.); [1990] Q.B. 993.

108. Purchas L.J. at p. 66; Ralph Gibson L.J. at p. 79.

between the three parties gave the contractor an alternative route by which he could recover his losses, namely by taking action against the employer (in this case under the arbitration clause in the FIDIC contract). In a later case, *Leon Engineering and Construction Co. Ltd* v. *Ka Duk Investment Co. Ltd,*[109] Bokhary J. regarded the principle of *Pacific* as being as follows:

"Where, first, there is adequate machinery under the contract between the employer and the contractor to enforce the contractor's rights thereunder and, secondly, there is no good reason at tender stage to suppose that such rights and machinery would not together provide a contractor with an adequate remedy, then, in general, a certifying architect or engineer does not owe to the contractor a duty in tort coterminous with the obligation in contract, owed to the contractor by the employer."

Logically, the same points should apply to a sub-contractor or any other party affected by the supervising officer's negligence.

Of course, where the employer is impecunious or insolvent, the alternative route would be of no value to the contractor. Only when such an alternative route is unavailable in principle will a contractor be able to avoid the principle of *Pacific*. Such cases will be rare. They could arise in poorly drafted or badly amended forms of contract, however, where the contractor is deprived of the power to ask the court or arbitrator to open up, review and revise architect's or engineer's certificates.

A leading commentator has suggested that liability may be founded where an architect or engineer makes a representation to the contractor, which is then relied upon, which is *outside* his duties under his terms of engagement. This could fall within the *Hedley Byrne* principle, and the *Pacific* restrictions would not apply.[110] The example given is the negligent assurance by an architect to an unpaid sub-contractor that ample money will be owing to the main contractor to meet the sub-contractor's account, in reliance upon which the sub-contractor continues to carry out work.

109. (1989) 47 B.L.R. 139.

110. I. Duncan Wallace Q.C., "Charter for the Construction Professional?" (1990) 6 Const. L.J. 207.

3.6.4.3 Provision of tender information etc

If the contractor is given pre-tender information which is incorrect—e.g. an incorrect soil survey—the question then arises whether the contractor has any rights against the person who provided the information. Often such information would be incorporated into the contract. When that happens the contractor has a right, if any, against the employer under the building or engineering contract and, it seems, following the principles of *Pacific* outlined above, that no collateral action could be brought against the architect or engineer who prepared the survey. Where the survey, however, is not incorporated, the contractor may have an action under the *Hedley Byrne* principle if the architect or engineer can be said to have "assumed a responsibility" towards the contractor (*Henderson* v. *Merrett Syndicates*[111]—and see paragraph 3.6.2 above). In *Dillingham Ltd* v. *Down*[112] the possibility of such an action was mooted, although liability was not in fact found on the facts in that case. The person providing site information to the contractor (in this case the employer) was not negligent because the specification required the contractor to satisfy himself about site conditions; the contractor made no inquiries of the employer and took no independent advice from anyone else; and the contractor was clearly anxious to obtain the contract.

Similarly the Canadian Supreme Court held in *South Nation River Conservation Authority* v. *Auto Concrete Curb Ltd*[113] that an engineer owed no duty to advise a prospective contractor of the need to obtain a work permit for the particular form of dredging that he proposed to carry out (which was unconventional, but not barred by the contract). The court regarded it as well-established that the method by which a contractor decides to carry out work (i.e. where a discretion is allowed to him) is within his sphere of responsibility.

3.6.4.4 Exception for deliberate acts

The contractor will generally have an action, however, where an architect or engineer *deliberately* misapplies the contract or acts

111. [1995] 2 A.C. 145.
112. (1972) 13 B.L.R. 97.
113. (1995) 11 Const. L.J. 155.

fraudulently. This is apparent, for example, from the discussion in *Lubenham Fidelities & Investments Co. Ltd* v. *South Pembrokeshire District Council*,[114] although in that case it was held that the breach by the architect was not deliberate but merely a case of the architect doing his "incompetent best".

The evidential difficulties in such cases will nevertheless be formidable. In *John Mowlem & Co. Plc* v. *Eagle Star Insurance Co. Ltd*[115] a contractor alleged that the project architect had conspired with an insurance company to have the contractor removed from its position on the project. The contractor overcame the employer's initial attempts to strike its action out, but was forced to abandon its allegations altogether some six months after the substantive trial began.[116]

3.7. DAMAGES

3.7.1 Introduction

In awarding damages for breach of contract, the courts attempt to put the innocent party in the position that he would have been in if the contract had been performed properly.[117] The basis for damages in tort is that the injured party must be placed, so far as possible, in the position that he would have been in had the negligent act not taken place (the principle of *restitutio in integrum*).[118]

The plaintiff must of course establish a causal link between the breach of contract and the loss suffered. In *Hill Samuel Bank Ltd* v. *Frederick Brand Partnership & Others*[119] the court held that although a firm of structural engineers was negligent in failing to obtain calculations from the designers of proprietary cladding, it was unlikely that its clients would have decided not to proceed with the installation of the cladding even if they had obtained the calculations. Thus, it was held, the loss suffered was not caused by the negligence.

Remoteness must also be considered. In order to be recoverable

114. (1986) 33 B.L.R. 46 (C.A.), especially at p. 75.
115. (1992) 62 B.L.R. 126.
116. *The Times*, 2 August 1995.
117. *Robinson* v. *Harman* (1948) 1 Exch. 850.
118. See, e.g., *Livingstone* v. *Rawyards Coal Co.* (1880) 5 App. Cas. 25.
119. (1994) 45 Con. L.R. 141.

the plaintiff must generally show that the loss arose naturally in the usual course of things, or was within the actual or presumed contemplation of the parties at the time when the contract was made as being the probable result of any future breach. These alternatives are often referred to as the first and second limbs of the rule in *Hadley* v. *Baxendale*.[120]

It should be noted that where deceit or fraudulent misrepresentation is proved the plaintiff is entitled to recover damages in principle corresponding to *all* his losses suffered, without regard to foreseeability or remoteness. This principle was reiterated by the House of Lords in *Smith New Court Securities Ltd* v. *Scrimgeour Vickers (Assessment Management) Ltd.*[121]

3.7.2 South Australia Asset Management Corporation v. *York Montague*

It is likely that the House of Lords' reasoning in this case[122] will be of wide significance in the area of causation and recoverable loss. Indeed, an Official Referee has suggested extra-judicially that the decision establishes a new test of liability in professional negligence cases.[123] Three cases on appeal involve plaintiffs who had advanced loans on the strength of what turned out to be negligent valuations. The main issue was whether they could recover, as part of their damages, losses that they had suffered only because of a fall in the property market in the early 1990s (which drastically reduced the value of their security when they came to repossess).

The House of Lords held that they could not. Lord Hoffman drew a distinction between cases where the professional advises as to a particular course of action, and cases where he merely gives information. In the first, he is liable (if negligent) for the foreseeable consequences following from that course of action being adopted; in the second, only for the foreseeable consequences of the information being wrong. Since the valuers only provided information, they were liable only for damages corresponding to the difference between the security that the plaintiffs thought they had

120. (1854) 9 Exch. 341.
121. [1996] 4 All E.R. 769 (H.L.).
122. (1996) 80 B.L.R. 1 (H.L.).
123. H.H. Judge Thornton Q.C., "Current Official Referee Practice" (1998) 14 Const. L.J. 3 at 4.

(the valuers' figure) and the security that they actually had (the actual values at the time of the valuation).

Architects and engineers sometimes provide information only (e.g. proposing designs, submitting plans or drawings etc.) and sometimes advise on a course of action (regarding procurement strategy, whether to terminate a building contract, whether to engage a particular trade specialist etc.). Indeed the distinction may sometimes be difficult to apply.[124] In the light of *South Australia* they should exercise particular care where their work falls within the "advice-giving" category.

3.7.3 Damages for negligent design leading to a defective building

In general, where a plaintiff has suffered loss relating to a defective building, there are two principal ways in which that loss can be assessed. One is based on the diminution in value of the building. For example, in cases of surveyors' negligence in relation to pre-contract surveys, the measure of damages will be the difference between the value of the property as indicated in the negligent survey and its actual (lower) value.[125]

Conversely, in cases where an employer has sued for negligent building work undertaken by a contractor, a second method is appropriate. Here the employer recovers the cost of repair, or reinstatement, of the defective work.[126]

In cases of negligent design by architects and engineers the "cost of repair" basis appears to be the usual starting point. For example, in *Bevan Investments* v. *Blackhall & Struthers* a businessman instructed an architect to design a recreation centre comprising an ice rink, squash courts and sauna facilities. During construction, the design was found to be at fault and the businessman's new advisers proposed a modified design to which the work could be completed. The plaintiff businessman claimed, among other things, the cost of completion to the modified design.

The New Zealand Court of Appeal held that the *prima facie* rule in actions against architects and engineers was that damages would

124. As noted by H.H. Judge Thornton Q.C., *op.cit.*, at 8, and by the Building Law Reports editors commenting on this case at 80 B.L.R. 6E.

125. *Watts* v. *Morrow* [1991] 4 All E.R. 937.

126. *East Ham Corporation* v. *Sunley (Bernard) & Son Ltd* [1966] A.C. 406.

be assessed on the cost of reinstatement basis, although this rule was not inflexible. The decision has often been cited in English cases.

The House of Lords decision in *Ruxley Electronics and Construction Ltd* v. *Forsyth*[127] may provide the basis of a third measure of damages. A contractor contracted to build a swimming pool at Mr Forsyth's home. Although Mr Forsyth stipulated a requirement of a depth of 7'6", the pool as built was only 6'9" at its deepest point. It was found as a fact, however, that this did not in any way hinder diving, nor did it affect the value of the property. The pool could not be repaired and either had to be left as it was or completely replaced at a cost of £21,560, which was more than the contract sum.

Mr Forsyth succeeded on liability and asked for £21,560 in damages. The House of Lords, in upholding the trial judge's original decision, awarded him only £2,500 for loss of amenity representing the lost depth. It held that it was not forced to give him £21,560 or nothing at all.

Thus, in a designer's negligence case, it is open to a court to award damages representing the loss of amenity to someone who has suffered from the defective design, rather than awarding either nil damages or complete replacement costs. Such damages will be particularly appropriate in domestic cases (as *Ruxley* was) rather than commercial ones; and also in cases where the plaintiff required something that has subjective or idiosyncratic value. In *Ruxley*, for example, the court gave examples of the person who stipulates a design that most people would regard as having no objective value (e.g. someone who requires a lurid set of bathroom tiles or contracts for the building of a grotesque folly).

3.7.4 Negligent design leading to other losses

In *Turner Page Music Ltd* v. *Torres Design Associates Ltd*[128] the judge found that the defendant's design of a cinema was negligent, in that there was inadequate provision for a fire escape. It was held that a correct design would still have led to an increase in the contract sum, but that the plaintiff was entitled to claim for the *extra* costs

127. [1995] 3 All E.R. 268 (H.L.).
128. [1997] C.I.L.L. 1263.

in connection with having to arrange for the work to be priced separately and by way of variations.

3.7.5 Where the design misleads the client as to cost etc

Where a designer gives an incorrect estimate of a project, a good deal depends on what the plaintiff does in reliance upon the estimate. One difficulty for the plaintiff is that he may often be able to show no loss, even when there is negligence. This is because, if he proceeds with the works, he faces the argument that the works would always have cost the higher figure, and he has paid for and received the value of them. In such cases damages would be limited to such matters as reasonably foreseeable consequential costs, e.g. administrative and refinancing costs.

The situation is different where the plaintiff can show that he would have taken a materially different course of action had the correct advice been given. In *Gable House Estates Ltd* v. *The Halpern Partnership & Bovis Construction Ltd*[129] an architect provided his client with a schedule which led the client to believe that there would be more available office space in a building than in fact there was. The judge found on the facts that, had the client been given the correct figures, he would probably not have proceeded with the course of action that he in fact took, namely to redevelop the building. In these cases the usual measure of damages will be the wasted expenditure regarding the works carried out, although if the client later sells the building other factors may need to be considered.

3.7.6 Damages for errors during a construction phase

In general, plaintiffs on the construction phase will often take action against their architects and engineers for the following failures:

(a) Failure to spot contractor's defects. Here, the damages are generally the cost of repair. The architect or engineer will often be able to recover a contribution from the contractor.

(b) Failure to give timeous or correct information, or negligence in relation to the giving of instructions, where (in

129. (1995) 48 Con. L.R. 1—the case takes up the entire volume. It is discussed at para. 3.4.11.2 above.

either case) the employer has to pay damages or loss and expense to the contractor under the building contract.[130] *Prima facie*, the damages will be the loss and expense paid.

(c) Overvaluation. Here the employer may be unable or unwilling to recoup monies paid to the contractor on overvalued certificates. Valuation is generally the function of the quantity surveyor under the standard forms of building contract.[131] The architect or engineer will often be able at least to recover a contribution from the quantity surveyor, if one is appointed.

3.7.7 Betterment

What is the plaintiff's position where he corrects a defect in building works that has been caused by the architect's or engineer's negligence, but recovers some sort of windfall by repairing to a particularly high standard? The test is whether the plaintiff acted reasonably. In *Board of Governors of the Hospitals for Sick Children* v. *McLoughlin & Harvey plc*[132] the court noted:

"The mere fact that the result of the plaintiff's work is to produce a better building than he had before ... does not necessarily mean that he had acted unreasonably or unforeseeably. ... A change in, say, the building regulations ... may have required the plaintiff to build to a higher standard."

The judge said that it was not for the court to consider *de novo* what costs should have been incurred as a check upon the reasonableness of the plaintiff's action or otherwise. The court will thus not be over-critical of the plaintiff's course of action.

Similarly, in *Richard Roberts Holdings* v. *Douglas Smith Stimson*[133] the judge said:

"I think that the law can be shortly summarised. If the only practicable method of overcoming the consequences of a defendant's breach of contract is to build to a higher standard than the contract had required, the plaintiff may recover the cost of building to that higher standard. If, however, a plaintiff needing to carry out works because of a defendant's breach of contract, chooses to build to a higher standard than is strictly necessary, the courts will, unless the new works are so different as to break the chain

130. *East Ham Corporation* v. *Sunley (Bernard) & Son Ltd* [1966] A.C. 406.
131. See, e.g., cl.13.4.1.1 of JCT 80.
132. (1987) 19 Con L.R. 25.
133. (1988) 46 B.L.R. 50 at 69.

of causation, award him the cost of the works less a credit to the defendant in respect of betterment."

Of course, if the plaintiff *chooses* to improve the building unnecessarily he will have to give credit.[134] In *Board of Governors of the Hospital for Sick Children* (above) Judge Newey held that in certain cases "a plaintiff's own action in failing to mitigate his loss by, for example, carrying out more remedial work than he needs, may in itself break the chain of causation".

3.7.8 Mitigation and the plaintiff's impecuniosity

An impoverished employer may often plead that he is unable to carry out important repair or remedial work, following an architect's or engineer's negligence, because of lack of funds. The House of Lords in *Liesbosch Dredger (Owners)* v. *SS Edison*[135] held that, in general, losses arising because of the plaintiff's impecuniosity are not recoverable. However, in subsequent cases this principle has been somewhat weakened.

—In the *Bevan* case referred to above, the court accepted that the owner had acted reasonably and commercially in awaiting the outcome of the litigation on liability before embarking on costly reinstatement work, and expressed some doubt whether the *Liesbosch* case still represented good law.

—In *Dodd Properties (Kent) Ltd* v. *Canterbury City Council*,[136] a case in tort, the Court of Appeal distinguished *Liesbosch* by holding that the decision to postpone reinstatement was not to be regarded as a product of impecuniosity, but to be seen as a decision based on commercial good sense.

—In *Perry* v. *Sidney Philips*[137] Kerr L.J. felt that the authority of certain statements emanating from the *Liesbosch* case was "consistently being attenuated" by more recent decisions and said:

"If it is reasonably foreseeable that the plaintiff may be unable to

134. *British Westinghouse Electric & Manufacturing Co. Ltd* v. *Underground Electric Railways Co. of London Ltd* [1912] A.C. 673.
135. [1933] A.C. 449.
136. [1980] 1 W.L.R. 433.
137. (1982) 22 B.L.R. 120 (C.A.).

mitigate or remedy the consequence of the other party's breach as soon as he would have done if he had been provided with the necessary means to do so from the other party, then it seems to me that the principle of the *Liesbosch* no longer applies in its full rigour."

—In *Mattocks* v. *Mann*[138] it was held that only in exceptional circumstances could the impecuniosity of a plaintiff be isolated as a separate cause so as to bring the *Liesbosch* principle into consideration.

3.7.9 The relationship between causation, betterment and mitigation

The judge in *Skandia Property (UK) Ltd* v. *Thames Water Utilities Ltd*[139] undertook an examination of these three areas. In this case, a fracture occurred in one of the defendant water company's underground mains in Pall Mall, which caused a flood in the plaintiff's basement. There was no dispute about the defendant's liability pursuant to the Water Act 1981. However, it was held that the plaintiff could not recover for the cost of making the basement watertight, because there was no causal link between his making it so and the defendant's admitted breach—in other words, what caused the plaintiff to act was not the defendant's wrongdoing, but "a sensible desire to have a watertight building".

The judge noted that causation was a matter of fact, to be determined by the judge's common sense. It was up to the plaintiff to prove causation and, if he relied on a decision of his which he said was reasonable, it was for him to prove its reasonableness. Conversely, it was up to a *defendant* to plead and prove, if he wished to, the arguments of betterment and/or mitigation. The judge said:

"The distinction between betterment and mitigation is not one of mere characterisation or nomenclature. The theory of betterment requires a plaintiff to give credit as an absolute obligation, while the duty to mitigate loss requires him to act reasonably, the onus being on the defendant in both cases to plead and prove either his entitlement to a credit or the plaintiffs' failure to act reasonably."

138. [1993] R.T.R. 13.
139. [1997] C.I.L.L. 1293.

3.7.10 The impact of contributory negligence

To what extent is it open to an architect or engineer, found liable to his employer for negligent administration or supervision of a building contract, to argue that the employer is contributorily negligent—for example in failing, through his clerk of works, to notice defective work—and should have his damages reduced accordingly? Such a defence was successful in *Kensington and Westminster and Chelsea Area Health Authority* v. *Wettern Composites*[140] where His Honour Judge Smout Q.C. reduced the employer's damages by 20 per cent where his clerk of works failed to notice poor workmanship. However, this case may be regarded as not representative of the current trend.

Contributory negligence was given a statutory foundation in the Law Reform (Contributory Negligence) Act 1945, section 1 of which states:

> "Where any person suffers damage as the result partly of his own fault and partly of the fault of any other person or persons, a claim in respect of that damage shall not be defeated by reason of the fault of the person suffering the damage, but the damages recoverable in respect thereof shall be reduced to such extent as the court thinks just and equitable having regard to the claimant's share in the responsibility for the damage."

The defence is frequently raised in road traffic or personal injury cases, but fits less easily into contractual situations. In *Barclays Bank plc* v. *Fairclough Building Ltd*[141] Nourse L.J. said:

> "It ought to be a cause of general concern that the law should have got into such a state that a contractor who was in breach of two of the main obligations expressly undertaken by him in a standard form building contract was able to persuade the judge in the court below that the building owner's damages should be reduced by 40 per cent because of his own negligence in not preventing the contractor from committing the breaches . . . It ought to have been perfectly obvious that the [1945 Act] was never intended to obtrude the defence of contributory negligence into an area of the law where it has no business to be."

Contributory negligence is thus restricted to the third of the following three categories of contractual obligation formulated by the court in *Forsikringsaktieselskapet Vesta* v. *Butcher*:[142]

140. (1984) 31 B.L.R. 57.
141. [1995] 1 All E.R. 289 (C.A.).
142. [1988] 2 All E.R. 43 (C.A.).

(i) where a party's liability arises from breach of a contractual provision which does not depend on negligence (this could, for example, apply to an obligation to design to a set standard);

(ii) where the liability arises from an express contractual obligation to take care, but which does not in fact correspond to any duty which would exist in tort (for example, an obligation to design using reasonable care and skill but again to a set standard);

(iii) where the liability for breach of contract is the same as, and co-extensive with, a liability in tort independently of the existence of a contract.

In fact, most architects' and engineers' cases will be within the third category, so that the defence would be available in principle (even if the plaintiff pleads breach of contract only, and does not specifically allege negligence).[143] This does not mean that it will be applicable in practice. In *E. H. Cardy & Sons Ltd* v. *Paul Roberts & Associates*[144] Judge Bowsher Q.C. rejected the argument that the client should have checked his architect's survey in the words:

> "There is little point in hiring a professional to do work if it is to be said that the client has a duty to check the professional's work. . . . You do not hire a dog and bark yourself."

It may thus be that architects and engineers will, in practice, not readily be able to persuade courts to reduce their damages by reason of this defence.

3.7.11 Miscellaneous heads of damage

The substantive relief recoverable by a client in a professional negligence action against an architect or engineer has already been discussed earlier in this section. Here we briefly examines miscellaneous possible heads of damage.

143. For an argument that contributory negligence should in principle be capable of being raised in the other two categories as well, see a note by A. Burnett on *Schering Agrochemicals Ltd* v. *Resibel Nusa* at (1993) 109 L.Q.R. 175. See also Law Commission Working Paper No 114 (1990), "Contributory Negligence as a Defence in Contract".

144. (1994) 38 Con. L.R. 79.

3.7.11.1 Lost profits

Subject to the usual rule as to foreseeability and remoteness, this head of damage may be recovered in principle. If the professional cannot reasonably be expected to know at the time when the contract was made of any special loss that the client might suffer, he may only be liable for notional lost profits corresponding to what was reasonably foreseeable at the time when the contract was made.[145] In *Bevan* v. *Blackhall & Struthers*,[146] the facts of which are discussed at paragraph 3.7.3 above, the New Zealand Court of Appeal had to make an assessment of what the profits of a plaintiff's recreation centre might have been had the architect carried out his design obligations properly, and took into account the plaintiff's enthusiasm and business ability in reaching its figure.

3.7.11.2 Damages for inconvenience, distress and loss of amenity

The courts have generally taken a restrictive view of the extent to which such damages are recoverable in contract cases.[147] However, they may be recoverable in three areas:

(i) Where the object of the contract is the provision of pleasure. Holiday contracts are typical of this category. But construction contracts will rarely be included. In *Knott* v. *Bolton*[148] the Court of Appeal declined to hold that a contract by which an architect was to build a couple their "dream home" with a wide and impressive staircase (which he did not do) was within this category. However, a contract to build a games room or something of purely aesthetic value could conceivably qualify. In *Hutchinson* v. *Harris*[149] the Court of Appeal declined to award damages for distress following a finding of architect's negligence, for a plaintiff who had lost the use of her premises, since

145. *Victoria Laundry (Windsor) Ltd* v. *Newman Industries Ltd* [1949] 1 All E.R. 997.
146. (1977) 11 B.L.R. 78.
147. *Addis* v. *Gramophone Co. Ltd* [1909] A.C. 488 (H.L.).
148. (1995) 45 Con. L.R. 127 (C.A.).
149. (1978) 10 B.L.R. 19 (C.A.).

she was intending to convert and renovate her house for commercial purposes.

(ii) In cases where other means of assessing damages are inappropriate. Damages for loss of amenity may be awarded in cases, particularly those having some "domestic" element, where the usual measure of damages may be felt to over-compensate the plaintiff—see *Ruxley Electronics & Construction Ltd* v. *Forsyth*, discussed above at paragraph 3.7.3.

(iii) Where the distress etc. is directly related to physical inconvenience and discomfort caused by the professional's breach.

In *Watts* v. *Morrow*,[150] a case of surveyor's negligence, Bingham L.J. summarised the position relating to damages for distress and inconvenience as follows:

> "Where the very object of a contract is to provide pleasure, relaxation, peace of mind or freedom from molestation, damages will be awarded if the fruit of the contract is not provided or if the contrary result is procured instead. If the law did not cater for this exceptional category of case it would be defective. A contract to survey the condition of a house for a prospective purchaser does not, however, fall within this exceptional category.
>
> In cases not falling within this exceptional category, damages are in my view recoverable for physical inconvenience and discomfort caused by the breach and mental suffering directly related to that inconvenience and discomfort. If those effects are foreseeably suffered during a period when defects are repaired I am prepared to accept that they sound in damages even though the cost of the repairs is not recoverable as such. But I also agree that award should be restrained."[151]

3.7.11.3 Costs of alternative accommodation while repairs are being carried out

These are frequently allowed in actions by tenants for landlords' breaches of repairing covenants (e.g. *Lubren* v. *Lambeth LBC*).[152]

150. [1991] 4 All E.R. 937 (C.A.).

151. For reviews of quantum of damages for these types of cases see K. Franklin, "Damages for Heartache: The Award of General Damages for Inconvenience and Distress in Building Cases" (1988), Const. L.J. 4 and "More Heartache: A Review of the Award of General Damages in Building Cases" (1992) Const. L.J. 8.

152. (1987) 20 H.L.R. 165.

There seems no reason in principle why they cannot be made in architects' and engineers' negligence cases in appropriate circumstances.

3.7.11.4 Managerial time and costs

These costs were recovered by a corporate plaintiff in *Babcock Energy Ltd* v. *Lodge Sturtevant Ltd.*[153] In this case, however, the plaintiff was able to provide detailed records of the time claimed, and the judge noted that "an untoward degree of time" had been spent by the manager who had otherwise been employed to sort out problems of the nature that had arisen. It should be noted, however, that the costs incurred by the corporate bodies' staff dealing with litigation arc not recoverable, except to the extent that one of their staff acts as an in-house expert in litigation, in which case some costs (excluding profit) may be recoverable.[154]

3.7.11.5 Lost opportunity to obtain cheaper quotations

In *Corfield* v. *Grant*[155] a hotelier successfully argued that because of the architect's delay in progressing matters, he had lost the opportunity to obtain competitive quotations, since he had had to work speedily and obtain whatever quotations he could in the time available. The judge awarded £500 to represent the lost opportunity of obtaining cheaper quotations.

3.7.11.6 The cross-claim for fees

A finding of negligence against an architect or engineer does not mean that the client gets away with paying nothing. For one thing, the architect's or engineer's contract will often be in severable parts, so that he is entitled to be paid to the extent that he has performed a certain part properly. Further, if a client has the defective professional work re-done by someone else, and claims that other person's fees as part of his damages, he must give credit for the fact that, had the negligent architect performed properly, the client

153. [1994] C.I.L.L. 982.
154. *Re Nossen's Patent* [1969] 1 All E.R. 775.
155. (1992) 59 B.L.R. 102 (Q.B.D.).

would still have had to pay that architect's fees. This is an application of the principle expounded at paragraph 3.7.1 above and is exemplified in *Hutchinson* v. *Harris*[156] where the court held that the plaintiff had to give credit for the architect's fees in her successful damages claim, so as to avoid double recovery.

It now seems likely that despite some reservations in the Court of Appeal decision in *Hutchinson*[157] there is no reason why the fees of a professional cannot be abated, i.e. reduced to reflect the work that simply has not been done by the professional in question. Judge Hicks Q.C. reduced the architect's right to fees accordingly in *Turner Page Music Ltd* v. *Torres Design Associates Ltd.*[158]

156. (1978) 10 B.L.R. 19 (C.A.).

157. Waller L.J. was influenced by the fact that abatement was not pleaded or argued in the court below and held that it could lead to a double recovery for the plaintiff. Stevenson L.J. had "the greatest difficulty" in applying the principle of abatement to a claim for professional services. However, none of these reasons are particularly cogent, it is submitted.

158. [1997] C.I.L.L. 1265.

CHAPTER 4

QUANTITY SURVEYORS AND CLAIMS CONSULTANTS

4.1. INTRODUCTION

This chapter concerns those professionals whose primary functions are concerned with the financial aspects of construction projects. Although quantity surveying and claims consultancy are discussed as separate professions, the services provided by each of them very often overlap, principally because, while quantity surveying is a relatively old profession, the profession of construction claims consultancy is a relatively modern one which evolved from the practice of quantity surveying, so that the large majority of claims consultants practising today are quantity surveyors, and claims consultants' practices nowadays usually offer traditional quantity surveying services as well as various other types of services, mainly legal in nature.

4.2. QUANTITY SURVEYORS

4.2.1 Definition

The traditional function of a quantity surveyor as defined in 1870 in *Taylor* v. *Hall* was "taking out in detail the measurements and quantities from plans prepared by an architect for the purpose of enabling builders to calculate the estimates for which they would execute the plans".[1] The functions of quantity surveyors have developed considerably since this case in the last century in line with the development of the construction industry and the way

1. *Taylor* v. *Hall* (1870) 4 I.R.C.L. 467 at 476.

in which projects are carried out and administered and with the development of the contracts that govern such matters into the present-day construction industry.

Generally speaking, a quantity surveyor's functions cover three stages of a construction project. These stages are, first, during the development and procurement stage prior to the building contract being entered into, secondly during the construction of the project, and thirdly after its completion. Although independent quantity surveyors will, usually, be retained by an employer to carry out their various functions, with contractors or sub-contractors usually employing their in-house staff to deal with financial aspects on behalf of the contractor or sub-contractor, in some circumstances contractors or sub-contractors will also employ independent quantity surveyors to carry out quantity surveying functions on their behalf.

Work carried out by a quantity surveyor prior to the building contract being entered into will include advising the employer of the estimated cost of the project; preparation of a detailed bill of quantities from the architects' and engineers' drawings for the purposes of submitting to contractors to submit a tender; preparing schedules for contractors to tender, and doing costs comparisons of submitted tenders and advising the employer upon submitted tenders; and negotiating with one of more of the tendering contractors. Other ancillary tasks may include advising the employer upon the form of contract to be used or on the rate of liquidated and ascertained damages to be inserted into the contract. If acting for a contractor, a quantity surveyor's functions may include pricing a bill of quantities or estimating from tender documentation submitted what would be the cost of the works, advising the contractor upon an amount to tender and, similarly, negotiating with an employer.

During the construction of the project, the role of a quantity surveyor retained by the employer may be one of administering the building contract in its entirety, although this is usually carried out by an architect or engineer.[2] Usually, however, the quantity surveyor's role during the construction phase of a building contract will be subordinate to that of the architect administering the project generally, and will be confined to measuring work at periodic

2. See Ch. 3, para 3.5.

intervals for the purposes of valuing work properly carried out by the contractor for the purposes of interim payments, including valuing variations, assessing claims by the contractor, valuing nominated sub-contractors' accounts or advising the architect on the calculation of liquidated damages for late completion, particularly where partial possession is taken or there are phased or sectional completion requirements. In most standard forms of building contract in use today, the precise functions which the quantity surveyor is to carry out are described in detail.

After the completion of the project, the quantity surveyor will value the contractor's final account and determine the loss and expense and damages to which a contractor may be due as a result of permissible claims under the contract and advise the employer as to these matters.

No professional qualifications are required for a person to practise as a quantity surveyor. The Royal Institution of Chartered Surveyors, however, provides professional training and examinations for quantity surveyors and has a prescribed code of conduct for its members. It has disciplinary procedures and makes professional indemnity insurance and continuing education compulsory. The Royal Institution of Chartered Surveyors provides professional qualifications at Fellowship and Associate level (FRICS and ARICS respectively). The term "quantity surveyor" is used to describe those carrying out the usual functions of quantity surveyors across the whole range of experience and qualifications from junior level up to qualified Fellows of the Royal Institution, and whether in independent practice or employed by an organisation such as a contractor or sub-contractor. However, only RICS-qualified surveyors may use the expression "chartered quantity surveyors".

The Royal Institution of Chartered Surveyors provides a standard form of appointment. For many years, quantity surveyors' remuneration was based upon recommended fee scales. Commercial bargaining resulted in their gradual fall into disuse over the past 20 years and they were finally abolished in May 1998 as a result of concerns that they were anti-competitive and might offend the impending enactment of the Competition Act. The level of remuneration is, therefore, a matter entirely for negotiation and agreement. Under the Housing Grants Construction and Regeneration Act 1996, the retainer contracts of quantity surveyors are subject to its provisions. The Act is discussed in more detail in

Chapter 9[3] but, in brief, its essential provisions so far as quantity surveyors are concerned are the right to interim payments, restrictions on the right of an employer to make set-offs against fees due, and a statutory right to adjudication in the event of a dispute.[4]

4.2.2 Standard of care

The obligation of the quantity surveyor, like all other professionals, will be to use reasonable skill and care in the performance by him of his duties. This obligation is imposed by section 13 of the Supply of Goods and Services Act 1982 into a quantity surveyor's contract of retainer (in the absence of any express term to the contrary) and will also be implied by common law so far as any possible tortious obligations of a quantity surveyor are concerned. The starting point for the degree of skill and care and how that should be exercised will, as always, be the terms of the quantity surveyor's contract and the definition of the duties which he is required to perform under that contract. The general standard required will, however, be that of a reasonably competent quantity surveyor. Since the levels of expertise, experience and qualifications vary greatly across the range of those offering quantity surveying services, is the exercise of reasonable skill and care to be judged by reference to the level of quantity surveyors which the client chooses to engage? For example, will a different level of skill be required from a relatively junior surveyor offering routine quantity surveying services to a professionally qualified chartered surveyor? Although it could be said that different standards of quantity surveying services are likely to be expected according to the level of surveyor selected, the same general principles are applied whatever the level, in accordance with the test as laid down by McNair J. in *Bolam* v. *Friern Hospital Management Committee*:[5]

> "Where you get a situation which involves the use of some special skill or competence ... the test is the standard of the ordinary skilled man exercising and professing to have that special skill. A man need not possess the highest expert skill ... it is sufficient if he exercises the ordinary skill of the ordinary competent man exercising that particular art."

3. Below, p. 211.
4. See RICS Form of Enquiry and Fee Quotation for the Appointment of a Quantity Surveyor and RICS Professional Charges for Quantity Surveying Services (July 1988).
5. [1957] 1 W.L.R. 582 at 586.

Generally, therefore, and in accordance with general principles, where a professional professes to have a special skill, he will be judged by the level of competence exercised by those who ordinarily exercise that skill. In the case of a quantity surveyor, therefore, this means that in determining whether there has been a breach of the obligation of the use of reasonable skill and care, he will be judged by the level of a reasonably skilled and competent quantity surveyor, whatever his actual level of experience and competence. The situation may be different if, for example, the contract of engagement is somehow limited to fix a level of services which would enable a particular level of skill to be exercised rather than that which would be applied by the test of the reasonably skilled and competent practitioner. This, however, could be considered to be no more than allowing a level of service to be provided which would be considered "reasonable" in the exercise of skill and care within the definition of the implied obligation. In *Cardy* v. *Taylor*,[6] an unqualified person practising as an architect was judged by the standards of a reasonably competent architect. An extension of the general principles will be likely to cover the situation where quantity surveyors carry out functions exercised by members of other professions, for example, architects and lawyers, which they frequently do, especially so in the case of claims consultants, which are dealt with later in this chapter. Although there are no English cases directly on the point, a leading textbook[7] suggests that in such circumstances the quantity surveyor should be judged by the standards of the other professions, which would appear to be a logical application of the general principles laid down by the courts and is in line with what could be considered to be the reasonable expectations of the parties as to the performance by the quantity surveyor of those functions which he contracts with his client to provide. This is, however, a question of degree. Thus, if a quantity surveyor agrees to give advice in the nature of legal advice, for example, upon the terms of an appropriate form of building contract and he advises negligently, it will be no excuse for him to argue that, although the legal advice was wrong, he was nevertheless not negligent because he was not a lawyer. The reason for this result is that it would be open to the quantity surveyor to express an opinion

6. (1994) 38 Con. L.R. 79.
7. *Jackson & Powell* (4th ed.), 2–87.

but, in the discharge of his obligation to use reasonable skill and care, to advise the client that he did not carry the particular level of legal expertise required and advise the client to seek specialist advice. On the other hand, however, there may be certain circumstances where, by virtue of the tasks carried out by the quantity surveyor, he would be deemed to have a sufficient knowledge of certain principles of law to be able properly to discharge his obligation and exercise reasonable skill and care. Thus, in the case of *B. L. Holdings Limited v. Robert J. Wood & Partners*,[8] where it was accepted that when an architect acts in a field of activity commonly carried out by architects, in which knowledge and understanding of certain principles of law were required, the architect must have sufficient knowledge of those principles. Again, in *West Faulkner Associates* v. *London Borough of Newham*,[9] an architect misconstrued a provision in a standard form of building contract which deprived the client of a right or opportunity to determine a building contract, and the court held that the architect's construction of the clauses was not one which a reasonably competent architect could or should have held, in that at the very least he ought to have advised his client to seek legal advice. It seems to be expected that in certain of the functions carried out by quantity surveyors, for example administration of a building contract, a quantity surveyor would similarly be required to have a sufficient knowledge of the legal principles and would not be excused from liability if his application or understanding of sufficient principles of law to enable him to properly discharge his functions proved to be inadequate.

The connotation of reasonable skill and care means that not every error will be negligent. The law recognises that all professional work requires, at times, the exercise of judgement and that judgement is not infallible; furthermore, that the work carried out by professionals is constantly developing and, by its nature, is not an exact science. In *Whitehouse v. Jordan*[10] an error of judgement by a consultant surgeon was held not to be negligent because the surgeon's actions were still within the scope of what a reasonably competent surgeon could have done, so there had not been a failure to exercise reasonable skill and care.

8. (1979) 10 B.L.R. 48.
9. (1994) 74 B.L.R. 1.
10. [1981] 1 W.L.R. 246.

There have been remarkably few cases reported over the years where a quantity surveyor has been held to be negligent. This is probably for a number of reasons. First, the nature of the work carried out by quantity surveyors is often such that, even where there has been negligence, this may not give rise to actual loss. Alternatively, the contractor or employer will have a direct remedy against the party with whom he contracts, and against whom he may prefer to take action. For example, if a quantity surveyor underestimates the cost of a building, then, in theory at least, his developer client will have obtained a building equivalent to the actual cost and therefore will have suffered no loss. If a quantity surveyor negligently overvalues the amount of a payment due to a contractor, the employer will usually have a right to litigate or arbitrate against the contractor for the recovery of sums overpaid. Secondly, the role of the quantity surveyor often tends to be subordinate to that of the other professionals engaged on the project, for example an architect or engineer, and the quantity surveyor's role where he is not responsible for administering the building contract will result in his having far fewer functions likely to affect his client's interests. Thirdly, since the work of a quantity surveyor only, generally, involves the secondary aspect of the project, namely the cost of it, rather than the primary aspect, namely its design and construction, it could be said that there is probably less room for quantity surveyors to make errors of great significance, as opposed to, say, an architect who negligently designs a building with the possibility of catastrophic consequences resulting from such negligence. Fourthly, and in any event, there is usually an opportunity for the quantity surveyor, by the very nature of the work he carries out, to remedy any errors either before or during the course of the construction project. Fifthly, the nature of the work carried out by quantity surveyors is usually only likely to have an impact directly upon his client, and although situations may arise whereby a quantity surveyor assumes some voluntary responsibility to a third party so as to subject him to a tortious liability for his negligence, such circumstances are unlikely to be common. Under the Defective Premises Act 1972, a duty is imposed upon a quantity surveyor to see that, in relation to work for or in connection with the provision of a dwelling, the work he does is done in a professional manner so that as regards the work the dwelling will be fit for habitation when completed.[11] This duty applies to all subsequent owners of the property and, while it is possible to conceive of circumstances where a quantity surveyor could be found liable apart from under his contract of retainer with his client, it is considered that this is most unlikely. Quantity surveyors are undoubtedly under a general common law duty to take reasonable skill and care so that their acts and omissions do not cause damage to property or personal injury to a third party. However, because the work of quantity surveyors does not involve the production of a three-dimensional object such as a building, but rather only concerns the cost of that project, quantity surveyors are extremely unlikely themselves directly to create a situation where that three-dimensional project could cause damage to property or personal injury to a third party so as to give rise to tortious liability. As a result, any tortious claims that are likely to be made against the quantity surveyor will be for purely economic loss where, in accordance with the principles discussed in Chapter 1, the ingredients of a voluntary assumption of responsibility and reasonableness will be required.[12] Finally, certain of the work carried out by quantity surveyors is in the nature of advice, for example, an estimate of the cost of a project, which is only one of a number of factors which the quantity surveyor's client will take into account before deciding whether or not to embark on a particular course of action. This situation, that of the provision of advice, should be contrasted with that of a warranty being given, which in practice is unusual, and where the legal consequences are significantly different if the warranty turns out to be incorrect rather than merely the advice being incorrect. Thus, there may be difficulties in proving a causative link between the damages claimed and the alleged negligence. Each of these factors are expanded upon in more detail in relation to the specific tasks carried out by quantity surveyors, which are detailed below, but they serve briefly to explain why quantity surveyors are and have been, compared to other professionals, the profession that has largely managed to keep clear of the legal process.

11. Defective Premises Act 1972, s. 1(1).
12. See Ch. 1, para 1.2.1.

4.2.3 Pre-contract work

4.2.3.1 Cost estimates

The quantity surveyor's initial involvement with the project will, when acting for the employer, usually be after the outline design has been prepared by an architect. The quantity surveyor will be passed the drawings carried out by the architect and/or the engineer and asked to provide an estimate of the costs of carrying out the project. The purpose of this exercise will be obvious, namely to enable the employer to have some idea of the probable costs to enable him to budget accordingly, to organise finance, and to implement increases or reductions in the quality or quantity of the proposed works so as to fit in with his available budget. If this exercise is carried out negligently by the quantity surveyor, whether he is liable may depend upon what happens subsequently. If the employer, in reliance upon the inaccurate estimate, enters into a contract with a contractor on a cost-plus profit basis, such as the JCT standard form of Prime Cost Contract,[13] or if a number of variations become necessary to enable the works to be properly carried out, so that in either case the employer becomes liable to pay the contractor a substantially greater sum than the estimate, the employer may look to the quantity surveyor to recover the difference. There will, however, be difficulties in establishing liability in terms of proof of causation of loss. First of all, it is necessary to ascertain precisely what it is that the quantity surveyor is doing. A distinction needs to be drawn between the provision of advice and the provision of a warranty. When he provides an estimate of costs, the quantity surveyor will usually be under a duty to take reasonable care to provide an accurate estimation, and if he negligently breaches that duty, the measure of damages is the loss attributable to the inaccuracy of the information which the employer suffers by reason of his having entered into the transaction on the assumption that the information was correct. The quantity surveyor does not usually give a warranty that the project can be constructed at the cost which he has estimated. Damages for breach of warranty would be measured by reference to a comparison between the employer's position as a result of entering into the building contract with what it would have been if the information had been accurate.

13. JCT Standard Form of Prime Cost Contract, 1992 ed.

Moreover, it is necessary also to ask precisely what advice the quantity surveyor is giving. He is not advising the employer to take a specific course of action, such as to proceed with the proposed project. He is effectively providing information which is then one of a number of factors which the employer may take into account in deciding whether or not to proceed with the project, for example how much available capital and finance he has, whether he is looking at the project as a long-term investment or whether he intends to sell and has a potential buyer, what kind of rental income may be obtained and so forth.[14] Unless, which would be unusual, the quantity surveyor did give a warranty, the employer's loss would only be that which is attributable to the inaccuracy of the cost estimate. Whether any loss can be shown will obviously depend upon the facts of the individual case, but the quantity surveyor will argue that although the ultimate project cost more than his estimate, even had he provided an accurate estimate the employer would still have proceeded by reason of other factors, and, furthermore, the employer has actually ended up with a building of a greater value, equivalent to the cost, so that there is no loss. As against this, however, it will usually be possible for an employer to say that had he been provided with an accurate estimate, he would have had the opportunity of altering the design in terms of quality or quantity so as to effect savings, so that the consequences of the inaccuracy of the estimate were having to spend more than would have been actually spent. Such was the position in *Wilks v. Thingoe Rural District Council.*[15] Furthermore, the employer may have had to raise additional finance at a higher cost than he would have done had he been provided with an accurate estimate and been able to plan his finance accordingly.

Usually, after the initial design has been completed and the quantity surveyor has given the employer his estimate, tenders will be invited, and on most projects at least one contractor will be asked to give a quotation or estimate other than administrative expenses and fees of other professionals arising from the tender process. If this is substantially greater than the quantity surveyor's negligent cost estimate, the employer will have the option of aban-

14. See *South Australian Asset Management Corporation* v. *York Montague Limited* (1996) 80 B.L.R.1, a valuer's negligence case, particularly Lord Hoffman at 10A and 16A–D where these principles are discussed.

15. (1954) 164 E.G. 86.

doning the project and so he will suffer no loss as a result of the negligent estimate other than administrative expenses and fees of other professionals arising from the tender process. On the other hand, if the employer decides to enter into the project with the contractor at the likely contract price, there will be no reliance upon the negligent estimate and, consequently, no liability on the part of the quantity surveyor. In these circumstances, however, the quantity surveyor may not be entitled to any fees if his estimate is negligent to the extent that it is so far short of the likely costs so that the employer has received no value from the quantity surveyor's services.

In *Moneypenny v. Hartland*[16] an engineer was held not to be entitled to his fees where the actual cost of a project greatly exceeded the engineer's estimate. Best C.J. said:

> "If a surveyor delivers an estimate greatly below the sum at which a work can be done, and thereby induces a private person to undertake what he would not otherwise do, then I think he is not entitled to recover".

Similarly, in *Nye Saunders & Partners* v. *Alan E. Bristow*[17] an architect was held by the Court of Appeal to be unable to recover his fees because the estimate he provided failed to take into account the likely effect of inflation. The architect provided a schedule of costs, which he had obtained from a quantity surveyor, in the sum of £238,000 to carry out certain works. This was during a very high inflationary period, but the schedule did not contain any figure for likely increases in inflation. After planning permission was granted, the quantity surveyor then produced an up-to-date statement which showed likely costs of completion during the 18-month contract period as £440,000 after taking into account inflation. The client cancelled the project and the architect's claim for fees was rejected.

The legal basis behind the decisions in the above cases appears to be that there was a total failure of consideration for the quantity surveyor's fees, in that in each case the client received no benefit whatsoever from his services. Whether this is correct has been doubted by a leading textbook.[18]

Generally speaking, quantity surveyors are regarded as being more likely to know what the current trends are in costs of materials

16. (1826) 2 C. & P. 378.
17. (1987) 37 B.L.R. 92.
18. See *Jackson & Powell* (4th ed.), 2–111.

or wages, and more about the effect of inflation on the building industry. The quantity surveyor should therefore advise as to the possible effects of price variables upon his estimate or make it plain that his estimate is based upon current prices. Similarly, the quantity surveyor should ensure that he advises upon the incidence of Value Added Tax, which may be due in respect of some aspects of the works but not others.

Whether or not an estimate has been prepared negligently cannot simply be determined by looking at the size of the gap between the estimate and the tendered or actual building costs. There may be other explanations for the size of the gap. In *Copthorne Hotel (Newcastle) Limited* v. *Arup Associates*[19] an estimate was given of the cost of piling works in the sum of £452,000 and the successful tender was in the sum of £930,000. Judge Hicks Q.C. held that there was no onus of proof upon the quantity surveyor to explain his underestimate; the onus of proof was on the plaintiff to prove negligence in the usual way. In his judgment, the judge explained that while culpable underestimation was one of the possible explanations of such a discrepancy, there were other possible explanations, such as the contractor having over-specified from excessive caution, or to obtain a greater profit, or to suit the drilling equipment available or for some other reason. Market conditions may have changed or have been subject to some distortion outside the knowledge and foresight of a reasonably competent professional adviser. The judge held that the plaintiff had failed to discharge the onus of proof of negligence which was upon it.

When a quantity surveyor is engaged by a contractor, the damages that would be incurred by the contractor would be likely to be in the nature of a lost opportunity. Where a quantity surveyor provides a contractor with an estimate for the purposes of a tender which is then accepted, if the estimate proves to be a negligent underestimate, the contractor's case would be put upon the basis that if a proper estimate had been provided, it would have submitted a tender at the higher price which would then have been accepted, and that its loss, on a lump sum contract, would be represented by the difference. This would require the contractor to prove, on the balance of probabilities, that the higher-priced tender would have been accepted and this may be difficult, especially if the higher price

19. (1996) 12 Const. L.J. 402.

would not then have been the lowest tender. In these circumstances, however, the contractor would clearly be entitled to recover his actual loss on the project upon the alternative basis that he would not have entered into the transaction at all, and therefore the losses incurred were all incurred as a consequence of the inaccuracy.

The cases referred to above have dealt with situations where information was provided by the quantity surveyor in the form of estimates. The position is different if the advice given by the quantity surveyor is in the nature of a warranty, namely that a project can be built for a particular sum or that the costs will not exceed a particular sum. Where a quantity surveyor provides a warranty as to cost, he will be liable for any difference between the figure in his warranty and the actual cost if he has been negligent. In practice, it is unusual for quantity surveyors to give estimates which are in the nature of warranties as opposed to estimates which are in the nature of advice. There may be circumstances, however, where a warranty will be given. Where a client tells a quantity surveyor that he has a financial limit, the quantity surveyor's duty will be to exercise reasonable skill and care in advising the client whether or not that limit will be exceeded. If the quantity surveyor, however, provides an assurance that the necessary works can be carried out within that limit, that will amount to a contractual warranty given to the client, and he will be liable for the extra costs if the warranty given proves to be inaccurate.

4.2.3.2 Bills of quantities

After the client has decided to proceed to tender, the quantity surveyor will prepare a detailed Bill of Quantities. Bills of Quantities evolved from the practice of sending out drawings to different trades who then submitted detailed priced schedules of work and materials. Bills of quantities are prepared, usually, using standard methods of measurement in accordance with universal practice. These methods of measurement are the Royal Institution of Chartered Surveyors' Standard Method of Measurement, 7th Edition ("SMM 7") and the Civil Engineering Standard Method of Measurement, 3rd Edition 1991, approved by the Institution of Civil Engineers and the Federation of Civil Engineering Contractors in association with the Association of Consulting Engineers ("CESMM 3"), or the Method of Measurement for Highway Works

(July 1987) ("MMHW") published by Her Majesty's Stationery Office. The standard methods of measurement are recognised in all of the standard forms of building contract. The Joint Contracts Tribunal standard form of Building Contract, 1980 Edition, with Quantities or with Approximate Quantities, expressly states that the contract bills are to be prepared in accordance with SMM7.[20] Similarly, the Institute of Civil Engineering Conditions of Contract, 6th Edition ("ICE 6"), indicate that the bill of quantities should be deemed to have been prepared and measured in accordance with the latest edition of CESMM.[21] Where MMHW is used, the relevant condition of ICE 6 is amended. The standard forms of contracts contain further provisions whereby any errors or misdescriptions in the bill are to be corrected and they will be treated as variations under the particular contract in question. The consequence of variations entitles the contractor to bring claims for additional sums, not just for the extra or different work carried out, but also for the consequences of the impact of the variations upon progress of the works.

It is believed that the most common forms of error that appear in bills of quantities are processing errors. A bill of quantities is a very detailed document and the preparation is routinely checked by quantity surveyors, but errors can slip through. For example, where there are repetitive calculations which are to be applied to several floors, a floor might be missed out, or some pages from the architect's specification could be omitted accidentally. This could have serious consequences if, for example, the bill remains silent in the event of what might be likely to be the discovery of hazardous or dangerous substances, for example asbestos. Further processing errors may be where a quantity is stated as "500" instead of "50". Any of these errors may give rise to a claim by the contractor for additional sums or, indeed, by the client if the carrying out of the works leads to intervention by statutory authorities.

The losses that may result from negligence in the preparation of a bill of quantities will depend upon the nature of the contract subsequently entered into. If the bill is of approximate quantities, errors, whether of processing or otherwise, which merely affect the approximate quantities stated, are unlikely to cause the employer

20. Cl. 2.2.2.1.
21. Cl. 57.

any loss since the contract is and always was going to be a remeasurement contract, and it may be difficult for a client to argue that he has suffered any loss as a result of the actual quantities being greater than anticipated in what, after all, is a contract where the final price was always going to be uncertain. Even where the contract that is subsequently entered into is a lump sum contract and similarly the errors relate merely to the quantities, the situation can in some way be compared with the situation where a negligent under-estimate of costs is prepared. In such instances, the extra costs resulting from any extra quantities required following rectification of the errors in the bill will not necessarily prove damage, because the employer will still have works carried out to the value of that which he has paid. Moreover, unlike in the case of estimates, the client may have difficulty in proving reliance in relation to a negligently prepared bill of approximate quantities where the quantity of work is, at that stage, not finally determined. Whether the contract is a lump sum contract or a remeasurement contract, it is more likely to be the consequence of the bill being inaccurate, giving rise to claims permissible by the contractor under the contract, that is likely to cause the employer loss which may not have been incurred had the bill not been negligently prepared and, in these circumstances, if the employer is able to show that had the bill been correctly prepared in the first instance, so that there would have been no claims in the nature of loss or expense or enhanced rates, the causative link will be established and the quantity surveyor will be liable. A leading textbook commentator has in fact criticised the universal use of the English standard methods of measurement upon the basis that they are globally damaging to owners, permitting a variety of claims for additional payment by the contractor.[22] However, the use of the standard methods of measurement is so universally used by reasonably competent quantity surveyors that its use would be difficult to establish as negligence *per se*.

Minor errors in the preparation of a bill may not be sufficient to establish negligence. In *London School Board* v. *Northcroft, Southern Neighbour*[23] errors in the calculations resulting in overpayment of two sums of £118 and £15 were held not to have been negligent, which suggests that to some degree errors are permissible. Whether

22. See *Hudson's Building and Engineering Contracts* (11th ed.), 2.161 *et seq.*
23. *Hudson's Building Contracts*, (4th ed., 1914), Vol. 2, p. 149.

this result would be the same today is considered to be unlikely if the errors resulted from carelessness.

4.2.3.3. Advising upon and negotiating tenders

After tenders have been received the quantity surveyor will draw up comparisons and advise the employer. In larger projects, the process of tenders is usually followed by negotiations between the chosen (usually the lowest priced) tendering contractor and the employer with a view to reaching agreement on contract price. In tenders which have involved pricing a bill of quantities, the successful tenderer will be asked to submit a copy of his priced bill, which will then form the basis of negotiations to agree either the contract price in a lump sum contract or the rates in a remeasurement contract. During these negotiations, the employer will look for possible savings. The quantity surveyor will also be asked to advise upon the contractor's priced bill as part of this process. If the quantity surveyor failed to spot an obvious error in the contractor's priced bill, which then leads to an unnecessarily higher contract price than would be likely to have been negotiated had the error been pointed out, the quantity surveyor will be liable to the employer for damages. In the case of *Tyrer* v. *District Auditor of Monmouthshire*[24] the quantity surveyor was held negligent when he approved excessive quantities and prices. Conversely, if a quantity surveyor representing a contractor were to agree to, or advise the contractor to agree to, a reduction from the tender price based upon a negligent misunderstanding of the contractual requirements, he could be liable to the contractor for any loss consequential upon the agreement to reduce.

4.2.3.4. Recommending builders or form of and terms of contract

Usually speaking, especially in larger projects, these functions will be carried out by an architect or engineer, but where a quantity surveyor is carrying out these functions, which is more likely in smaller, domestic, projects, he will have the same duties as regards exercising reasonable skill and care as would an architect/engineer. These duties are dealt with in Chapter 3 relating to architects/

24. (1973) 230 E.G. 973.

engineers and the principles discussed there apply equally to quantity surveyors.[25]

4.2.4 Functions during the performance of the contract

4.2.4.1 Administering the contract

The role of the quantity surveyor can vary considerably according to the nature of the contract in question. Under a traditional form of building contract, the architect will usually administer the terms of the building contract and will retain responsibility for design, giving instructions to the contractor, approval of selection of subcontractors and materials, inspection of quality of work, the issuing of formal certificates and the like. The quantity surveyor's role will be subordinate to that of the architect and, during the carrying out of the works, will be limited to the carrying out of valuations for the purposes of interim payments, the valuation of variations and to assessing the value of the contractor's claims. In addition to his role under the contract, the quantity surveyor will, however, usually be required to keep the client up to date with the likely cost of the project by the submission of regular cost estimates and cashflow forecasts and, in this respect, the principles discussed at paragraph 4.2.3.1 above will apply. Particularly, a negligent cost estimate provided during the course of the project may deprive the employer of the opportunity to make savings that he would otherwise have had the opportunity of making had an accurate estimate been given, so that a provable loss could result.

Where the project is to be carried out on a design and build basis, the quantity surveyor will probably not have a defined function under the contractual arrangements. Under the JCT standard form for design and build projects, there is no provision for a quantity surveyor to assume a valuation role, but invariably the employer will employ a quantity surveyor to advise him upon the contractor's applications for interim payments, which is the mechanism under the terms of that contract by which interim payments to the contractor are determined.[26]

Where the contract is on a construction management basis, the

25. See Ch. 3, para. 3.4.5.

26. JCT Standard Form of Building Contract with Contractor's Design 1981 Edition, esp. cl. 30.

client will directly employ a series of separate trade contractors and provide the co-ordination of the management of the project through a construction manager who, under the trade contracts, will be named as having responsibility for the administering of each of the trade contracts. In terms of the possible consequences of a quantity surveyor's negligence where he acts as a construction manager, the financial consequences of misadministration of the building contract will fall upon the client and, generally speaking, the same principles that apply to the administration of the contract under a traditional build arrangement will apply to a construction management contract, since the consequences of negligence will be the same in each case, namely the payment by the client to the contractor of extra sums of money.

Management contracting is a further form of contractual arrangement whereby the client enters into a contract with the construction manager and he in turn enters into direct contracts with the works contractors. Generally speaking, the contract between the client and the management contractor will be for the payment of a sum representing all the sums that are due to be paid under the separate contracts between the management contractor and the works contractor together with an additional sum in the form of a fee for the works carried out by the management contractor. While every management contract will depend upon its terms, generally speaking the risks will be shared between the client and the management contractor. In particular, where the management contractor is responsible for ensuring due completion, and he negligently fails to achieve this, the consequence of this will be that he bears the costs himself. Otherwise, so far as certain risks in a management contract lay with the employer, then again, applying usual principles, the quantity surveyor, in the exercise of his duties on behalf of the employer, will have to take reasonable skill and care when he does so, so as not to cause the client to suffer a loss.

In smaller traditional build projects, the quantity surveyor may be employed generally to administer the contract. To this extent he will be required to carry out all of the functions that an architect or engineer usually carried out. These duties are detailed in Chapter 3 above and generally apply equally to quantity surveyors if they carry out these functions.[27] These functions cover the prevention,

27. See Ch. 3, para. 3.5.

detection and correction of defective work, to intervene in the case of default by the contractor in his obligations as to time and method of performance, and the issuing of certificates. This chapter only deals with those tasks which the quantity surveyor carries out in his role as a subsidiary consultant to the architect.

4.2.4.2 General responsibility

The quantity surveyor's general responsibility where an architect is administering a building contract is effectively to provide advice or information. He is not there to act as a check upon the actions of the architect. In *Aubrey Jacobus & Partners* v. *Gerrard*,[28] Judge Stabb Q.C. said:

> "it is suggested that the quantity surveyor was under a duty to monitor or control the costs and advise the client. I am satisfied that no such duty exists. The architect is the team leader: he is primarily responsible for design and for the cost of it. If called upon, the quantity surveyor is there to provide information as to cost but not in my view to monitor or control it by carrying out checks at regular intervals as was suggested."

The terms of his retainer may impose a requirement upon the quantity surveyor to provide regular cost reports, but it is unlikely that this could impose an obligation upon him to proffer opinions on the incurring of the cost. Thus, for example, if it appears to the quantity surveyor that the architect is incurring extravagant expenditure in the ordering of variations, it would seem that it is not the quantity surveyor's responsibility to question such. He would be entitled to assume that the architect had the authority of the employer.

There may be instances, however, where a quantity surveyor may, by reason of the acquisition of some particular knowledge, also acquire some responsibility in relation to a matter which is the responsibility of the architect under the contract. For example, the responsibility to detect defective work is that of the architect and not the quantity surveyor (see *Sutcliffe* v. *Chippendale & Edmondson*[29]). On the other hand, if a quantity surveyor noticed defective work while attending a site, it may be difficult for him properly to suggest that he was under no duty to draw the matter

28. 1981, unreported.
29. (1971) 18 B.L.R. 149 at 162 *et seq.*

to the architect's attention, especially if it became apparent that the architect was unaware of it.

4.2.4.3 Negligent valuations

The quantity surveyor will usually be retained to carry out interim valuations for the purposes of certifying interim payments due to the contractor at regular intervals, usually monthly. The contract will usually provide that the amount to be certified will be the value of work properly executed as well as the value of unfixed goods and materials on site and, in some circumstances, the value of goods and materials off site.[30] The quantity surveyor will usually carry out a cursory examination of the site sufficient to enable him to provide a valuation in accordance with the terms of the contract and which he then passes on to the architect with a recommendation for payment. The architect will then issue a certificate which creates an obligation upon the employer to pay. In addition, the quantity surveyor will be required to assess and value from time to time permissible claims by the contractor during the carrying out of the works.[31]

The nature and the responsibilities of the role carried out by the quantity surveyor in relation to his valuation functions are dual ones. On the one hand the decisions of the quantity surveyor affects the financial interests of both the contractor and the employer. In such matters, the obligation is upon the quantity surveyor to carry out his valuations impartially and fairly, having regard to the interests of both the contractor and the employer. The building contract between an employer and a contractor will usually contain an implied warranty that the quantity surveyor will reach his valuation decisions fairly; furthermore, in order for him to do so, that he will do so free from interference by the employer. On the other hand the quantity surveyor has an obligation to the employer under his professional terms of engagement to use all reasonable skill and care in the carrying out of his valuation functions.

In *London Borough of Merton* v. *Leach*[32] Vinelott J. stated, when discussing similar discretionary powers of an architect:

30. See JCT 80, cl. 30.2.1; ICE 6th Edition, cl. 60(2).

31. See para. 4.2.5, *infra*, for the obligation to ascertain loss and expense under JCT 80.

32. (1985) 32 B.L.R. 51 at 78.

"The contract also confers on the architect discretionary powers which he must exercise with due regard to the interests of the contractor and the building owner. The building owner does not undertake that the architect will exercise his discretionary powers reasonably; he undertakes that although the architect may be engaged or employed by him he will leave him free to exercise his discretion fairly and without improper interference by him."

The nature of the certifying functions, where a balancing exercise between the interests of the employer and contractor has to be carried out, was held by the Court of Appeal in 1901 (*Chambers* v. *Goldthorpe*[33]) to be of a quasi-arbitral nature so that the certifier was entitled to immunity from negligence in the performance of those duties. This was upon the basis that a requirement to act fairly creates the status of quasi-arbitrator. This principle was, however, rejected when *Chambers* v. *Goldthorpe* was overruled in *Sutcliffe* v. *Thackrah*[34] where a certifier was held to be liable to his employer under an obligation to his employer to use reasonable skill and care in carrying out his certification functions.

On the basis that the quantity surveyor will be potentially liable to the employer if he negligently overvalues work carried out, a quantity surveyor must therefore exercise reasonable skill and care in carrying out his valuation. This then leads on to the question of the extent of the enquiries that he should make. Interim certificates at, for example, monthly intervals are primarily designed to facilitate cashflow for the contractor, who cannot reasonably be expected to wait until the end of the project before receiving any payment at all. Because of the regularity of interim valuations, the whole process provides an opportunity for self-correction so that an error in an interim valuation can possibly be corrected when the next or subsequent valuations are carried out. This opportunity obviously depends upon the degree of overvaluation and/or the number of remaining interim certificates, which may provide an opportunity of self-correction after the error is discovered. If the overvaluation is large and possibly greater than the remaining value of the work to be carried out, only a negative valuation will be possible, so that the only option open to the employer to try and recover the overpayment from the contractor would be outside the contractual machinery, namely by proceedings or the threat of proceedings.

33. [1901] 1 K.B. 624.
34. (1974) 4 B.L.R. 16.

This will particularly be so if the overvaluation occurs at practical completion, when there will be no further work to be carried out by the contractor, the value of which could then be used to claw back the overvaluation, and the only opportunity to correct will be if further sums are identified as being due to the contractor during the subsequent process of computation of the contractor's final account for measured works or in the process of ascertainment of loss and expense. Otherwise the employer will have to look to the usual amount of 2.5 per cent retention that will only become payable upon the issue of the final certificate.

Because the process of interim certificates is for the purposes of cashflow and usually offers an opportunity of self-correction, with the final account being the definitive exercise which the quantity surveyor carries out to determine the amount to which the contractor is properly entitled (in respect of which see paragraph 4.2.5 below), this does not lessen the degree of diligence which the quantity surveyor must exercise in discharging his obligation to the employer to carry out interim valuations with all reasonable skill and care. In *Sutcliffe* v. *Thackrah* when heard at first instance (*Sutcliffe* v. *Chippendale & Edmondson*[35]) expert evidence was called to the effect that an interim valuation was more of an approximation of the value of the work as it was progressed, assessed by the quantity surveyor without any detailed inspection of the work, the object being simply to provide a reasonable progress payment for the contractor based upon a comparatively cursory examination of the site. It is doubtful whether simply carrying out these tasks will, by itself, be sufficient to discharge the obligation of reasonable skill and care. Much may depend upon the particular circumstances prevailing at the time. If the contractor is found to be, or is suspected of, submitting inflated or exaggerated applications for payment, the quantity surveyor may consider it necessary to exercise a greater degree of vigilance. Similarly, where doubts may be raised about the immediate solvency of the contractor, the quantity surveyor will want to ensure that the payments to be made to the contractor are as precise as can be.

Having said this, it is recognised that valuation is not an exact science, and there will always be possible parameters of a valuation within which any valuation will not be negligent. Indeed, the same principle that applies to cost estimates as is discussed at paragraph

35. (1971) 18 B.L.R. 149.

4.2.3.1 above appears to apply to valuations, so that the mere size of the overvaluation will not, by itself, establish negligence.

Even where overvaluations are carried out which are then corrected by subsequent valuations, the client may still have a claimable loss against the quantity surveyor in the form of loss of interest on or of financing the amount of overpayment between the time when it was paid until the time when it eventually and properly became due to be paid. Where, however, the opportunity to recover the overpayment is lost, such as where the contractor goes into liquidation, then the quantity surveyor will be liable for the full amount of the overpayment resulting from the negligent valuation.

A more difficult situation is where the opportunity to recover the amount overpaid as a result of a negligent valuation by means of self-correcting interim certificates is not available but, similarly, neither is the opportunity to recover through litigation or arbitration proceedings lost forever. Thus, where there has been a negligent overvaluation carried out at practical completion in favour of a solvent contractor, one of the employer's options would be to seek to commence arbitration or litigation against the contractor with a view to recovery of the monies. However, he will not be obliged to do so, and instead may simply decide to bring proceedings against the quantity surveyor for negligent overvaluation. There may be a number of reasons which may make it preferable to bring proceedings against the contractor—the more difficult requirement of proving want of reasonable skill and care against the quantity surveyor compared with simply proving a correct valuation against the contractor, or whether any other claims may have also to be brought against the contractor, for example in respect of defects. Equally, there may be reasons why it is considered preferable to bring proceedings against the quantity surveyor, for example if the contractor has a counterclaim that is likely to attract liability. If the employer chooses to sue the quantity surveyor first, the quantity surveyor will not be able to suggest that the employer has failed to mitigate his loss by first attempting to recover the payment from the contractor. In *Wessex RHA* v. *HLM Design*[36] the employer engaged in expensive arbitration proceedings against the contractor, which were settled, and the employer then sued the architect for his losses. The architect alleged that the compromise which the

36. (1995) 71 B.L.R. 32.

employer reached was unreasonable. His Honour Judge Fox-Andrews Q.C. said:

"There would appear to be much to be said for contractual arrangements which require the employer to pursue his remedy against the contractor who had been overpaid and only gave him limited rights against his architect. But if in the absence of such contractual arrangements there are untrammelled independent causes of action, then unless the procedure of law declines to assist in the enforcement of the cause of action against the architect, it is difficult to see how it is relevant whether the employer acted competently or incompetently in the arbitration or whether the settlement reached was reasonable or unreasonable. The employer can sue either or both and in the case of the latter, in such order as he wishes."[37]

Thus, it can be seen that, by virtue of the concurrent causes of action which a client will have in relation to an overpayment, it is irrelevant whether or not the client takes proceedings against the contractor and, if he does, what portion of the loss, if any, is recovered. Obviously, the client will have to give credit for sums actually recovered to reduce his outstanding loss. As Judge Fox-Andrews Q.C. said, however, it is up to the client which party he chooses to sue. In *Townsend* v. *Stone Toms*,[38] Oliver L.J. said:

"But whether something is a breach of duty cannot depend upon whether or not the builder remains solvent or not. If it was a breach when it occurred, it remains a breach of duty, although the subsequent course of events may clearly affect the quantum of any damage."

Where the employer chooses to take proceedings against the contractor first, in these circumstances, if the employer establishes the overvaluation he will recover an arbitration award or a judgment from the courts in his favour and, usually, will recover an order for costs in his favour. However, he will inevitably have to pay an element of his solicitor/own client costs which will not be recoverable from the contractor, and a further question is then whether these costs can be recoverable from the quantity surveyor as damages resulting from the negligent overvaluation. It would appear possible that such irrecoverable costs could be recovered as damages, applying general principles of recoverability. Because of the concurrent tortious and contractual duties that will generally be imposed, these losses could be recoverable either under the

37. *Ibid*, at p.63B.
38. (1984) 27 B.L.R. 26 at 46.

contractual measure under the second limb of *Hadley* v. *Baxendale*[39] as being reasonably foreseeable as a consequence of the breach, or under the tortious measure of damages, which would be the amount necessary to put the employer in the same position as he would have been in if he had not sustained the wrong for which compensation is sought. Part of His Honour Judge Fox-Andrews' reasoning in *Wessex RHA* v. *HLM* suggests that the costs under consideration will still retain a causative link to the breach resulting in the overvaluation and they will not be considered to be too remote.

Again, if the employer commences proceedings against the contractor to recover the amount overpaid and then enters into a settlement at less than the full value of his claim (after taking into account the incidence of costs), he is perfectly entitled to then bring an action to recover the shortfall against the quantity surveyor. Arguments based upon breaks in causation of loss or remoteness of damage or a failure to mitigate are unlikely to succeed.[40]

4.2.4.4 Obligation to contractors

The converse of overvaluation is, of course, undervaluation. Where a quantity surveyor, during the course of a contract, negligently undervalues the amount of work carried out by a contractor with the result that the contractor recovers less than he is properly entitled to, the question is whether he can bring an action against the quantity surveyor for negligence. Upon the basis of the principles discussed above, so that if the contractor has a cause of action in negligence against the quantity surveyor this will be concurrent with any cause of action to recover further sums due from the employer, whether by way of arbitration or litigation, the answer to this question depends upon the existence of a duty of care on the part of the quantity surveyor to avoid causing economic loss to the contractor. In *Pacific Associates* v. *Baxter*,[41] it was held that no such duty of care existed. That case concerned the actions of an engineer in relation to a claim by the contractor for extra costs arising from hard materials. It was held that there had been no voluntary assumption of responsibility by the engineer sufficient to give rise

39. (1854) 9 Ex. 341.
40. See *Wessex RHA* v. *HLM Design* (1995) 71 B.L.R. 32.
41. (1988) 44 B.L.R. 33.

to a liability to the contractor in respect of economic loss. This will apply equally to a quantity surveyor carrying out valuation functions. The very nature of the contractual arrangements in which a quantity surveyor is employed to carry out valuations would appear to exclude circumstances arising where it could be said that, by those arrangements, the quantity surveyor had assumed a duty of care to a contractor. The quantity surveyor is employed to protect the owner's interests and not to provide a protection or safeguard to the contractor. As discussed at 4.2.4.3 above, while the owner warrants that the quantity surveyor will carry out his tasks impartially and fairly, he does not warrant that he will do so competently. In these circumstances, the contractor's remedy lies only within the contract, namely to arbitrate or litigate against the employer. The Court of Appeal held that although there was a degree of proximity in the obvious sense that the contractor relied upon the engineer performing his duties there was not the same quality of proximity required to establish an actionable duty of care. Although the Court of Appeal said that the decision depended upon the particular facts of that case, the line of later cases beginning with *Murphy* v. *Brentwood District Council*[42] and continuing, discussed in Chapter 1 above,[43] would, when the additional factors of reasonableness in the imposition of a duty were also considered, make it improbable, except in special circumstances, that in carrying out his valuation functions a quantity surveyor will be held to have assumed a duty to the contractor to take reasonable care.

So far, the discussions have centred on the duties and obligations imposed upon a quantity surveyor when employed by the owner. It is not uncommon for contractors, however, particularly subcontractors, to engage the services of independent quantity surveyors to carry out quantity surveying services relating to valuations for interim payment or final account purposes, quantification of variations and so forth. In these circumstances, the claims that are likely to be made will result from the submission of negligently prepared applications for interim payments or final accounts, or for agreeing sums for variations which are too low, whereby the contractor or sub-contractor concerned becomes bound by such

42. [1991] A.C. 398.
43. Ch. 1, paras. 1.2.1 *et seq.*

agreements. The contractor or sub-contractor concerned will, to establish his claim in negligence, have to prove a causative link by establishing, on the balance of probabilities, that had correctly valued interim payment applications or a proper final account been submitted, they would have resulted in higher payments, or, in the case of variations, that the contractor or sub-contractor has been deprived of an opportunity to obtain the correct, higher value.

4.2.5 Post-completion works

Following practical completion, the quantity surveyor is usually given specific functions that are somewhat inquisitorial in nature. These are the valuation of the final account for measured work and variations, and the ascertainment of loss and expense and other claims which are permissible under the terms of the contract. Under JCT 80, these functions are to be carried out by the architect or the contract administrator unless he delegates the tasks to the quantity surveyor, which is what usually happens in practice. As far as loss and expense are concerned, the obligation to ascertain is not limited to doing so simply after completion, but from time to time during the contract. Clause 26.1 of JCT 80 contains the following provision:

> "If the Contractor makes written application to the Architect/the Contract Administrator stating that he has incurred or is likely to incur direct loss and/or expense in the execution of this Contract for which he would not be reimbursed by payment under any other provision in this Contract due to deferment of giving possession of the site under clause 23.1.2 . . . or because the regular progress of the Works or of any part thereof has been or is likely to be materially affected by any one or more of the matters referred to in clause 26.2; and if and as soon as the Architect/the Contract Administrator is of the opinion that direct loss and/or expense has been incurred or is likely to be incurred due to any such deferment of giving possession or that the regular progress of the Works or of any part thereof has been or is likely to be so materially affected as set out in the application of the Contractor then the Architect/the Contract Administrator from time to time thereafter shall ascertain, or shall instruct the Quantity Surveyor to ascertain, the amount of such loss and/or expense which has been or is being incurred by the Contractor; provided always that:
>
> . . .
>
> .3 the Contractor shall submit to the Architect/the Contract Administrator or to the Quantity Surveyor upon request, such details of such loss and/or expense as are reasonably necessary for such ascertainment as aforesaid."

Clause 26.2 details the matters which entitle the contractor to claim loss and expense in the event that they materially affect the regular progress of the works.

Clause 30.6.1.1 of JCT 80 contains the following provisions:

"30.6.1.1 Not later than 6 months after Practical Completion of the Works, the Contractor shall provide the Architect/the Contract Administrator, or if so instructed by the Architect/the Contract Administrator, the Quantity Surveyor, with all documents necessary for the purposes of the adjustment of the Contract Sum including all documents relating to the accounts of Nominated Sub-Contractors and Nominated Suppliers.

.1.2 Not later than 3 months after receipt by the Architect/the Contract Administrator or by the Quantity Surveyor of the documents referred to in clause 30.6.1.1.

.2.1 The Architect/the Contract Administrator, or, if the Architect/the Contract Administrator as so instructed, the Quantity Surveyor shall ascertain (unless previously ascertained) any loss and/or expense under clause 26.1, 26.4.1 and 34.3; and

.2.2 The Quantity Surveyor shall prepare a statement of all adjustments to be made to the Contract Sum as referred to in clause 30.6.2 other than any to which clause 30.6.1.2.1 applies.

..."

The clause then sets out in detail the nature of the adjustments that will be made to the contract sum.

These provisions impose upon the quantity surveyor obligations of the following nature:

(a) to call for documentation or information necessary to enable him to carry out his functions;
(b) to carry out the functions of ascertainment and adjustment to the contract sum; and
(c) to do so within a specific time.

In carrying out the quantification exercises of the amount of loss and expense and of the adjustments to the contract sum, the quantity surveyor is doing no more than carrying out valuations of contractual entitlements, and he will be under a similar duty to take reasonable skill and care in dealing with these matters as he is in the case of interim valuations, so that the similar principles discussed above will apply. However, a different approach, that requiring more certainty, will be required. For example, whereas in *Sutcliffe* v. *Chippendale & Edmondson* referred to above, expert evidence on interim valuations was that they were carried out as an approximation of the value of works based upon a cursory examination of the site, the expert evidence in that case was also that interim certificates assumed greater importance as the works got nearer to completion. The provisions of the contract which provided for the adjustment of the balance due either way between employer and contractor at final certificate stage showed that possible overpayments were contemplated, and so it was at this stage that the exercise was carried out with more precision.[44] Indeed, the provisions of clause 26.1 of JCT 80 specifically require the quantity surveyor to "ascertain" loss and expense due to the contractor, which means, by the dictionary definition, "to find out for certain" and not, therefore, to make an approximation or unproven assessment. It can be seen, therefore, that the obligation upon the quantity surveyor is not to make some judgmental or instinctive approach, but to require the contractor to prove his entitlement and, for that purpose, to require the contractor to provide such details that he requires to enable him to do so. If the quantity surveyor curtails this exercise, so that the contractor has certified sums which have not strictly been ascertained and which he is not, therefore, entitled to under the terms of the contract, the quantity surveyor may be liable to the employer for negligence.

Contractors frequently complain that after they have submitted details of loss and expense or documents necessary for the final adjustment of the contract sum, the quantity surveyor then delays in carrying out his tasks beyond the three-month period specified in the contract. The quantity surveyor's defence is usually that he has not been provided with either the details that he requests under clause 26.1.3 or the documents necessary under clause 30.6.1.1. Nevertheless, contractors make claims for financing charges upon the amounts they seek by way of financing the (alleged) shortfall. If, in fact, there has been a delay by the quantity surveyor which is not justifiable, so as to make the employer liable to the quantity surveyor for finance charges, the quantity surveyor could be liable to the employer for damages for negligence in the form of additional finance charges which the employer becomes liable to pay to the contractor.

44. (1971) 18 B.L.R. 149 at 165.

4.3. CLAIMS CONSULTANTS

4.3.1 Introduction

Claims consultants evolved from the historical ability of contractors to make claims of a variety of natures under construction contracts. During the twentieth century, as construction contracts grew in terms of their complexity and the design and management of the projects also became more complex and difficult, an environment was created for variations, delays and disruption resulting in the contractor incurring extra costs. The result was that quantity surveyors employed by contractors enlarged their skills from their traditional role of measuring for the purposes of interim valuations and the final account for measured work, and so acquired a greater awareness of the ability to pursue legitimate claims and became more sophisticated in their advancement of such claims under the contract. Similarly, quantity surveyors employed by the employer developed equal skills in dealing with contractors' claims and ascertaining their legitimacy.

The Royal Institute of British Architects and, subsequently, the Joint Contracts Tribunal have produced standard forms of building contract throughout the twentieth century.[45] These standard forms contained a framework for dealing with the most common type of situations encountered during a construction project that gave rise to possible claims by the contractor for an extension of time and financial loss and contained mechanisms for determining the entitlement or otherwise of the contractor in respect of such matters. The current version of the standard form is the JCT Standard Form of Building Contract 1980 Edition, and this standard form of contract, in its variant forms, is still the most common standard form of contract in use today. Similarly, the standard forms of engineering contract published by the Institution of Civil Engineers detailed the circumstances in which claims could be made and the mechanisms for dealing with them when they arose. The current version of the ICE Conditions of Contract is the 6th Edition, published in 1991. Sub-contractors quickly followed the lead of main contractors to become more conscious about the ability to

45. The first one was produced in 1903 "under the sanction of the RIBA and in agreement with the Institute of Builders and the National Federation of Building Trades Employers of Great Britain".

bring claims, and most of the standard forms of sub-contract also contain mechanisms for dealing with claims for extensions of time and financial loss.[46] In the late 1970s and early 1980s, the proliferation of construction claims led to the development and subsequent growth of independent claims consultants who, primarily, were quantity surveyors who had been employed by contractors or who had been operating in independent practices. These surveyors started setting up their own practices to advise and prepare claims for and on behalf of contractors or to advise employers and resist claims made against them. Although no statistics are available, there is currently a very considerable number of independent claims consultants operating throughout the country. Indeed, in a case in 1992, a Court of Appeal judge was led to remark:

> "It seems to be the practice in the construction industry to employ consultants to prepare a claim almost as soon as the ink on the contract is dry."[47]

The evolutionary process of quantity surveyors to claims consultants has continued, so that many claims consultants currently offer an even greater variety of services relating to construction contracts, such as advice upon contract terms at procurement stage or during the course of the project; advising upon claims as they arise during the project including on compliance with any terms regarding claims, e.g. notice requirements, preparation of loss and expense and extension of time claims; litigation and arbitration management support in the form of assistance to lawyers in relation to the preparation and pursuit of legal or arbitral proceedings; and the provision of expert witness services. Furthermore, although the High Court requires a company to be represented by a qualified lawyer, both in the pre-trial stages (by a solicitor) and at any hearing (either by a barrister or a solicitor with higher courts' rights of advocacy) there is no such restriction in arbitration proceedings. A party can choose who he wishes to represent him in arbitration proceedings, irrespective of whether the appointed person has any qualifications at all. Since the vast majority of standard form contracts and sub-contracts contain arbitration clauses, in the event of

46. See BEC form DOM/1/, JCT form NSC/C/, and FCEC Blue Form and Green Form.

47. Lloyd L.J. in *McAlpine Humberoak* v. *McDermott International* (1992) 58 B.L.R. 1.

a dispute one or both parties to these contracts may choose not to be represented by lawyers, and some claims consultants offer and provide a full range of services from commencement of the arbitration through all of the preliminary stages, including drafting of pleadings and gathering of evidence, up to and including advocacy at the hearing. Alternatively, because professionals other than lawyers have been able to have direct access to barristers since the Bar's Code of Conduct was first relaxed in April 1989, by which the rule that barristers could only accept instructions from a solicitor was abrogated, barristers may now receive instructions from, among others, quantity surveyors, architects or engineers, so long as they are qualified and paid-up members of their appropriate professional institution.[48] Accordingly, a qualified professional from an approved body operating as a claims consultant in arbitration services may take Counsel's advice and instruct Counsel to appear at the arbitration hearing. Thus, it can be seen that, apart from representation in High Court proceedings, claims consultants are able to, and many do, offer a full range of legal services that solicitors and barristers have traditionally carried out. Indeed, a body known as the Institute of Commercial Litigators was set up, primarily consisting of claims consultants who were not qualified lawyers, and in 1993 an attempt was made by claims consultants to continue their evolution in the form of an application by the Institute of Commercial Litigators seeking rights under the Courts and Legal Services Act 1990 of advocacy in the High Court. This was only recently rejected by the Lord Chancellor's Advisory Committee.[49] The situation prevailing today is that claims consultants can be regarded as a separately recognised profession. They cover the full range of construction industry professionals—architects, engineers and, predominantly, quantity surveyors. The larger consultancies offer a full range of services of all these professions combined, as well as qualified lawyers, so as to offer a multi-disciplinary service.

48. See statement of the Bar Council on Direct Professional Access, March 1989. The current approved list of direct professional access bodies includes the Architects and Surveyors Institute, the Association of Consultant Architects and the Royal Institute of British Architects; the Royal Institution of Chartered Surveyors and the Institute of Civil Engineering Surveyors; the Institution of Chemical Engineers, the Institute of Civil Engineers, the Institute of Electrical Engineers, the Institution of Mechanical Engineers and the Institution of Structural Engineers.

49. Advice of the Lord Chancellor's Advisory Committee on Legal Education and Conduct to the Institute of Commercial Litigators, 2 February 1996.

Claims consultants operate under a variety of different names—construction contract consultants, construction claims consultants, construction cost advisers and similar, but they are, collectively and colloquially, usually referred to as claims consultants.

This section of this chapter is principally concerned with those services relating to the preparation and prosecution of claims under construction contracts, but also touches upon the other activities which consultants become involved in apart from those of their more traditional calling, which have already been dealt with elsewhere in this book. The nature of these services is, generally, legal services and, as a consequence, the cases which are referred to have all concerned solicitors or barristers since, until relatively recently, such matters were almost exclusively within their province.

4.3.2 The degree of skill and care required

Where a claims consultant, for example a qualified quantity surveyor, offers legal advice or prepares a pleading in an arbitration case, is he to be judged by reference to the standards of the reasonably competent quantity surveyor or by those of the reasonably competent claims consultant or by those of the reasonably competent lawyer? A leading textbook on professional negligence suggests that if a practitioner carries out tasks usually carried out by the members of another profession, he will be judged by the standards of that other profession.[50] This is in line with the general principles laid down by the courts when determining the test of reasonable skill and care that is to be applied.

Upon this basis, if a person is unqualified in a particular field but holds himself out as possessing a skill in that field, he will be judged by the standards of a reasonably competent person qualified in that field. Claims consultants who hold themselves out as being in a position to give legal advice or to pursue arbitration proceedings which are legal in nature and which have traditionally been carried out by lawyers, hold themselves out as possessing the skill of a reasonably competent lawyer to do so and, as such, will be relied upon by their client as having such skills. It would be likely to be held to be unreasonable for a claims consultant to assert that his actions or omissions were consistent with the level of skill to be

50. See *Jackson and Powell*, (4th ed.), 2–87.

exercised by reasonably competent quantity surveyors, for example, even if not consistent with the level of skill that would be exercised by reasonably competent lawyers. This is especially so since many claims consultancies have one or more members with some legal qualification, including fully qualified barristers and solicitors. This, therefore, gives rise to a variety of different levels of legal skills being offered by different claims consultants which, first, would make it difficult to assess precisely what was the skill level of a reasonably competent claims consultant and, more importantly, would import a subjective element into the exercise of looking at the act or omission under consideration. This is contrary to the general approach which applies to all professionals when considering whether negligence is established, namely an objective test in relation to the act or omission in question. Accordingly, the claims consultant, when he provides legal services, will be judged by the standards of the reasonably competent lawyer. This is perhaps reinforced by the fact, as mentioned above, that construction professionals do have direct access to a barrister, so that if they are in any doubt, they can always seek the specialist advice of a barrister or indeed a solicitor.

One question to be considered is whether a claims consultant may dilute the level of skill required of him by stressing the limit of his knowledge, notwithstanding that he still holds himself out as possessing an ability to provide a legal service. For example, a quantity surveyor may advise the client that he is not a qualified lawyer but express what his opinion is upon a particular point. In these circumstances, the client may still, nevertheless, be inclined to rely upon the consultant's advice. It is submitted that for the consultant to avoid liability for the consequence of any advice or action being wrong, he should inform the client accordingly and either decline to offer any advice or take the action concerned, or advise the client to seek specialist advice and assistance of a lawyer so as to discharge the obligation to exercise reasonable care and skill.[51]

51. See *Moresk Cleaners Ltd* v. *Hicks* [1966] 2 Lloyd's Rep. 338.

4.3.3 The taking of legal advice

Where a claims consultant, acting upon his client's instructions, seeks legal advice from either a solicitor or a barrister, almost certainly he will not be liable in negligence for acting upon such advice if it turns out to be incorrect. The situation is not the same as that of architects who delegate or rely upon the advice or work of specialists, where they may still be liable in negligence.[52] The consideration in such cases that the client may be left without remedy against either the architect or the specialist, in the absence of a direct agreement between the client and the specialist, will not apply where a claims consultant seeks the advice of a solicitor or barrister because, except in unusual circumstances, the claims consultant will clearly be instructing the solicitor or barrister as agent for his client, which will give the client a direct right of action against the lawyer concerned.

The law as it applies to seeking the advice of a barrister is summarised in *Locke* v. *Camberwell Health Authority*:[53]

"(1) In general, a solicitor is entitled to rely upon the advice of counsel properly instructed.

(2) For a solicitor without specialist experience in a particular field to rely on counsel's advice is to make normal and proper use of the Bar.

(3) However, he must not do so blindly, but must exercise his own independent judgement. If he reasonably thinks counsel's advice is obviously or glaringly wrong, it is his duty to reject it."

Where a claims consultant takes it upon himself to act in matters beyond his competence, or to advise on points which ought to be referred to a solicitor or barrister, in these circumstances he will be creating unnecessary risks and acting "at his peril".[54] Generally speaking, therefore, it would appear that if a claims consultant acts in accordance with the advice of solicitors or counsel whom he has properly instructed, the claims consultant will not be held liable in negligence, even if the legal advice proves to be mistaken or misconceived. This will not assist the claims consultant, however, where he has failed to give adequate instructions to the lawyer or where he has instructed a lawyer who was obviously not competent to advise upon the particular point in question.

52. See Ch. 3 at para 3.4.7.

53. [1991] 2 Med. L.R. 249 at 254.

54. *Ireson* v. *Pearman* (1825) 3 B.M.C. 799 which concerned a solicitor's failure to obtain Counsel's opinion on a matter of construction of some deeds.

On the other hand, the actions that the claims consultant may take will be subject to the overriding obligation to comply with his client's instructions even if they are in the face of advice to the contrary. The claims consultant's duty will be only to inform and advise, ensuring that the information and advice was understood by the client. It is not part of his duty of care to force his advice on the client, with the effect that the client can pursue a hopeless claim or enter into an onerous contract if that is what he wishes to do (see *Dutfield* v. *Gilbert H. Stephens & Sons*[55]).

4.3.4 Advice upon contract terms

Many claims consultancies, as part of an overall service offered, give advice on contract terms at the procurement stage and during the performance of the contract, in addition to advice relating to possible claims. If a legal adviser gives incorrect advice on a point which is clear, he will be liable in negligence. On the other hand, as in the case of all professions, an error of judgement is not, of itself, negligence. Construction contracts are notorious for being one of the most complex forms of document upon which legal advice can be expected to be given, and the construction of obligations under construction contracts is a frequent and common source of disagreement between lawyers. If advice is given on the effect of a contract clause or clauses, the claims consultant will not be negligent if his view turns out to be in error if such view was a reasonable one. Similarly, where advice is sought from a claims consultant upon a difficult point, he will not be negligent if the opinion he expresses is a reasonable one. It is not clear whether a claims consultant should qualify his advice by stating that the matter was in doubt. It would appear prudent to do so in any event, but Canadian authorities have held that a lawyer is not liable for failing to expressly state that his advice is no more than an expression of opinion on a debatable point:

> "The lawyer's advice in matters of statutory interpretation can never be more than opinion ... he is not, I think, normally required to warn experienced business clients of the possibility that the opinion, although firmly held, may not in fact prevail."[56]

55. (1988) 18 Fam. Law 473.

56. *Ormindale Holdings Limited* v. *Ray, Wolfe, Connel, Lightbody & Reynolds* (1981) 116 D.L.R. 3(d) 346 and (1982) 135 D.L.R. 3(d) 557, British Columbia C.A.

Claims consultants may be liable in negligence if they fail properly to advise their client upon the effect of particularly onerous contract terms. Construction contracts usually have a large number of contractual terms contained in a series of interlinked documents, and it is not uncommon for onerous terms to be tucked away in one document or even not actually included in the contractual documents but incorporated by reference. The most common examples are the incorporation of a main contractor's standard terms and conditions into a sub-contract. Careful diligence is needed to ensure that any onerous contractual terms are properly discovered and their effect, or potential effect, brought to the client's attention. A failure to do so may well result in the claims consultant being negligent if the client is deprived of an opportunity to act differently. Examples of common onerous terms in construction contracts are the exclusion of a right to payment or additional payments or of a right to claim such in the event of certain occurrences, or of the need to comply with certain conditions precedent, or of a right to require a sub-contractor to work to the will of and at the direction of a main contractor or an onerous determination clause. Further examples include clauses requiring notices or time limits or restrictions upon, for example, the submission of claims or the bringing of arbitration or litigation proceedings.

Of particular relevance to claims consultants, when dealing with claims prior to commencement of formal arbitration proceedings, is the need to ensure that the client is properly advised whether or not claims can be brought under the terms of the contract. If advice is given to a client that, for example, he is liable for a claim when the contract expressly excludes a claim of the sort being made, he could be liable in negligence.

Where negligent advice is given or, perhaps, where advice is not given when it should have been, in order to establish causation, the court will have to assess on a hypothetical basis what the client would have done had the correct advice been given and then compare that with the actual situation which the client found himself in. If the client establishes, on the balance of probabilities, that he would have taken a different course of action thus avoiding or reducing the loss suffered, then he will be entitled to recover damages.

4.3.5 Arbitration proceedings

4.3.5.1 Generally

The procedure for actions in the High Court and County Court is governed by Rules of Court and solicitors and barristers of reasonable competence are expected to have a reasonable knowledge of the procedures of the courts. In arbitration proceedings, there is no universal practice and each arbitration will be dealt with by the particular procedure laid down by the arbitrator's directions from time to time. This is subject, however, to any institutional rules which the parties have, by their contract, incorporated into the arbitration clause. For example, JCT forms of contract presently incorporate the Construction Industry Model Arbitration Rules[57] and the ICE contract and FCEC sub-contracts incorporate the ICE arbitration procedure.[58] Each of these sets of rules contains provisions for the arbitrator to make peremptory orders against a party in default of compliance with a direction or rule.[59] Additionally, the Arbitration Act 1996 gives the arbitrator power to make certain peremptory orders against a party who fails to comply.[60] Furthermore, many aspects of arbitration procedure mirror, to a certain extent, those procedures of the courts. For example, usually a party will not be permitted to present a case which has not been pleaded. Principles such as this derive from the overriding principles of natural justice, which apply equally to arbitration proceedings as they do to proceedings in the courts, whereby a party is entitled to know in advance the case it has to meet. Thus, it can be seen that in arbitration proceedings a number of actions or omissions may occur which could result in the client and his opportunity of presenting his case being disadvantaged. A claims consultant should therefore have sufficient knowledge of arbitration law and procedure generally, and of any applicable institutional rules, if he is to discharge his obligation of exercising reasonable skill and care in the furtherance of arbitration proceedings.

57. JCT 1988 edition of the Construction Industry Model Arbitration Rules.

58. The current edition is the ICE Arbitration Procedure (1997).

59. See, e.g. rule 11 of the Construction Industry Model Arbitration Rules and rules 8.4 and 8.5 of the ICE Arbitration Procedure.

60. Arbitration Act 1996, s. 41.

4.3.5.2 Commencement of arbitration proceedings

In the field of construction contracts, consultants need to be especially aware of the possible need to take timeous action. The very nature of construction projects with their possible long-term obligations, has meant that, in an effort to achieve some finality, a system has developed whereby, after a certain period of time, obligations under the contract will either cease or be stated to have definitively been exhausted. By and large, these contracts revolve around the principle that once practical completion is achieved, there then follows a definitive period of time within which defects are, under the law of probability, expected to occur, and that, after remedying all defects within this expected period, a final certificate is issued. Clause 30.9.1 of JCT 80 provides that the final certificate shall have conclusive effect in any proceedings as evidence of certain aspects of workmanship, adjustments to the contract sum, extensions of time and the reimbursement of direct loss and expense or of other claims, unless an arbitration is commenced by either party within 28 days after the final certificate is issued. The effect of this was graphically illustrated in *Crown Estates Commissioners* v. *John Mowlem & Co. Limited*,[61] where it was held that while there was no bar to commencement of proceedings seeking to re-open any of the decisions or certificates made during the contract, the "conclusive evidence" proviso of the contract meant that there was, in practice, nothing that a party may do in terms of adducing evidence to dispute the integrity of the final certificate after the 28-day period had expired.

In addition to the more commonly known clauses contained in the standard forms, claims consultants should be especially alert to the possibility that the contract or sub-contract in question may also contain certain time limits within which a claim has to be submitted or arbitration proceedings commenced or the like. This is more likely where a contract or sub-contract is under a party's standard terms and conditions (usually a main contractor's).

Finally, even if there is no contractual term governing the time for the taking of certain proceedings, the Limitation Act 1980

61. (1994) 70 B.L.R. 1. The effect of this decision was partly modified by the introduction of Amendment 15 to JCT 1980 in July 1995 with similar amendments to the rest of the family of JCT contracts and sub-contracts.

will apply. Under that Act, arbitration proceedings have to be commenced within six years from the date on which the cause of action arose.[62]

Limitation clauses, whether contractual or statutory, will mean that the possibility of a claim being lost are great, and the claims consultant needs to ensure that he examines the contractual position very carefully and, where necessary, takes precautionary steps to prevent limitation periods operating. In the event of a claim being lost as a result of a failure to observe a limitation period, the consultant almost certainly will be liable for negligence if he ought reasonably to have been aware of the possible limitation, and if he does not take sufficient steps to protect his client's interests as a consequence of a limitation period operating.

Where proceedings, or a remedy, are *prima facie* barred as a result of either a contractual time-bar or a failure to take some other step prescribed in one party's standard conditions of contract, the Unfair Contract Terms Act 1977 may apply. The effect of the provisions of this Act is that any contract term which restricts or prejudices the ability of one party to pursue a remedy for breach of contract cannot be relied upon unless the party who has the benefit of the clause is able to satisfy the tribunal as to its reasonableness. If the inability to pursue a legitimate claim results from a claims consultant's negligence, the question is whether there is an obligation on the part of the client to take proceedings to attempt to overturn the effect of the relevant contractual provision. The legal position is not entirely clear. While the clause may ultimately be set aside for want of reasonableness, however, the claims consultant could well be liable on the basis that the client has an option in the form of the availability of concurrent causes of action, as discussed earlier at paragraph 4.2.4.3.[63] An argument may be put forward that the client has failed to mitigate his loss by not taking proceedings that might have prevented the loss of the claim or remedy in question. However, in *Pilkington* v. *Wood*,[64] Harman J. stated that the duty to mitigate:

62. S.2 applies to claims in tort and s.5 applies to claims in contract, unless the contract is under seal, when, by virtue of s.8, the limitation period will be 12 years. S.34 provides that an arbitration will be commenced when one party serves on the other party a notice requiring the agreement to the appointment of an arbitrator.

63. See pp. 137–139.

64. [1953] Ch.770.

"does not go so far as to oblige the injured party, even under an indemnity, to embark on a complicated and difficult piece of litigation against a third party."

4.3.5.3 Errors in pleadings

Generally speaking, and subject to the right which a party will always have to seek leave to amend, a party will be restricted to his pleadings, even in arbitration. Although a much more flexible attitude is taken in arbitration, principles of natural justice apply so as to require a party fully to plead his case with such particularity as will enable his opponent to know the case he has to meet. Arbitrators generally will not allow a party to put forward a case that has not been pleaded. The general principles that the courts apply to applications for leave to amend are likely to be imposed by the arbitrator. Sometimes, because of lateness or prejudice or a combination of both, it may not be possible to bring forward a plea that should and could have been made at an earlier stage in the proceedings. If a claims consultant were to fail to pursue an obvious remedy, or to put forward an erroneous basis of case that becomes unsustainable in the form in which it is pleaded, and it is likely that if the client loses the opportunity of recovery of a sum to which he would otherwise have been entitled had the case been correctly pleaded, the claims consultant will be negligent. Even if leave to amend is given, almost certainly the party amending will be ordered to pay the costs thrown away, which could result in a costs liability for the client for which the consultant will be responsible, if he should reasonably have put forward the alternative plea at an earlier stage.

The converse may possibly be true where a hopeless case is pursued or pleaded. While the consultant's obligation will always be subject to the overriding instructions of the client, if the consultant does advance a claim which should never have been brought, and is not brought upon the specific instructions of his client, the claims consultant is likely to find himself liable to the client in damages in the form of the other party's costs and the client's own costs. Simply because a claim or defence fails, however, does not imply that it was hopeless. As was said in *Orchard* v. *South Eastern Electricity Board*:[65]

65. [1987] 1 Q.B. 565.

"It must never be forgotten that it is not for solicitors or counsel to impose a pre-trial screen through which a litigant must pass before he can put his complaints or defence before the court."

There is the possibility of a middle course, whereby a claim is brought that is successful overall, but the claim may include hopeless elements or be greatly exaggerated. This, unfortunately, is a common feature of the majority of construction claims. By and large, the practice is and has been for many years, both in court and in arbitration proceedings, to award the net winner his costs. The underlying reason is that in the High Court there is the option of a payment into court available,[66] and in arbitration proceedings the equivalent is available in the form of a "*Calderbank* offer".[67] In both methods, the option is open to both parties to make what is the equivalent of a formal offer of settlement of the claim (or counterclaim as the case may be), the contents of which are not made known to the tribunal until after a decision has been given. Subject to matters of form, if the offer is rejected, and at the hearing the claiming party fails to recover more than the amount offered, the general rule is that he will pay the costs incurred since the offer or payment in was made. However, in cases where an unreasonable amount of time or costs may be spent on a particular issue, which the claiming party loses but nevertheless still succeeds overall, there is a danger that the client could be ordered to pay the costs relating to that particular issue. There has been a tendency for many years to include all possible claims—some good, some arguable, and some hopeless—when a claim is advanced, upon the basis that even if the hopeless claims are rejected, the claiming party will not be penalised upon the "winner-takes-all" philosophy as to costs. This practice may well have to change, however, as a result of the hardening attitude of the judiciary and executive to the ever-spiralling costs involved in disputes. Following his enquiries into the civil justice system in England and Wales, which followed many years' complaints about excessive delays and costs, Lord Woolf included among his recommendations to the Lord Chancellor that, rather than a "winner-takes-all" rule as to costs, a successful claimant should not be free of risk as to costs and an approach should be

66. See Rules of the Supreme Court 1965, Ord. 22.
67. The procedure derived from the divorce case of *Calderbank* v. *Calderbank* [1975] 3 All E.R. 333.

adopted whereby a case is divided into a number of different issues with different orders for costs being made on the different issues involved.[68]

Hitherto, the courts have shown a reluctance to make split costs orders except in clear cases.[69] However, the courts may well, at least gradually, start to apply the spirit of Lord Woolf's reforms in the near future. Arbitrations, similarly, may, once they routinely start to apply the provisions of section 1(a) of the Arbitration Act 1996,[70] develop a philosophy to avoid unmeritorious points being taken, with the penalty of a costs order in relation to that issue if appropriate. Certainly, a philosophy has been developing in the courts for a number of years, whereby since the introduction of section 51 of the Supreme Court Act 1981, now replaced by section 4 of the Courts and Legal Services Act 1990, the courts have been given powers to order solicitors personally to pay the costs of an opponent if they are "wasted". While this jurisdiction derives from the control of the courts over their own officers, if applied analogously to those involved in the conduct of arbitration proceedings, it would inevitably mean that the claimant in an arbitration could be made liable for an opponent's costs incurred as a result of raising claims or issues unnecessarily or unreasonably. In such circumstances, the claims consultant who advanced, or exaggerated, unnecessarily or unreasonably, any claim would expose his client to an order for wasted costs and, if such exposure was done and without properly informed instructions, the consultant may be liable in negligence.

4.3.5.4 Gathering of evidence

The evidence that is to be called at the arbitration hearing is, perhaps, the most important pre-hearing preparation in any arbitration.

It will be negligent if a claims consultant fails to take reasonable steps to obtain proofs of evidence from factual witnesses who are

68. Interim Report to the Lord Chancellor on the civil justice system in England and Wales by Lord Woolf, June 1995, Ch. 25, para. 22.

69. See also the cases referred to in Ch. 8, para 8.2.4.

70. S. 1(a) of the Arbitration Act 1996 provides:

"1. The provisions of this Part are founded on the following principles, and shall be construed accordingly—

(a) the object of arbitration is to obtain the fair resolution of disputes by an impartial tribunal without unnecessary delay or expense."

likely to be called and who can give material evidence. As far as expert evidence is concerned, which is an almost inevitable feature of construction litigation and arbitration, the decision on which expert to instruct can sometimes be crucial. Providing the consultant's choice of expert is reasonable, he will not be held negligent if, in fact, the expert's evidence turns out to be incorrect or even inadequate. On the other hand, a consultant may be held negligent if he instructs an expert whose qualifications or experience make him an inappropriate choice as an expert witness.

4.3.5.5 Protection against costs

Upon the general basis that costs follow the event, as discussed above, the burden of costs upon the loser of arbitration proceedings is likely to be very substantial. Construction disputes are notorious not only for their complexity but also for their cost. It follows that it will be prudent, when acting for a respondent in an arbitration, to try and establish, at as early a stage as possible, whether there is likely to be some liability and, if so, to advise the client to take steps which may protect him. In arbitration proceedings this is known as a "*Calderbank* offer".[71]

Assessing how much a claim is worth and, therefore, what offer should be made and when it should be made, is generally very difficult in construction claims. Often it will not be until a late stage in the proceedings that the likely value of the claim can be accurately assessed, by which time the costs which would have to be paid by the likely loser will be very large. The claims consultant's duty will, therefore, be to advise at the earliest moment of the possible costs consequences and the availability of the *Calderbank* procedure and advise the client that if there is a *possible* liability, the client should assess this, even if only on a rough basis, and put forward a *Calderbank* offer. If the claims consultant fails to consider this and advise the client, or does not do so until a late stage in the proceedings when a large amount of costs have already been incurred, the consultant may be liable in negligence if the client has not been able to take steps which he otherwise would have been able to do so as to adequately protect his position in good time.

Even when a decision is made to put forward a *Calderbank* offer,

71. See p. 156.

great care needs to be taken to ensure that it is written in such terms as to provide adequate protection for the offering party. It must, therefore, leave the offeree in no doubt about exactly what is offered. Particularly, it is essential that the offer also includes an offer to pay also the offeree's and the arbitrator's costs, for if it does not do so, so that the offer is inclusive of these (as yet) indeterminable amounts, it will not be possible readily to identify how much the offer is worth in net terms, and, consequently, may not offer effective protection.[72] The *Calderbank* offer should therefore make it clear whether all of the claims made are encompassed by the offer or, if not, which are intended to be covered by the offer; and whether, and if so to what extent, any counterclaims have been taken into account, and if so which ones. Of particular note is the need to deal with the question of VAT and whether it is to be inclusive or paid in addition. Because of the tendency of the construction industry to speak in VAT-exclusive terms, this aspect often becomes overlooked both in settlement negotiations and in *Calderbank* offers, despite the fact that VAT is almost always claimed in the formal pleadings. The failure to deal with this may then give rise to a possible dispute whether the *Calderbank* offer is effective if the amount awarded by the arbitrator exclusive of VAT is less than the amount offered, but with the addition of VAT makes the claimant recover more than the amount offered.

4.3.5.6 Negotiations and settlements

Like a solicitor, a claims consultant will be bound to exercise reasonable care in the conduct of settlement negotiations and in advising on the merits of any settlement proposed. It may be difficult to prove negligence in relation to a settlement by virtue of the fact that advice in relation to settlement negotiations contains many imponderables which, like advocacy, are incapable of forensic analysis with hindsight. A claims consultant should be aware, however, of the fact that, when involved in settlement discussions, he will have, at least ostensibly, authority from his client to agree a matter which may then bind his client, whether in terms of his substantive rights or his procedural rights. If the consultant reaches an agree-

72. See *Tramountana Armadora SA* v. *Atlantic Shipping Co. SA* [1978] 2 All E.R. 870.

ment which binds his client and is either negligent when compared to the client's likely recovery or liability (as the case may be) or which is in excess of the client's authority, the claims consultant will be liable in negligence. Therefore, if the consultant advises the client to accept a settlement which is on far less favourable terms than would reasonably be expected to result if the matter proceeded to a hearing, and such advice, again taking into account the many imponderable factors that will be involved in reaching an opinion, could not be considered to be reasonable, the claims consultant will be liable in negligence.

4.3.5.7 Advocacy at the hearing

As a result of section 62(1) of the Courts and Legal Services Act 1990, claims consultants (as, indeed, will anyone) will be immune from actions for negligence arising out of their advocacy conducted at arbitration hearings. Section 62(1) provides:

> "A person:
> (a) who is not a barrister;
> (b) who lawfully provides any legal services in relation to any proceedings.
>
> shall have the same immunity from liability for negligence in respect of his acts or omissions as he would have as if he were a barrister lawfully providing those services."

This immunity devolves from the immunity given to barristers against damages for negligence as a result of their actions in court, which has been recognised for centuries. The reasons for the immunity have been summarised in a leading textbook[73] as:

(i) The administration of justice required that a barrister should be able to carry out his duty to the court fearlessly and independently. This might be affected if he had a conflicting duty to his clients.

(ii) Actions for negligence against barristers would only involve re-trying the original actions. This would prolong litigation, and create the risk of inconsistent decisions, which would bring the administration of justice into disrepute.

(iii) Because of the "cab-rank" rule, a barrister was obliged to

73. See *Jackson & Powell* (4th ed.), 5–11.

accept any client, however difficult. It would encourage breaches of this rule if barristers did not have immunity.

(iv) A barrister's immunity for what he says and does in court is part of the general immunity, which attaches to all persons participating in court proceedings: judges, court officials, witnesses, parties and solicitors.

Point (iii) above has no applicability to arbitration advocates other than barristers, but the other three points carry equal force. The general purpose of the immunity, with its extension to other advocates as provided by the Courts and Legal Services Act 1990, is one of public policy.

The immunity given to barristers and, by section 62 of the Courts and Legal Services Act 1990, any advocate involved in arbitration proceedings not only covers the actual advocacy at the hearing itself, but also includes some pre-trial work if the particular work is so intimately connected with the conduct of the case in court that it can fairly be said to be a preliminary decision affecting the way that the case is to be conducted when it comes to a hearing. Thus, where a decision is made not to call a particular witness or not to adduce a particular piece of evidence, an advocate will not be liable in negligence, whatever the result may otherwise have been. The general philosophy relating to the conduct of a hearing is that it is perhaps the least scientific of all legal services offered, requiring the exercise of judgement as the case progresses and in respect of which it is inapplicable to impose forensic hindsight.

4.3.5.8 After the hearing

If there is a possibility of appeal or of other relief arising from the arbitrator's award, claims consultants will have to advise their clients on the possibility of an appeal and, particularly, the time limits for bringing such. Under section 70 of the Arbitration Act 1996, the time limits for seeking relief from the courts are very short, namely 28 days from the date of the arbitration award. Moreover, claims consultants will need to be mindful of the fact that in certain circumstances leave to appeal may be required, but in others, such as in relation to disputes under the JCT standard forms of contract and their related family of sub-contracts, there is already a pre-consent to an appeal which satisfies the requirements of section 69(3) of the Arbitration Act 1979.[74] If a client were to fail to lodge an appeal in time or seek other relief available under the Act as a result of not being advised of his rights to do so, a consultant might be liable if an appeal might have given him a chance of a different result or at least mitigated against the consequences of the award.

74. See, e.g., 74 JCT 80, cl. 41.6 or DOM/1, cl. 38.7.

CHAPTER 5

LIABILITIES OF ARBITRATORS, MEDIATORS, ADJUDICATORS AND EXPERTS

Arbitrators, mediators, adjudicators and expert witnesses all make their contribution to the various aspects of the dispute resolution processes. Parties to the construction industry are not hidebound to litigating their grievances through the courts, and mediation, adjudication and arbitration are perceived as viable alternatives. Whereas construction professionals may elect to resolve any of their own disputes by any of these methods, they also provide very useful and valuable work opportunities—acting within any of the aforementioned capacities—in the disputes of others. The question must, however, be asked about the extent, if any, to which the law should accord immunity from any action to those parties involved in the dispute resolution process. It may be that by their conduct they have fallen below the standard of care and expertise that may reasonably be expected of them. On the other hand, the law did recognise that parties so involved should to some extent be able to conduct their activities without fear of being sued. There is inevitably one party to any dispute who is disappointed by the outcome, and occasionally both parties may be disappointed. It would be wrong to place arbitrators, mediators, adjudicators and experts in the position in which they are to be held responsible for an unfavourable or unsatisfactory outcome.

5.1. LIABILITY VERSUS IMMUNITY

Public policy interests prevent judges from being sued by any parties to the litigation process. Why should not this same protection also apply to arbitrators? Formerly, it was not clear whether or not an arbitrator was immune. In *North Eastern Co-operative Society Limited*

v. *Newcastle-upon-Tyne City Council and another*,[1] a decision involving the appointment of a surveyor to arbitrate in a dispute, the court expressly refused to comment on whether or not the surveyor was immune from action for negligence in his capacity as an arbitrator. In *Arenson* v. *Arenson*[2] a majority of the House of Lords was prepared to assume that arbitral immunity existed, but the point was not one on which a decision was directly called for. The matter would now appear to have been resolved beyond doubt as a consequence of the introduction of section 29 of the Arbitration Act 1996. All the provisions of the Act have been in force since January 1997 and the Act applies to all arbitration proceedings that are commenced following this date. Section 29 of the Act states that:

> "29—(1) An arbitrator is not liable for anything done or omitted in the discharge or purported discharge of his functions as arbitrator unless the act or omission is shown to have been in bad faith.
>
> (2) Subsection (1) applies to an employee or agent of an arbitrator as it applies to the arbitrator himself.
>
> (3) This section does not affect any liability incurred by an arbitrator by reason of his resigning (but see section 25)."

The importance of the role of an adjudicator within the construction industry has received impetus as a consequence of the enactment of the Housing Grants Construction and Regeneration Act 1996. Section 108 of the Act contains a specific adjudication procedure. This is discussed in greater detail in Chapter 9.

Section 108(4) of the Act states:

> "The contract shall also provide that the adjudicator is not liable for anything done or omitted in the discharge or purported discharge of his functions as adjudicator unless the act or omission is in bad faith, and that any employee or agent of the adjudicator is similarly protected from liability."

In other words, an adjudicator appointed pursuant to the Act will be immune from any action which could otherwise be brought against him.

Mediation is a form of alternative dispute resolution ("ADR"). A number of specialist organisations have been formed for the specific purpose of facilitating the introduction of mediation and the training of mediators. Mediators are often successful in resolving

1. [1987] 1 E.G.L.R. 142.
2. [1977] A.C. 405.

more complicated disputes where there are a number of parties. Standard terms of engagement in use by mediators will normally provide for the immunity of the mediator himself. This means that he cannot be sued by one or any of the parties. However, it is most unlikely that any liability would apply to a mediator in any event, since his function is to seek to persuade as opposed to compel the parties to resolve their differences by appreciating each other's argument and thus ultimately effecting some compromise which both parties consider acceptable. Whether the attempts at mediation are successful or not entirely depends upon the parties' willingness themselves to discuss and attempt a compromise.

The role of the expert witness is different from that of the mediator, adjudicator or arbitrator. A major difference is that the expert witness is engaged on behalf of his professional client only, whereas the other categories are engaged by both. Thus, it must follow that if an expert witness is to be sued at all, it is only by his own client who has engaged him. Repeated warnings have been issued by the courts of the dangers to the parties and their expert witnesses involved in disputes. In *The University of Warwick* v. *Sir Robert McAlpine and Others*[3] Garland J. gave useful guidelines on the nature of expert evidence and the manner in which it should be introduced. The judge recalled observations of Lord Wilberforce in *Whitehouse* v. *Jordan*:[4]

> "It is necessary that expert evidence presented to the Court should be and should be seen to be, the independent product of the expert, uninfluenced as to form or content by the exigencies of litigation. To the extent that it is not, the evidence is likely to be not only incorrect but self defeating."

Furthermore, in *National Justice Compania Naviera SA* v. *Prudential Insurance Co. Limited* ("The Ikarian Reefer"),[5] Cresswell J. set out seven separate points or guidelines for the appointment of an expert. One of these emphasised the importance of the independence of the expert, who should provide not only his client but also the court with objective unbiased opinion in relation to matters within his expertise. An expert witness in the High Court, the judge said, should never assume the role of an advocate.

Things can and do, however, go wrong in an action and a client

3. (1988) 42 B.L.R. at 22.
4. [1981] 1 W.L.R. 246 at 256.
5. [1993] 2 Lloyd's Rep. 68.

may often feel that his expert has not performed as he should have and that this has caused or contributed to the court concluding in favour of his opponent. A more obvious example of communication breaking down between a client, his advisers and an expert may be found in the decision of *Richard Roberts Holdings Limited* v. *Douglas Smith Stimson Partnership & Others (No. 2)*[6] where an expert instructed by a party in litigation proceedings entered into a binding agreement with his opponent which it was argued he had no authority to do. Whereas an expert is engaged ultimately to give evidence in the proceedings themselves this is not the whole of his services, and in the preliminary stages he will, in all probability, be advising his client. This is especially so in the case of claims brought against professionals where the early involvement by the specialist expert witness is invaluable. In *Palmer and another* v. *Durnford Ford (a firm) and another*,[7] Mr Simon Tuckey Q.C., sitting as Deputy High Court judge, had to decide whether or not a claim commenced against an expert should be allowed to stand or whether, in the alternative, it should be struck out as not giving rise to a reasonable cause of action. The expert in question was an engineer who had been asked to prepare a report on the cause of the breakdown of an engine. The court commented that experts were usually liable to their clients for advice given in breach of their contractual duty of care, and that any immunity conferred was based upon public policy and should therefore only be conferred where it was absolutely necessary to do so. The court concluded that no immunity should be conferred on the preliminary advice by the expert, that is, the advice given which was preliminary to his giving evidence in court. While it followed that the prime purpose of the preparation of the expert's report was ultimately for his opinions to constitute opinion evidence this could be contrasted with the initial advice given to his client. This distinction had to be identified in order to decide in the first instance whether or not there were claims which could properly be made. The judge concluded that he did not think that it was difficult in most cases to decide where the line should be drawn.

6. (1989) 47 B.L.R. 113.
7. [1992] 2 All E.R. 122.

5.2. LIABILITIES OTHER THAN IN CONTRACT AND TORT

Notwithstanding that such person may not be sued on the grounds of immunity, there may nonetheless be some financial consequences of a failure properly to perform responsibilities, at least in the case of an arbitrator. In the case of an expert witness the matter of his fees will be governed by his terms of engagement by his employer, and if it may properly be maintained that there has been a complete or partial failure of consideration on the part of the expert witness, in the sense that he has not done all or part of what he has been asked to do, the employer will have a strong argument for the reduction of the expert's fee or the total extinguishment of any liability in respect thereof. It is to be doubted whether or not there is any mechanism for the reduction of the fees of mediators or adjudicators. If they can demonstrate that they have properly spent the time in the conduct of the reference they should be entitled to receive payment.

The position of arbitrators is different. The court ultimately reserves the right to remove the arbitrator on the ground of misconduct. Such a right is now to be found embodied in section 24 of the Arbitration Act 1996. In the event of an arbitrator being removed by the court on the ground of misconduct or incapacity, listed in that same section, the court can make such order in respect of the arbitrator's entitlement to fees or expenses, including those already paid, as it sees fit. Thus, some or all of the arbitrator's fees may be forfeited in the event of misconduct. In any event the court reserves the power to be able to tax the fees and expenses of arbitrators pursuant to section 64 of the Arbitration Act 1996. It will only allow the recovery of such reasonable fees and expenses as are appropriate in the circumstances.

CHAPTER 6

BONDS AND WARRANTIES

Note: Throughout this chapter, reference is made to the CoWa/F and CoWa/P&T forms of collateral warranty. These warranties are reproduced in full at Appendix 3 (at p. 247) and Appendix 4 (at p. 259) respectively.

Those involved in the construction process are often called upon by an employer to provide agreements which are additional to their primary contracts governing the terms of their engagement. The purpose of this chapter is to have regard to these additional agreements, be they bonds or warranties, and to analyse their typical content and to explain the legal position in relation to them.

6.1. BONDS

The House of Lords in its decision of *Trafalgar House Construction (Regions) Limited* v. *General Surety and Guarantee Co. Limited*,[1] laid down important guidance for the interpretation of a typical bond which had been given to a main contractor by its sub-contractor. Of the major conclusions reached by the House of Lords, the first was that the bond was in effect a contract of guarantee. To this extent, it reversed the earlier conclusion of the Court of Appeal.[2] A guarantee is usually a promise to accept liability for a failure to perform legal obligations and is thus to be contrasted with an indemnity. Whereas an indemnity provides an obligation by the indemnifier to pay a sum of money, whatever that may be, thus indemnifying against a loss, a guarantee, by way of contrast, relates to performance. Thus a contract of indemnity involves two parties. A contract of guarantee involves three parties, with the guarantor agreeing to perform the work on the part of the principal should he fail to do so.

1. (1995) 73 B.L.R. 35.
2. (1996) 66 B.L.R. 42.

In deciding that the bond was but a contract of guarantee, Lord Jauncey, who gave the leading judgment in *Trafalgar House*, was influenced by the many earlier decisions of the courts when dealing with wording similar or identical to that before it in which they had concluded that the contract was one of guarantee. The Court also referred to the specimen bond included in the ICE Conditions of Contract, which was in identical terms. The bond itself contained indications that it was intended to be a guarantee. The appellant, General Surety and Guarantee Company Limited, was described in the agreement as "the surety".

There are a number of consequences of the court concluding that the bond was a guarantee. These are:

(i) In the event of there being any material change in the primary contract, the surety may regard himself as being discharged from obligations under the guarantee unless there is a specific clause which preserves liability in this event. This broad principle was developed in the nineteenth century and is referred to as the rule in *Holme* v. *Brunskill*.[3] This rule was relied upon successfully by the surety in *Wardens and Commonalty of the Mystery of Mercers of the City of London* v. *New Hampshire Insurance Co. Limited*.[4] In this decision the court explained the reasoning behind the rule, which was that a surety ought not to be bound to a guarantee which was different in content from that to which he had expressly consented.

(ii) The guarantor is placed in exactly the same position as the original party and may avail himself of the benefit of any defences, including those by way of set off to which the original party may have been entitled.

(iii) Unless it is specifically stated otherwise (see *post*) the beneficiary must establish both a liability and a definitive loss before it is entitled to seek recovery of that sum from the guarantor.

The wording of a conditional bond may appear antiquated and difficult to understand for those who are not familiar with its typical wording. The wording of the conditional bond before the court in

3. (1877) 3 Q.B.D. 495.
4. (1992) 60 B.L.R. 26.

Trafalgar House is typical and suggests that there is liability but this liability will not be actionable and shall be null and void unless there is default. This wording was the subject of the decision by the Court of Appeal in *Trafalgar House*, in which it stated that this was in essence an "on demand" bond and not a conditional bond. The only requirement necessary to instigate payment under an on demand bond is the written demand itself. As discussed, the decision of the Court of Appeal was reversed by the House of Lords.

The antiquated form of wording typically used in conditional bonds, which caused the difficulty at the Court of Appeal stage of *Trafalgar House*, was again the subject of criticism by the House of Lords. Thus Lord Jauncey stated[5] that the "archaic nature of the bond" had indeed been the subject of comment by Lord Atkin in *Workington Harbour Dock Board* v. *Trade Indemnity Co. Ltd (No. 2)*:[6]

> "I may be allowed to remark that it is difficult to understand why businessmen persist in entering upon considerable obligations in old-fashioned forms of contract which do not adequately express the true transaction."

Although this harsh but justified criticism is now over 60 years old, such antiquated forms of wording continue to be used. All parties should avoid giving "on demand" bonds since it is considered to be analogous to a cash payment. The difficulties were graphically explained by Lord Denning in *Edward Owen* v. *Barclays Bank*[7] when referring to the prospect of a demand being made:

> "The possibility is so real that the English supplier, if he is well advised, will take it into account when quoting his price for the contract."

Whereas "on demand" bonds were formerly reserved for international contracts, many of which had a Middle East connection, they have now become increasingly common.

Whichever kind of bond is given, however, be it a conditional or an "on demand" bond, there is nonetheless an immediately identifiable cost to the provider. Bonds may be provided by insurers or banks. If provided by an insurer, the premium payable will directly be reflected by the underwriters' perception of the risk. If provided by a bank, the bank will ensure that there will always be

5. At p. 45.
6. [1937] A.C. 1 at 17.
7. (1977) 6 B.L.R. 1.

clearly identifiable funds to the credit of the provider's account which will be set aside to deal with any possible call on the bond. In the interim, these identified funds will effectively have been frozen.

Whereas conditional bonds are actionable in the event of default, care should always be taken when drafting to ensure that a call may be made, not only where there has been a breach of contract or a default but also where there is insolvency. This ultimately is the most important benefit to be derived from any bond. If there has been a default or breach the party responsible and primarily liable can always be called upon to take steps to remedy the situation. This is not so in cases of insolvency. The employer will then have to engage another party to perform these same obligations in its place. This process, together with the employer's consequential costs, must be the true justification for the provision of a bond. However, professionals must be contrasted with contractors and the perception of risk by an employer of engaging professionals must be different. Professionals usually operate by way of a partnership. Partners are and remain jointly and severally liable for each others' acts or omissions. If a partnership were to dissolve, inevitably some of the partners would wish to retain the right to perform its professional services, no doubt for financial benefits or reward. If none of the partners were to do this ultimately an employer would be entitled to regard the contract as having been repudiated in the face of continued default and could engage another party in substitution. Consequently, any claim for losses would be recoverable from each of the partners of the old firm, all of whom would be jointly and severally liable. Whereas this process may appear to be more protracted than making a call under a bond, it nonetheless provides a powerful argument why bonds should not be sought from professionals.

6.2. WARRANTIES

It is now the norm rather than the exception for construction professionals appointed to deal with a project to give warranties extending their contractual liabilities to a completed project. These typically include the funders, the tenants and purchasers. Thus, a new building, in the eyes of the consumer, is to be compared to a chattel which is sold with the benefit of a specific warranty entitling the owner to claim repair or replacement if the chattel develops a fault within a specific period of time. The difficulty with a construction professional is that this warranty may not be for a period of 12 months, as is typically the case with a chattel, and could even be for a period of 12 years if the warranty is executed under seal. Furthermore, the warranties are expected to be delivered at no additional cost, albeit that the cost to the professional is real enough and takes the form of increased premiums and increased potential for uninsured liabilities, such as under a typical policy of professional indemnity insurance where the professional bears a certain portion of the loss himself.

Warranties have been given by architects, engineers and surveyors for some considerable time, albeit that the trend toward the giving of warranties received added impetus as a consequence of the decisions in *D & F Estates* and *Murphy* v. *Brentwood* (as discussed in Chapter 1). Whereas formerly, and prior to these decisions, there was a possibility that a claim in the tort of negligence might succeed, this is not the situation following these two landmark decisions. While the professional bodies initially resisted the giving of warranties by their members, they ultimately perceived that this was no longer tenable. There was thus an advantage in producing standard forms with the active co-operation of the professional bodies, which would seek to standardise the use of warranties. It was believed that this would lead to less wastage of time and costs in agreeing warranties on a project-by-project basis, each with its own particular wording. In 1988 the Royal Institute of British Architects published its warranty form to be given to funding bodies. Subsequently, in May 1990, the British Property Federation published its own, not dissimilar, form of warranty (CoWa/F) to be given to funders. The form was approved for use by the RIBA (and its Scottish equivalent), the Association of Consulting Engineers, the Royal Institution of Chartered Surveyors and the Association of British Insurers. This was then followed in February 1992 by a second standard warranty (CoWa/P&T), again approved by the same bodies, to be given to purchasers or tenants of the proposed development. Whereas these have undoubtedly seen extensive use, more commonly employers tend to produce their own bespoke forms of warranty. The argument used by employers is that they are entitled to impose whichever form of wording they wish and consultants have to accept this if they are to be engaged in relation to the project. They may also draw some comfort from their familiarity with their own forms, which undoubtedly have been written in order to afford them maximum protection.

There have been many powerful arguments in favour of the adoption of insurance on a project-by-project basis. This may be termed "project cover" or "decennial insurance". The origin of this term is that the cover typically lasts for a period of 10 years. This operates on the basis that insurers insure the building in return for a premium which is usually calculated by taking a percentage of the project sum. In return for this premium, the insurers underwrite the risk of any defects howsoever occurring within the building for a specific period of years, usually 10 years, and waive any rights of subrogation against any parties who may have a liability for the causes themselves. The advantage of this form of insurance is that it provides the owner with a definitive remedy and does not compel him to sue any of the parties in order to obtain a remedy. The waiver of the subrogation rights, furthermore, removes any element of culpability whatsoever. The obvious disadvantage is cost, and at a time when employers are desirous of reducing cost liabilities wherever possible, they are content to pursue their legal remedies themselves if they perceive that they have a grievance. Thus, at least for the time being, the perceived need for collateral warranties remains unabated. It must be stated, however, that there is a significant advantage to be derived from the obtaining of project insurance. This advantage lies in the avoidance of the causation exercise in order to ascertain culpability. If there are, for example, substantial cracks in the superstructure there can be a claim under the policy or the commencement of legal proceedings followed by an exhaustive analysis of who is to blame and to what extent.

The term "collateral warranty" is not a term of art. It commonly denotes an agreement given to parties who have or may assume an interest in the completed structure. The significance of the term "collateral" is that the warranty must exist side by side with the principal agreement which governs the terms of engagement of the construction professional. Thus, this may often be used as a powerful argument against any attempt to impose more onerous obligations in the collateral warranty than those which in any event exist within the principal terms of engagement contract.

6.3. TYPICAL CLAUSES TO BE FOUND WITHIN WARRANTIES

It would be very difficult, if not impossible, to reproduce every variant clause found in every warranty. Without wholesale and fundamental acceptance of the standard forms which have been produced, the ability of the legal draftsman to prepare variations to any legal wording is not to be underestimated. However, there are specific clauses which may typically be found within warranties, albeit that, as stated, the precise wording will vary. Thus it is possible to look at specimen wordings in this section and the principles of law that apply to their application and interpretation. Reference is made to the clauses to be found in the Standard Forms of Warranty, which are analogous to those wordings as set out below.

"The professional shall have no greater liability to the [funder, tenant, purchaser, etc.] by virtue of this agreement that it would have had if the company had been named as a joint client in accordance with the terms of the professional's engagement."

This clause is of fundamental importance to the professional, and it should not be omitted. To do otherwise gives rise to the suggestion that the warranty may not be regarded as being "collateral" to the principal contract at all. Furthermore, it is worthwhile insisting with this clause that, in the event of there being any conflict or discrepancy with any other clause in the warranty, this clause is to take precedence over all others. Thus the professional has the security of knowing that there is no greater extent of liability imposed than that which he has himself assumed under the terms of his own contract with his employer. The absence of any such provision can cause serious prejudice. Consider a warranty executed as a deed but a primary contract between the professional and his employer executed under hand. The period of limitation is 12 years in the former and six years in the latter. It would also be advisable to define "the extent of liability" not only within the context of its scope but also its duration. Without such careful consideration of the drafting, the liability on the part of the professional to enter into successive warranties may continue indefinitely.[8]

"The construction professional warrants that he has exercised and will

8. See Cl. 1 of both CoWa/F and CoWa/P&T.

continue to exercise all reasonable skill and care in the performance of his duties to the client and will at all times exercise his best endeavours."

The usual test of competence for a professional is that of reasonable skill and care only. This test as discussed by McNair J. in *Bolam* v. *Friern Hospital Management Committee*[9] has not been seriously questioned since this time. The test is of the "ordinary competent man exercising that particular art". The mere inclusion of the word "all" in this context seeks to impose a much more onerous responsibility and is suggestive of a stricter test of liability. It is for this reason that the professional should be wary of it. Furthermore, any suggestion of the design being fit for its intended purpose should be treated with some caution. It is clear from the authorities following from *Greaves (Contractors) Limited* v. *Baynham Meikle & Partners*[10] that the test for a designer who is producing the design only is that of reasonable skill and care. A later authority which affirms this principle may be found in *George Hawkins* v. *Chrysler (UK) Limited and Burne Associates.*[11] Whereas in *Greaves* the designer was subjected to a judicial test of "fitness for purpose" this decision has not been followed and is no longer regarded as good law. A notable exception arises however if the professional is responsible for the design of a "dwelling", as defined pursuant to the Defective Premises Act 1972. In such an instance, the designer is to be subjected to a requirement of "a fitness for habitation" test. The test imposed by the Act is consistent with the pre-existing case law as reflected by *Hancock* v. *Brazier.*[12] Similarly, any wording which imposes upon the professional the obligation to exercise its "best endeavours" must be treated with caution. The substitution of the term "reasonable endeavours" is to be preferred. The requirement to exercise "best endeavours" is an onerous requirement. This meaning was discussed by the Court of Appeal in *IBM (UK) Limited* v. *Rockware Glass Limited.*[13] The facts in this case related to an agreement for the sale of land to IBM for £6 million. The agreement provided that "the purchaser will make an application for planning permission and use its best endeavours to obtain the same". Although planning permission was sought, it was refused.

9. [1957] 2 All E.R. 118.
10. [1975] 1 W.L.R. 1095.
11. (1986) 38 B.L.R. 36.
12. [1966] 1 W.L.R. 1317.
13. [1980] F.S.R. 335.

Moreover, IBM did not appeal to the Secretary of State against the refusal. The Court of Appeal interpreted the responsibility as one to take all those steps in the purchaser's power capable of producing the desired result, namely the obtaining of planning permission, being a step which a prudent determined and reasonable owner acting in his own interests and desiring to achieve that result would take. Further, in *UBH (Mechanical Services) Limited* v. *Standard Life Assurance Company*[14] the court held that "reasonable endeavours" carried with it a lesser obligation than that of "best endeavours".[15]

"The professional agrees that it will not without first giving the [fund] not less than 21 days previous notice in writing exercise any right it may have to terminate its appointment or to discontinue its performance and involvement in the project."

Funding bodies usually insist upon such a clause, since it provides them with the opportunity of taking remedial action to maintain continuity in the event of default or insolvency on the part of the employer. Thus, on the one hand, there is an obvious benefit to the professional in the sense that he may have continuity of employment. It would be advisable, however, for there to be a provision for the payment of all outstanding arrears of fees by the fund prior to the agreement on the part of the professional for the continuation of the performance of its services. On the other hand, care will need to be taken to ensure that there is no prejudice which may befall the consultant by being compelled to continue working for a period of 21 days or so while the period of notice is running. It may not be compulsory for the fund to step in and take over, and significant irrecoverable costs may be incurred during this same 21-day period. Thus it must be seen as a fetter and obstruction against the exercise by the professional of his rights under the terms of his principal contract of engagement with his employer. Despite this caveat and concern, it is fair to say that these clauses have a general use and are usually considered acceptable.[16]

"The professional warrants that it will maintain professional indemnity insurance for any one occurrence or series of occurrences arising out of any one event for a period of . . . years from the date of practical completion of the works."

14. *The Times*, 13 November 1996.
15. See by analogy Cl. 1 of both CoWa/F and CoWa/P&T.
16. See Cll. 5 and 6 of CoWa/F.

Most warranties will contain such a provision. On the basis that professionals are, in any event, duty bound to insure against their liabilities, inclusion of such a clause will generally not create too much hardship. However, the level of cover is sometimes considered to be unrealistically high. Furthermore, it must be borne in mind that if the professional should retire or should the partnership cease to exist, "run-off" cover must be obtained in respect of those liabilities which had hitherto been assumed by him as well as the other partners irrespective of any ongoing arrangements of the partnership.

Whereas the inclusion of this clause is generally not considered to be too confrontational, it is interesting to note the consequences of any breach of any such clause. No loss will result from a failure to insure until and unless there is liability on the part of the professional which is not the subject of indemnity under any insurance policy and the professional cannot pay.[17]

"The copyright in all drawings, specifications and other similar documents produced by the professional shall remain vested within that same party but the [fund, purchaser or tenant] shall have a licence to copy and use such drawings and other documents and to reproduce them albeit limited for the purpose of the development only."

Architects, engineers and surveyors are involved in the issue of copyright in respect of two separate interests. On the one hand, there is a copyright issue in respect of the building itself, to which there is reference in section 4(2) of the Copyright Design and Patent Act 1988 in which there is a description of "building or fixed structures or any part of a building or fixed structure". Secondly, copyright is normally vested in the person who creates the artistic work and is thus its author as defined in section 9 of the Copyright Design and Patent Act 1988. Although the usual terms of engagement provide that the professional will maintain copyright in all documents and drawings which it has prepared, it appears likely that such a term would be implied in any event albeit that the person for whom the documents are produced must have a licence to be able to use those documents for the purpose for which they were intended. Thus, to extend a licence from the employer to other parties does not normally cause any difficulties in practice. Care must however be taken in order to ensure that any further

17. See Cl. 9 of CoWa/F and Cl. 6 of CoWa/P&T.

documents, which may be requested and which there is an obligation on the part of the professional to supply, could be subjected to a charge in respect of the professional's reasonable copying and administration costs. If the fund, purchaser or tenant is able, furthermore, to appoint its own professional team who may have an involvement in the project it is important that they should have the status of observers only.[18]

There will usually be a clause in the warranty whereby the professional warrants that no specifically referred to materials have been used in the construction. This may include, for example, high alumina cement or asbestos products. Ordinarily, there is no objection to such a clause.

The issue of assignment causes controversy. Whereas the ability to assign the warranty confers no benefit upon the professional who is called upon to assign, a more sinister innovation for professionals relates to the imposing of a continuing obligation to enter into new and successive warranties with any party who may be nominated at any given time. This, in the absence of any words of limitation, creates an open-ended liability which cannot be considered at all acceptable. The professional in this situation has no means of limiting the amount of warranties to be issued and those parties to whom they are to be given. Each new warranty would carry with it its own limitation period.

Finally, and inevitably, the professional must not be prepared to enter into any warranty if there is any possibility that he may in future be an uninsured litigant. There is never any guarantee of this situation being avoided, given that policies are underwritten on a "claims made" as opposed to an "events occurring" basis. However, professionals and their advisers would be well advised to consider carefully the terms of their current professional indemnity policies in order to see what restrictions or exclusions may apply. These are most likely to be of particular relevance when dealing with any obligation assumed by the professional to enter into successive warranties (as discussed above). Alternatively, any obligation to enter into successive assignment(s) of warranties already executed may be unacceptable to underwriters. This subject is discussed in detail below.

18. See Cl. 8 of CoWa/F and Cl. 5 of CoWa/P&T.

6.4. ASSIGNABILITY OF WARRANTIES

The issue whether or not a warranty may be assignable is a matter of some considerable importance. If it is, then another party may obtain the benefits under the warranty and the professional may find that a claim may be made against him some years in the future by a stranger, a party of whom the professional has had no prior knowledge. On the other hand, a party who receives the benefit of the original warranty will wish to maximise the saleability or marketability of the property by being able to pass on the same rights as he enjoyed to a subsequent purchaser or tenant.

It is important initially to understand that an agreement itself cannot be assigned. It is the benefit only which is capable of being assigned. Although the wording of the JCT Standard Forms of Building Contract as published by the Joint Contracts Tribunal[19] refers to the assignment of the contract, this is a legal nonsense and impossibility. The clause was the subject of some criticism by Lord Browne-Wilkinson in *Linden Gardens Trust Limited* v. *Lenesta Sludge Disposals Limited.*[20] He commented that:

> "Although it is true that the phrase 'assign this contract' is not strictly accurate, lawyers frequently use those words inaccurately to describe an assignment of the benefit of a contract since every lawyer knows that the burden of a contract cannot be assigned."

Staughton L.J. in giving judgment in the Court of Appeal[21] in the same decision was less complimentary of the JCT Drafting Sub-Committee when dealing with this same issue. He commented:

> "Lawyers know that one cannot assign a contract as a whole, if by that is meant both the benefit and the burden, without the consent of the other party and the assignee. So what was the point of saying that consent of the contractor would be required? If the intention was merely to prevent the employer assigning benefits under the contract without consent, why not say so?"

It is important to note that the benefits under a contract are freely assignable unless it can be argued that the contract is of a personal nature. It is unlikely that this would apply to many contracts involv-

19. I.e. 19.1.1 of JCT 80.
20. [1993] 3 All E.R. 417 at 427.
21. (1992) 57 B.L.R. 57 at 81.

ing a professional and his client. See *Tolhurst* v. *The Associated Portland Cement Manufacturers (1900) Limited*:[22]

"The benefit of a contract is only assignable in cases where it can make no difference to the person on whom the obligation lies to which of two persons he is to discharge it."

Of course, if a contract does prohibit an assignment of the benefit it cannot be assigned, since to do otherwise would be contrary to the obvious intention of the parties. Thus, if there is to be any restriction upon the right of the assignment of any warranty the warranty must expressly state this.

Two other rules are important to consider in relation to assignments. The first is that an assignee takes subject to equities. Thus, where a claim arises out of the warranty an assignee of the benefits arising from that warranty will take subject to any causes of action that may have been pleaded as a defence by the professional against the original beneficiary under the warranty. The second rule is that an assignee cannot recover more than an assignor.[23] Thus, the losses recoverable by an assignee cannot exceed those losses which the assignor would have been entitled to. However, does this mean:

(a) the assignor's loss and entitlement to damages would have to be calculated and the assignee's claim for damages would be capped at this level and could not exceed this sum, or
(b) this should not be construed as being necessarily the same quantum but for the same kinds of losses or heads of claim?

It may be argued with some force that the assignor's loss, especially if he has sold the property at a market value, albeit oblivious of any defects, is nil. If the former of the alternatives is accepted there will obviously be an iniquitous result, on the basis that the person who has obtained the benefit of the assignment and who thus has suffered the loss would not be able to recover anything. Thus, it is considered to be more than likely that the second proposition, as opposed to the first, would find acceptance by the court. This issue was a matter which could have been dealt with by the House of Lords in *Linden Gardens* but Lord Browne-Wilkinson indicated[24] that this was not an issue which arose for determination.

22. [1902] 2 K.B. 660 at 668.
23. (1992) 57 B.L.R. 108.
24. At p. 34.

However, even if it is this second proposition which is accepted there may nonetheless be serious implications for the assignee. This may easily be demonstrated by looking at the issue of design defects.

In the event that there are design defects, the issue of quantum of damages can, it is admitted, have far-reaching and significant relevance. If the assignor has divested its interest in the property, it could be argued with some force that the quantification of damages on the basis of the cost of repairing the defects would be wholly inappropriate on the ground that the assignor is most unlikely ever to undertake the repairs. To the contrary, the diminution in value formula which usually generates a lesser sum would give a much fairer and proper result. There is some judicial support for this proposition at first instance in the decision of His Honour Judge John Newey Q.C. in *IMI Cornellius (UK) Limited* v. *Alan J. Bloor & Others.*[25]

The findings of the House of Lords in *Ruxley Electronics & Construction Limited* v. *Forsyth*[26] may be of relevance. In this case, the House of Lords refused to award substantive damages where a swimming pool had not been constructed to the correct depth based upon the remedial costs of doing so. The court was not convinced that, were damages so awarded, these monies would be spent in the performance of this work. Whereas a court is not normally concerned directly about the manner in which any award of damages may be spent by a beneficiary it is always aware that in awarding a specific sum as damages it is not giving rise to a "windfall".

Whatever the argument may be, however, on the means of quantifying damages, the simple truth remains that professionals run a greater risk of claims by allowing successive assignments of warranties to take place.

Mindful of the arguments that relate to quantum, it is always advisable to define in the warranty the extent of the quantum for which there is liability. A good example may be found within Clause 1(a) of CoWa/P&T which states:

"The Firm warrants that it has exercised and will continue to exercise reasonable skill [and care] [care and diligence] in the performance of its services to the Client under the Appointment. In the event of any breach of this warranty:

25. (1992) 57 B.L.R. 108.
26. (1995) 73 B.L.R. 1.

(a) subject to paragraphs (b) and (c) of this clause, the Firm shall be liable for the reasonable costs of repair renewal and/or reinstatement of any part or parts of the Development to the extent that
—the Purchaser/the Tenant incurs such costs and/or
—the Purchaser/the Tenant is or becomes liable either directly or by way of financial contribution for such costs.
The Firm shall not be liable for other losses incurred by the Purchaser/the Tenant."

Thus it will be seen that this clause has the benefit of excluding liability for damages other than those based upon costs of repair, renewal or reinstatement, and only then upon proof of those costs being incurred or any liability being assumed for them.

CHAPTER 7

CAUSATION, ASCERTAINMENT OF LIABILITY AND QUANTUM

7.1. CAUSATION AND ASCERTAINMENT OF LIABILITY

The law has often to decide issues of causation, in other words the ascertainment of the reason for the occurrence of a particular loss. However, this issue more frequently arises in the tort of negligence than it does in contract. In deciding issues of liability in negligence the courts have often to consider a particular chain of events in the application of the test of reasonable foreseeability. In the construction industry, when one is considering the liability of its professions, the issue arises predominantly in the context of a breach of contract, although as previously discussed in Chapter 1 there will also be concurrent liability in negligence. The difficulty in construction cases is not so much due to the application of the legal principles, but to the complexity of the factual information, compounded by the number of different parties who have an input in any particular building contract. Claims by contractors and subcontractors for further monies due to a variety of reasons represent the norm rather than the exception. Complex situations often arise when building contracts are initially performed. The issue of disentangling cause and effect is not always performed with any degree of precision. It was stated by Lloyd L.J. in *McAlpine Humberoak* v. *McDermott International*[1] that:

> "It seems to be the practice in the construction industry to employ consultants to prepare a claim almost as soon as the ink on the contract is dry."

Claims for direct loss and/or expense are prepared by quantity surveyors, who are usually the first to be called upon by contractors

1. (1992) 38 B.L.R. 1.

who perceive that they have a legitimate grievance In the past they have tended to avoid complicated arguments of causation by pleading that all the claims for reimbursement arose by adopting the overall period of delay together with all of the constituent causes of that delay relied upon, with no attempt to demonstrate either the periods or durations of each individual delay caused by each. Thus, fundamentally, a rolled-up claim alleged that all of the factors of the delay, and/or alternatively of the disruption, caused the totality of the loss. This obviates the need for any precise investigation and analysis in any exhaustive detail which in due course gives rise to cost savings for the contractor. However, any such allegation is an inherently dangerous proposition to adopt.

Contractors may proceed with their claims against employers with or without a degree of necessary particularisation, but for whatever reason the employer may elect to conclude a settlement that does not apportion specific sums of money to the individual allegations advanced by the contractor. Such an occurrence is not unusual on the basis that the employer and the contractor may be anxious to conclude their particular disputes, which are thus compromised. The ability to insist upon any dispute between a contractor and employer being the subject of litigation, as opposed to arbitration, has all but disappeared, if the parties had earlier agreed to arbitrate, with the introduction of section 9 of the Arbitration Act 1996. The important implication this must have is that, even if the employer considers the architect or engineer to be liable in whole or in part for the contractor's additional entitlement, he cannot be enjoined as a party in those same arbitration proceedings in the absence of, in the first instance, an agreement providing for the reference of disputes to arbitration and, preferably, the same arbitration reference.

In *Mid-Glamorgan County Council* v. *J. Devonald Williams & Partners*,[2] Mr Recorder John Tackaberry Q.C. refused to strike out a claim pleaded on a rolled up basis. The claim was brought by the employer against its architects following the compromise between the employer and the contractor of the contractor's claims for further monies claimed under the contract. The employer simplistically considered that the architect was responsible for the employer's overspend and made a number of allegations against

2. (1992) 8 Const. L.J. 61.

the architect without being able to show what were the financial consequences of these alleged deficiencies. While the judge refused to strike out the claim, thus by inference stating that there was a cause of action, there were obvious evidential difficulties facing the employer. The judge commented that these meant that the employer was not likely to succeed, but that this was not a case of impossibility justifying the case being struck out. Notwithstanding the obvious difficulties of being able to pursue such a claim, this case demonstrates the vulnerability of architects to claims which would appear to be commenced upon purely commercial, as opposed to strictly legal, grounds.

In *ICI Plc* v. *Bovis Construction and Others*[3] His Honour Judge James Fox-Andrews Q.C. similarly rejected an application to have a statement of claim struck out, and instead ordered the delivery in a number of instances of further and better particulars. In this case, the management contractor (Bovis), the architect (GMW Partnership) and the consulting engineers (Oscar Faber & Partners) were all defendants to an action commenced by an employer. The employer's complaint was that the likely final cost of building works was £53,967,097 (exclusive of fees) against an original estimate of £29,082,000. The employer alleged that approximately £19 million was due to the fault of the defendants. However, the allegations of complaint against the defendants in the Statement of Claim were not sufficiently particularised. For example, the Statement of Claim said that each of the three defendants was responsible for the whole of the loss of the £19 million together with the professional fees. The judge, not surprisingly, concluded that this pleading was unsatisfactory and, although he refused to strike out the claim, made provision for the delivery of further particulars. Yet another example of the problems of causation may be found in *Wessex Regional Health Authority* v. *HLM Design Limited*.[4] The employer had resolved the claims brought by the contractor following the commencement of arbitration proceedings. The compromise concluded between the employer and the contractor included a payment of the sum of £1.65 million. The extensions of time of 74 weeks previously granted by the architect remained unaffected. The proceedings brought by the employer against the architect related to the alleged

3. (1992) 8 Const. J. 293.
4. (1995) 71 B.L.R. 32.

overpayment made to the contractor. Again, the court at first instance refused to strike out the claim on the ground that it did not disclose a cause of action. Two further cases dealing with global claims should be noted: *Bernhard's Rugby Landscapes Ltd* v. *Stockley Park Consortium Ltd*[5] and *Inserco Ltd* v. *Honeywell Control Systems.*[6] These decisions underline the message that whereas global claims will not be struck out, they should be advanced only as a last resort where there are no real alternatives.

The question of causation is more difficult to resolve where there is more than one cause, i.e. concurrent causes for a particular loss. The problem is not unique to building cases. Numerous insurance cases can be relied upon as guidance and in establishing the principles. See for example the following cases.

(a) In *Coxe* v. *Employer Liability Insurance*[7] the court had to decide whether or not the death of a military officer who was run over by a train when visiting the line was "directly or indirectly caused by, arising from, or traceable to ... war". If this was so, then the deceased's estate could not recover any proceeds from his policy of insurance which did not cover against death caused by such circumstances. The court concluded that the death was indeed indirectly caused by war.

(b) In *Leyland Shipping* v. *Norwich Union Fire Insurance Society,*[8] the court had to decide whether or not the cause of the total loss of a ship was storm damage or, alternatively, enemy action. The evidence before the court was that after the ship was struck by an enemy torpedo she was moored at Le Havre. She remained there for two days, grounding at each ebb tide but floating again with the flood, and finally her bulkheads gave way and she sank and became a total loss. It was held that the cause which was proximate in its efficiency was the torpedoing by the enemy German submarine. This cause had been preserved though other causes in the meantime had sprung up which had not yet destroyed it or truly impaired it, and thus the result was that the enemy action remained the real efficient cause to which the loss could be ascribed. Thus, underwriters were protected by the warranty against all consequences of hostility.

5. (1997) 82 B.L.R. 39.
6. Unreported, Court of Appeal, 12 February 1998.
7. [1916] 2 K.B. 629.
8. [1918] A.C. 350.

(c) Similarly, in *Yorkshire Dale Steamship Co. Ltd* v. *The Minister of War Transport*[9] the Privy Council had to decide whether or not the cause of damage to a ship was being involved in a warlike activity, being a deviation of course under naval orders to avoid apprehended submarine attack. The court emphasised that the choice of the real or efficient cause from out of the whole complex of facts had to be made by applying common-sense standards. The court emphasised that the interpretation to be applied did not involve any metaphysical or scientific view of causation. Viscount Simon L.C. stated[10] that one had to ask oneself what was the effective and predominant cause of the accident that happened whatever the nature of the accident may be. Furthermore, he drew the analogy with a doctor certifying the "cause of death", in which case the doctor looked for the thing which had predominantly operated to bring death about. The Privy Council concluded that the cause of the damage to the ship was a marine risk and not a war risk. A marine risk did not become a war risk merely because the conditions of war made it more probable that the marine risk would operate.

In *Leyland Shipping* Lord Shaw of Dunfermline[11] gave a very lucid account of causation. He stated thus:

"In my opinion, my Lords, too much is made of refinements upon this subject. The doctrine of cause has been, since the time of Aristotle and the famous category of material, formal, efficient and final causes, one involving the subtlest of distinctions. The doctrine applied to existences rather than to occurrences. But the idea of the cause of an occurrence or the production of an event or the bringing about of a result is an idea perfectly familiar to the mind and to the law, and it is in connection with that that the notice of *proxima causa* is introduced. Of this, my Lords, I will venture to remark that one must be careful not to lay the accent upon the word 'proximate' in such a sense as to lose sight of or destroy altogether the idea of cause itself. The true and the overruling principle is to look at a contract as a whole and to ascertain what the parties to it really meant. What was it which brought about the loss, the event, the calamity, the accident? And this not in an artificial sense, but in that real sense which parties to a contract must have had in their minds when they spoke of cause at all.

To treat *proxima causa* as the cause which is nearest in time is out of the question. Causes are spoken of as if they were as distinct from one another

9. [1942] A.C. 691.
10. At p. 698.
11. At pp. 368 and 369.

as beads in a row or links in a chain, but—if this metaphysical topic has to be referred to—it is not wholly so. The chain of causation is a handy expression, but the figure is inadequate. Causation is not a chain, but a net. At each point influences, forces, events, precedent and simultaneous, meet; and the radiation from each point extends infinitely. At the point where these various influences meet it is for the judgment as upon a matter of fact to declare which of the causes thus joined at the point of effect was the proximate and which was the remote cause."

Furthermore, Lord Dunedin[12] added:

"My Lords, we have had a large citation of authority in this case, and much discussion on what is the true meaning of *cause proxima*. Yet I think the case turns on a pure question of fact to be determined by common-sense principles. What was the cause of the loss of the ship? I do not think that the ordinary man would have any difficulty in answering she was lost because she was torpedoed."

Occasionally, it is not possible to decide which cause is the active, dominant or efficient cause, and thus it may be stated that the causes of the loss are of equal efficacy. In such a situation, it appears that, following the dictum of Devlin J. in *Heskell* v. *Continental Express Ltd*,[13] that the breach of contract is one of two causes, both co-operating and both of equal efficiency, it is sufficient to carry judgment for damages. Devlin distinguished cases of causation in contract and in tort. He stated that it was clearly settled that in tort the wrongdoer could not excuse himself by pointing to another cause. It was enough that the tort should be a cause and it was unnecessary to evaluate competing causes and ascertain which of them was dominant. The decision of Devlin J. in *Heskell* was approved by Steyn J. in *Banque Keyser Ullmann SA* v. *Scandia (UK) Insurance Co. Ltd and Others.*[14]

It is clear that where more than one party has caused or contributed to the same "damage" an apportionment of liability between them can arise as a consequence of the application of the Law Reform (Civil Liability) Act 1978. This applies particularly where there are two causes of the loss, each of equal effect. However, the wording of section 1(1) of the 1978 Act provides that "any person liable in respect of any damage suffered by another person may recover contribution from any other person liable in respect of

12. At p. 362.
13. [1950] 1 All E.R. 1033.
14. [1987] 2 W.L.R. 1300.

the same damage". It is important to note that the damage must be suffered by another person. Thus, in a situation where there are competing causes, one being contractor-related and the other being employer-related the Law Reform (Civil Liability) Act 1978 cannot, it is submitted have any specific application since it relates to "damage" caused to a third party. To this extent the principle of law in *Heskell* is not affected by the 1978 Act. This view would appear to be strengthened by the decision of the Court of Appeal in *Birse Construction Limited* v. *Haiste Limited*,[15] a decision involving allegations of liability against consultant engineers.

While it is difficult to disagree with the lucid judicial statements made by Lord Shaw in *Leyland*, lawyers and lay persons often have the difficulty of deciding issues of dominance. The principles of law may be the same but construction projects have the ability to create factual matrices infinitely more complex than the straightforward choices which confronted the court, for example, in the *Leyland, Coxe* or *Yorkshire Dale* decisions. For example in *ICI* v. *Bovis* the claim advanced by the plaintiff against the defendants exceeded £31 million and comprised in this total were a large number of heads of claim. While it was accepted in that decision that those particulars hitherto given were inadequate, the Scott Schedules were of not inconsiderable length. In the three quoted insurance cases factual questions which confronted the courts were easily defined and clear cut, such as "what was the cause of the loss of the ship?" or "why was the soldier killed?". In a building case, however, the delay to the project or the disruption is ongoing, with a number of active competing causes taking effect at various times. It is submitted that there is a twofold exercise to be performed in each claim situation. The first is the painstaking reconstruction of the contract with the analytical identification of the causes and identifying, where relevant, the extent of any concurrence. While this exercise is often undertaken with the aid of computer software it cannot hide the necessity for the understanding of the detailed history of the project. This exercise ought to be performed by interviewing the key witnesses of fact since it is most unlikely that the whole history will be obtained by reference to the written records alone.

It is only when this first task has been performed that it will then

15. (1995) 76 B.L.R. 26.

be possible to ask questions based on what was the "dominant" or active or efficient cause of the delay or disruption. This will be a crucial exercise where it may be shown that during the currency of the project there were also contractor-related or "neutral" causes of delay as well as those of the employer's or the professional's making. What distinguishes building cases from other cases involving questions of causation, such as the three aforementioned insurance cases, is that, first, there is invariably no necessity to perform the first analytical exercise as discussed above. There is no necessity to perform the detailed historical investigation since the facts are far less complex. Secondly, the cause and effect analysis, both in respect of extensions of time and more particularly in respect of direct loss and/or expense, given the detailed facts, can be exhaustive. Experts, usually quantity surveyors, have to analyse the effects of often hundreds of causes of delay and disruption, ascertain concurrency and eventually state what the financial consequences are.

The preceding problems, as discussed, all arise from claims by the contractor for either additional monies or additional time by way of an extension to the contract period and the issue as to the extent, if any, to which the professional has caused these losses. In the vast majority of cases, once the factual investigation has been thoroughly investigated it should be clear whether or not there is any culpability on the part of the professional. The more obvious dilemma arises from compromises of contractors' claims and subsequent attempts to analyse what any payments were in respect of.

Frequently, also, there are issues of causation arising from failures within the building structure itself. In a typical such instance, the problem is easily identified but the cause of the problem is not. Thus, to give a typical example, water may be entering the building but the cause of the leaks cannot be readily identified. This is compounded when the architect may be blaming bad workmanship on the part of the contractor and the contractor is blaming design deficiencies on the part of the architect as the cause of the water ingress. Either or both parties may indeed be responsible. The employer will, however, initially be dissatisfied on the ground that he knows he has a building which leaks but he does not know who is responsible and the extent thereof. Any such problem can ultimately be resolved only by employing an expert witness to investigate and to advise. Thus, in *Greater London Council* v. *Ryarsh*

Brick Company Limited and Another,[16] the employer, the GLC, brought an action against both the manufacturer of bricks (Ryarsh) and the main contractor (Gleeson) where bricks used to construct walls became dislodged. The court, having heard the evidence, however, dismissed both claims and, following the adducing of expert evidence, concluded that the failures were largely caused by deficiencies in the plaintiff's owns designs and its failure to review those designs in the light of criticisms of them made by the main contractor, Gleeson. In a situation where both the contractor and the designer are to blame, they will both be liable to the employer but will share liability *inter se* by operation of the Civil Liability (Contribution) Act 1978.

7.2. QUANTUM

The law which has developed is based upon the principle of compensation. Lord Blackburn in *Livingstone* v. *Rawyards Coal Company*[17] referred to damages in the context of compensation and of placing the innocent party in the same position, so far as was possible, as he would have been in if he had not sustained the wrong. This principle is further illustrated by *Radford* v. *Defroberville & Lange*,[18] a decision of Oliver J., where he stated:

> "Where a party sustains a loss by reason of a breach of contract, he is, so far as money can do it, to be placed in the same situation, with respect to damages, as if the contract had been performed. This decision related to a breach of a covenant to construct a wall and the issue was whether or not the damages should be based upon the cost of constructing the wall or whether, in the alternative, it should be based upon the diminution to the value of the land due to the wall not being constructed."

The court indicated that the measure of damages can be very frequently arrived at only be postulating and answering the question of what the particular plaintiff could reasonably do to alleviate his loss and what would be the cost to him of doing so at the time when he could reasonably be expected to do it.

The time for the calculation of damages for a breach of contract

16. (1985) 4 Con. L.R. 85.
17. (1885) App. Cas. 15.
18. (1977) 7 B.L.R. 35 at 43.

is the time of the breach itself. Thus, if the professional has been responsible for design defects, the measure of damages will inevitably be taken as being the cost of the repairs. It is important for a plaintiff at all times to take whatever reasonable steps he can in order to mitigate his loss. However, this does not translate into an obligation to undertake repairs immediately, and certainly before the commencement of an action claiming damages. In *Dodd Properties (Kent) Limited* v. *The City of Canterbury*,[19] the plaintiff decided not to undertake the cost of repairs in 1970 when the cause of action arose, and thought it more prudent to await the outcome of the hearing before undertaking the work. Thus, the issue which the court had to answer was whether or not the cost of repairs should be assessed as at 1970, with no doubt interest accruing on the damages thereafter, or, in the alternative, whether or not the damages should be assessed as at 1978 when the matter came before the court. The court said that where there was a material difference between the cost of repair at the time of the breach and the cost of repair when the remedial work could, in all the relevant circumstances, reasonably be undertaken, it was the latter time which was the relevant time for the purposes of assessing the damages. Thus, in this instance, the court decided that whereas the plaintiff could of necessity have performed the repairs at an earlier date, it was not to be criticised for failing to do so; given that there would have had to be measures of "financial stringency" imposed if the repairs had been undertaken, the court saw that it was consistent with commercial good sense to defer the repairs. Thus, the measure of damages was assessed as at the date of the trial in 1978, as opposed to the date when the breaches occurred.

The test for the recoverability of damages for breaches of contract relies upon the traditional twofold test discussed in *Hadley* v. *Baxendale*.[20] The decision requires damages to be considered within either of the following categories:

(a) there is an entitlement of recovery in respect of loss reasonably and naturally flowing from the breach;
(b) further losses can be claimed which would in the reasonable contemplation of the parties be incurred in the event of a breach.

19. (1979) 13 B.L.R. 48.
20. (1854) 9 Ex. 341.

The decision of the House of Lords in *South Australia Asset Management Corporation* v. *York Montague Limited*[21] has a bearing upon the tests of liability of professionals and the quantum of damages for which they may be liable. The substance of this decision, delivered in conjunction with that in *United Bank of Kuwait Plc* v. *Prudential Property Services Limited* and *Nykredit Mortgage Bank Plc* v. *Edward Erdman Group Limited*, related to the issue of whether or not valuers were liable for the losses sustained by the subsequent fall in the property market, notwithstanding that their valuations in themselves represented negligent overvaluations of properties offered as security for loans. In each of these decisions, the valuations had been relied upon by commercial lenders when considering whether to advance funds to borrowers on mortgages of real property. The borrowers defaulted and the lenders were forced to rely upon the security provided by the properties. The security was inadequate and the lenders suffered loss. The common features in the decisions were that, had the lenders known the true value of the properties, no funds at all would have been advanced. Secondly, the property market had fallen after the dates of the negligent overvaluations, and thus the losses suffered by the lenders were greatly increased above the level of losses that would have occurred had the market been static. The court commented in its judgment that a person under a duty to take reasonable care to provide information upon which someone else will decide upon a course of action is, if negligent, not generally regarded as responsible for all of the consequences of that course of action. He is responsible only for the consequences of that information being wrong. It was stated by Lord Hoffmann[22] that:

"[A person] is responsible only for the consequences of the information being wrong. A duty of care which imposes upon the informant responsibility for losses which would have occurred even if the information which he gave had been correct is not in my view fair and reasonable as between the parties. It is therefore inappropriate either as an implied term of a contract or as a tortious duty arising from the relationship between them.

The principle thus stated distinguishes between the duty to provide the information for the purpose of enabling someone else to decide upon a course of action and a duty to advise someone as to what course of action he should take. If the duty is to advise whether or not a course of action

21. (1996) 80 B.L.R. 1.
22. At p. 13.

should be taken, the adviser must take reasonable care to consider all the potential consequences of that course of action."

Thus, any fall in the market value of the property was an independent cause of the plaintiffs' losses, and these losses should not in themselves be recoverable from the defendants who had notwithstanding negligently overvalued the properties. Thus one can consider that the issue of a certificate of practical completion, or the issue of an interim certificate showing the main contractor's financial entitlement, are examples of providing information. If that information is wrong, an architect, engineer and, possibly also in the latter instance, a quantity surveyor are liable for the losses which may arise. There may be difficulties associated with the allocation of the functions into the two separate categories of providing information and providing advice. Thus, to choose the example of issuing certificates in addition to the primary purpose of issuing information, one can see that the architect is also giving advice on what should be done, i.e. for the employer to pay the amount of the certificate. On the other hand, where the professional is designing a building he is inevitably providing advice. He is advising that the building should be constructed in a specific way. In doing so, in the words of Lord Hoffman, he "must take reasonable care to consider all of the potential consequences of that action".

CHAPTER 8

PROFESSIONAL NEGLIGENCE LITIGATION AND ARBITRATION

8.1. THE CONDUCT OF MULTI-PARTY PROCEEDINGS

8.1.1 Jurisdiction

Litigation against professionals has, in the past, often involved a number of parties. Employers in particular sometimes adopt a "scattergun" approach, issuing writs against various members of their professional team, their contractor, and possibly against subcontractors or suppliers as well, under direct warranties. Until 1997, any professional who pointed to his arbitration clause with the client, and sought a stay to arbitration of the legal proceedings against him, under section 4 of the Arbitration Act 1950, would typically be met with cases such as *Taunton-Collins* v. *Cromie*[1] and *Berkshire Senior Citizens Housing Association Ltd* v. *McCarthy E. Fitt Limited and Another.*[2] In these cases the courts acknowledged a party's wish to rely on the arbitration clause appearing in his contract, but held that this was overridden by the undesirability of having multiple sets of proceedings and potentially several irreconcilable decisions from different tribunals. The position in international arbitrations was always different—there, section 1 of the Arbitration Act 1975 made a stay mandatory except in certain specified circumstances.

All this changed radically on 31 January 1997 when the Arbitration Act 1996 was brought into force. Apart from cases covered by the old law (arbitral proceedings commenced prior to 31 January 1997, or cases in which an arbitration application, including an application to stay court proceedings, was begun before that date)

1. [1964] 1 W.L.R. 633.
2. (1979) 15 B.L.R. 27.

the court now *must* uphold the right of a party to have a dispute referred to arbitration where that party wishes to exercise that right and where, of course, a valid arbitration clause exists.[3] This is so even if such a course of action would lead to a number of separate arbitration and/or litigation proceedings. The only exceptions are where the court is satisfied that the arbitration agreement is null and void, inoperative or incapable of being performed.

In any event, the party wishing to arbitrate must be careful not to take a "step" in the litigation proceedings or his right to arbitrate may be lost. Serving notice of intention to defend and taking out the summons to stay proceedings do not count as "steps". The position here is as it was under the old legislation.

Is there a further exception for cases where one party has no arguable defence to the claim? The argument for such an exception is that if in fact there is no proper defence (e.g. if the claim is capable of being the subject of summary judgment under R.S.C. Order 14 in the High Court) there is in reality no "dispute or difference" that can be referred to arbitration at all. However, the logic of this analysis has been attacked by Lord Saville in the first instance decision of *Hayter* v. *Nelson*[4] and extra-judicially.[5] The *Hayter* approach was endorsed by a majority of the Court of Appeal in *Halki Shipping Corporation* v. *Sopex Oils Ltd.*[6] In the light of these cases, it may be expected that the days of the six-or eight-party professional negligence action in the Official Referees' corridor are numbered, to be replaced, perhaps, with numerous separate arbitrations.

Against that somewhat alarming prospect, it should be said that the Arbitration Act 1996 expressly embraces, for the first time in English law, the concept of multi-party arbitrations, so long as the parties consent.[7] Whether such arbitrations will happen in practice

3. Arbitration Act 1996, s. 9. Ss. 85–87, which would have retained the "old" law for domestic arbitrations only, have not been brought into force, because it was felt that to do so would create an unacceptable distinction between domestic and international arbitrations and would potentially infringe Art. 6 of the Treaty of Rome. On this point, and on the thinking behind the Act generally see "The Arbitration Act 1996: What We Have Tried to Accomplish" (1997) 13 Const. L.J. 410 by Lord Saville, who was heavily involved in the preparation of this legislation.

4. [1990] 2 Lloyd's Rep 265.

5. (1997) 13 Const. L.J. 410 in "The Arbitration Act 1996: What We Have Tried to Accomplish".

6. 19 December 1997, unreported.

7. Arbitration Act 1996, s. 35.

depends upon those involved in a project (particularly the client's advisers) ensuring that the network of contracts contains compatible provisions for joint arbitrations in appropriate cases. Alternatively, the parties could agree, on an *ad hoc* basis after disputes have arisen, to have disputes dealt with in one arbitration (however this agreement will often not be forthcoming, since from the point of view of a typical respondent, it will often be advisable on grounds of costs, as well as tactically, to keep the dispute to a two-party one).

8.2. OFFERS, SETTLEMENT AND COSTS

8.2.1 The obstructive defendant

However acrimonious the relationship of co-defendants to one another, it will usually benefit them, if settlement is to be reached without trial, to present a united front to a plaintiff. In particular, if proposals are to be put to a plaintiff, they should be joint. Plaintiffs are often unwilling to settle with fewer than all of the defendants because of the possibility of the objecting defendant attacking at trial any settlement that they may reach; and because they lose the advantage of sitting on the sidelines at trial while the defendants attack each other's cases. From the defendants' point of view, the problem with any settlement that does not involve all of them is that the obstructive defendant may well haul some or all of them back into the litigation by serving a contribution notice under the Civil Liability (Contribution) Act 1978.[8]

What is to be done if one defendant will not settle? There is no easy answer. Things are particularly difficult if the obstructive defendant senses his own power to veto a settlement, and brings that into play as a bargaining chip. Two possibilities may be considered.

The first is to persuade the plaintiff to settle with one defendant alone. That defendant may have to run the risk of the obstructive defendant bringing him back by contribution proceedings (assuming the plaintiff is not willing to indemnify the settling defendant against this), but that may be a risky course of action for the obstructive defendant, who will now bear the full cost of those

8. See R.S.C., O. 16, r. 8.

contribution proceedings if they fail. Advantages to the plaintiff are the simplification of the litigation and a likely reduction in on-going costs.

Plaintiffs are sometimes unduly concerned about the obstructive defendant attacking the settlement. The courts have, however, been anxious to encourage settlement and there are various dicta (e.g. in *Biggin & Co Ltd* v. *Permanite Ltd*[9]) making clear that a plaintiff in this position need not defend his settlement to the last penny so long as it was reasonable to make it. In particular, the size of the costs saving will be a factor going to reasonableness of the settlement.[10]

There are conflicting Official Referees' decisions on whether the settling party can call evidence of legal advice given to it when settling, as evidence of reasonableness. It is submitted that the better view is that such advice is irrelevant.[11]

The second option involves the settling parties forming an unholy alliance to continue the litigation against the obstructive defendant. This extreme measure was successfully carried out in the following two cases. In *South East Thames Regional Health Authority* v. *W. J. Lovell (London) Ltd*[12] an agreement was reached by the plaintiffs and all of the defendants except one, under which one of the settling defendants agreed to pursue the plaintiff's case against the objecting defendant on behalf of all of the settling defendants and the plaintiff, and jointly at their cost. The objecting defendant's attempt to have this agreement declared void for maintenance or champerty was unsuccessful. In *Victoria University Manchester* v. *Hugh Wilson and Lewis Womersley and Another*[13] an agreement was entered into on the fifth day of the trial under which the first defendant agreed to pay to the plaintiffs £1.3 million on the condition that the *plaintiffs* continue the action against the second defendants, at the expense of the first defendants, and on the basis that any sum recovered in excess of £1.3 million would be paid to the second defendant.

9. [1951] 2 All E.R. 191. See also *Babcock Energy Ltd* v. *Lodge Sturtevant* [1994] C.I.L.L. 982.

10. *Oxford University Press* v. *John Stedman Design Group and Others* (1990) 34 Con. L.R. 83.

11. I.e. as stated in *DSL Group Ltd* v. *Unisys International Services Ltd* (1994) 67 B.L.R. 117. The judge in this case chose not to follow the earlier decision of *Society of Lloyd's* v. *Kitsons Environmental Services Ltd* (1994) 67 B.L.R. 102.

12. (1985) 32 B.L.R. 127.

13. (1984) 2 Con. L.R. 43.

Commenting on this case in the *South East Thames* case, Judge Newey Q.C. did not agree with the suggestion that the *Victoria* agreement could have been attacked as champertous, since the first defendant had a "genuine commercial interest" in it.

8.2.2 Difficulties with payments in

The payment in rules are not well adapted to multi-party cases and can pose problems for both plaintiffs and defendants.

8.2.2.1 Problems for plaintiffs

The plaintiff suing his professional and at least one other defendant can often proceed in the relatively safe knowledge that he is likely to succeed against one or the other. Provided that it was reasonable to sue both defendants, he may well obtain an order that the unsuccessful defendant should pay either directly (a "*Sanderson* order") or indirectly via the plaintiff himself (a "*Bullock* order") the costs of any successful defendant.[14]

If only one of two defendants pays into court, the plaintiff no longer enjoys such security. He cannot simply discontinue against the non-paying-in defendant (at least not without paying that defendant's costs) and may be unable to persuade the paying-in defendant to meet those costs.[15]

In *Carrs of Bury St Edmunds Ltd* v. *Whitworth Co. Partnership and The Barnes Group Ltd*[16] the plaintiff, suing its architect and contractor (both of whom blamed each other for condensation in a car showroom), did not accept a payment in made by one defendant. Approximately one month later (thus outside the High Court period of 21 days for accepting that payment in) the other defendant paid in a further figure. The combined total was now satisfactory, from the plaintiff's point of view, but he was by then out of time for accepting the first payment. The plaintiff argued that it should not have to bear any costs from the date of the first payment in. It was held, however, by the court that where defendants are sued severally (as in this case) there would have to be "exceptional and compelling reasons" why a

14. *Bullock* v. *London General Omnibus Ltd* [1907] 1 K.B. 264; *Sanderson* v. *Blyth Theatre Co.* [1903] 2 K.B. 533.
15. See *Magee* v. *Taymech Ltd* (1994) 13 Const. L.J. 5 (C.A.) p. 355.
16. (1996) 84 B.L.R. 117.

plaintiff applying out of time to accept a payment in could avoid the usual costs penalties. In this case, the plaintiff therefore had to pay the costs from the date of the first payment in.[17]

8.2.2.2 Problems for the defendant

Difficulty for the defendant who pays in alone has already been touched upon—other co-defendants may keep him in the action by way of contribution proceedings. The rule in High Court litigation is that, in general, the only way in which to put a plaintiff at risk as to costs is to make a payment in under Rules of the Supreme Court, Order 22. A "*Calderbank* offer" (i.e. a written offer made "without prejudice save as to costs") can only be used where a payment in is inappropriate, e.g. in cases where the plaintiff is claiming something other than money (in this respect, arbitration, where *Calderbank* offers are the norm, offers greater flexibility to the respondent).

In *Corby District Council* v. *Holst*[18] the defendant sought a declaration from the court that its *Calderbank* offer was a legitimate method *in principle* of protecting itself as to costs. In that case, the defendant did not wish to pay into court, having already provided an expensive bond as part of a previous arbitration settlement. The defendant therefore made a *Calderbank* offer to the plaintiff and asked the court to ratify the principle of the *Calderbank* offer by making an interim declaration. The court refused to make such a declaration, which it saw as usurping the function of the trial judge. The defendant was then faced with the problem of expending a further sum on the payment in, or trusting that its method of trying to protect itself on costs would be endorsed at trial, with potentially significant consequences in costs at trial if that were decided not to be the case.

However, the use of a *Calderbank* offer was endorsed in the different circumstances of *Padmanor Investments Ltd* v. *Soundcraft Electronics Ltd and Others*.[19] In this case a landlord sued its tenant for arrears of rent, and was met by a counterclaim alleging breach

17. The court thus followed an earlier decision in *Fell* v. *Gould Grimwade Shirbon Partnership and Malvern District Council* [1993] C.I.L.L. 861. See also *QBE Insurance (UK) Ltd* v. *Mediterranean Insurance and Reinsurance Company Ltd* [1992] 1 W.L.R. 573. For a decision the other way, see *Hodgson* v. *Guardall* [1991] 3 All E.R. 823.

18. (1984) 28 B.L.R. 35.

19. (1994) 77 B.L.R. 113.

of the lease agreement in relation to roofing works. The landlord joined its roofing contractor as a third party to the tenant's counterclaim (the tenant also claimed in negligence directly against the roofing contractor).

The roofing contractor offered the landlord the sum of £50,000 plus costs, on the basis that the landlord would secure the withdrawal of the counterclaim against it by the tenant (thus disposing of the third party action) *or* take over the roofing contractor's defence to the tenant's counterclaim. Judge Lloyd Q.C. held that the *Calderbank* offer was capable of giving the roofing contractor costs protection, and in fact did so. The judge, after noting that the policy of the courts was to encourage every proper means whereby a party should be made to realise that steps should actually be taken by him to bring litigation to an end praised the fact that the roofing contractor's letter gave the landlord more than one alternative:

"Indeed the writer [of the *Calderbank* offer] showed commendable foresight in presenting [the landlord] with some options. Settlements are usually only achieved if parties are prepared to be flexible. Since *Calderbank* letters will have to be justified in hindsight it is good practice for the party making the offer to show the extent to which the offer is susceptible to negotiation."

It is for this reason that *Calderbank* offers in arbitrations at least frequently contain invitations to the offeree to identify immediately any perceived technical inadequacies in the offer, so that, at the substantive award, the offeree has less opportunity to take purely technical arguments.

8.2.2.3 Reverse Calderbank offers

Plaintiffs may be encouraged by the endorsement of "Plaintiff's Reverse *Calderbank* Offers" in the Woolf report, "Access to Justice"[20] (details are in Lord Woolf's interim report of June 1995, chapter 24). Here, the plaintiff makes a written offer of the sum that it would be willing to accept on its claim. If at trial the plaintiff achieves less than this (so that the defendant should have accepted the offer) the judge may award the plaintiff its costs on an *indemnity* basis (i.e. all of its costs, except those that the paying party can show are unreasonable) from the date of the offer, rather than on the more usual standard basis. There is now judicial endorsement

20. HMSO, July 1996.

for this view in the personal injury case of *McDonnell* v. *Woodhouse & Jones & Others*.[21].

In conclusion, *Calderbank* offers in multi-party cases may be expected to be a more frequently used weapon in a defendant's armoury, possibly even in advance of the implementation of Lord Woolf's recommendations.

8.2.3 Alternative dispute resolution

Alternative dispute resolution or ADR is now firmly established in the United Kingdom.[22] The term is in fact a description used loosely of various types of dispute resolution not involving traditional trials, e.g. conciliation, mediation and "mini" trials. The most popular form appears to be mediation in one form or another, usually by the parties agreeing to appoint a mediator who will explore with them, separately or together, acting as a "shuttle diplomat" at times, the possibilities of settlement. Organisations such as the Centre for Dispute Resolution (CEDR) of 7 St Catherine's Way, London, E1 9LB organise mediations and appoint mediators promptly upon application by the parties.

Three judicial/governmental endorsements of ADR may now be noted:

(a) In the Queen's Bench and Chancery Divisions of the High Court, the parties must now lodge checklists with the court two months prior to the trial, stating whether the parties have considered ADR.[23] The Commercial Court has also issued a Practice Statement further endorsing ADR.[24]

(b) The *Practice Statement* on ADR in the Commercial Court of 10 June 1996 goes further:

   (i) The judge can adjourn the summons for direction to enable parties to consider ADR. If ADR is unsuccessful, the directions can be restored with a report on the progress (though not the substance) of the ADR discussions.

21. *The Times*, 25 May 1995.

22. For further reading about ADR see S. York, *Practical ADR* (Pearson Professional Ltd, 1996) and Philip Naughton Q.C., "Alternative Forms of Dispute Resolution: Their Strengths and Weaknesses" (1990) 6 Const L.J. 195.

23. *Practice Direction (Civil Litigation: Case Management)* [1995] 1 All E.R. 385.

24. *Practice Statement* [1994] 1 All E.R. 34.

(ii) The judge can order an "early neutral evaluation" either by himself or another judge, in which the parties are given some guidelines on the merits on an interim basis.

(iii) The judge can order that the costs of the ADR be regarded as costs in cause in the litigation.

Of the first 100 ADR orders made by the Commercial Court, only 5 per cent failed to result in settlement either through ADR or through further negotiations. In particular, an ADR order by the court brought a negotiated end in November 1997 to the 12-year litigation between the Government and Arthur Anderson, accountants, over the de Lorean car firm losses.[25]

(c) The Woolf Report[26] recommends that courts should become more aware of ADR and should raise it with the parties. It also recommends that judges should be able to take into account a litigant's unreasonable refusal to attempt ADR.

In the past, parties have sometime been reluctant to suggest ADR for fear of being perceived as showing a sign of weakness. However, the above endorsements may militate against this problem. A further possibility, in a multi-party case, is for an approach to be made to an appropriate body (e.g. CEDR), which can then make contact with the other parties, without disclosing the name of the "offeror", in order to establish whether there is any latent communal wish to try ADR.

8.2.4 Costs—partial or split orders

Costs are in the discretion of the court or the arbitrator. However, there is generally a rule that costs "follow the event".[27] Failure without reasons to apply this rule can result in a costs order being reversed on appeal.

There is *some* latitude for a court or arbitrator to make "split"

25. *Law Society Gazette*, 8 January 1998, p. 10.

26. The Interim Report of June 1995 (HMSO, 1995), Ch. 18.

27. In the High Court see Ord. 62, r. 3(3), which provides for this, in the absence of other circumstances. The Arbitration Act 1996 also enshrines this rule for the first time in arbitration, in s. 61.

costs orders in relation to various issues.[28] However this discretion should be exercised very carefully.

In *FKI Engineering plc* v. *Metro Cammell Hong Kong Ltd*[29] the High Court criticised an arbitrator who thought that he had "the widest discretion" on the award of costs, and stated that to deprive the net winner of its costs on the grounds that it had only been partially successful was to err in principle. Similarly in *Re Elgindata (No. 2)*[30] the Court of Appeal, while accepting that a successful party may be deprived of its costs (and even made to pay those of the other party) where it has raised issues improperly or unreasonably, allowed an appeal against the judge's order that had left the winning party bearing a large part of the overall costs even though no allegations of unreasonableness or impropriety had been made. Finally, in *Equitable Life Assurance Society* v. *Kenchington Ford plc and Others*[31] the judge was prepared to hold that cases in which the plaintiff had recovered some money but had been deprived of its costs were limited to those where recoveries had been extremely low in percentage terms (1.5 per cent, 2.2 per cent, 2.6 per cent etc.), which were nowhere near the 22 per cent figure in the case itself.

8.2.5 Costs on an indemnity basis

The difference between an order for costs on an indemnity basis and on the standard basis is that on the indemnity basis the receiving party gets all of his costs *except* those that are unreasonable, and the onus is on the paying party to prove unreasonableness. Such orders therefore tend to be reserved for situations where a party has behaved particularly badly or unmeritoriously. Two construction-related examples follow of orders for indemnity costs.

In *Connaught Restaurants* v. *Indoor Leisure Ltd*[32] the plaintiff landlord did nothing to repair its tenant's business premises, even though it must have known the financial and other hardship that

28. R.S.C., O. 62, r. 10, specifically allows this in the High Court. See also s. 47 Arbitration Act 1996.
29. (1996) 77 B.L.R. 84.
30. [1993] 1 All E.R. 232.
31. [1996] C.I.L.L. 1163.
32. (1992) 8 Const. L.J. 37.

this would cause. It resisted liability on the tenant's counterclaim and made no admissions until trial, even though its surveyors had made a number of admissions earlier. The plaintiff was held to have acted oppressively (without necessarily intending to do so) and unreasonably.

In *Munkenbeck and Marshall (a firm)* v. *McAlpine*[33] the trial judge found that the defendant had "done everything in his power to avoid payment to the last possible moment" and "cynically manipulated the court process to allow him the maximum amount of time". The defendant's tactics involved serving an original defence which was merely an attempt to delay matters and had to be completely amended; serving a counterclaim which was eventually abandoned; and forcing the plaintiff to bring a witness from the United States, instead of allowing his affidavit to be put in as evidence. The Court of Appeal agreed that the defendant had "exercised every ploy to avoid paying a valid claim".

8.2.6 Can costs orders be made against insurers direct?

Insurers who *take over and conduct* the defence of an action, may face having to pay the costs of successful parties themselves, particularly if their insured is unable to do so. The court has power to make a costs order against someone who is not a party to the litigation under section 51 of the Supreme Court Act 1981. There is no equivalent power in arbitration. The courts have now explored the criteria that should be applied.[34]

In *Pendennis Shipyard Ltd and Others* v. *Margrathea (Pendennis) Ltd (in liquidation)*[35] insurers were held to have taken over the defence of an action and conducted it for their own benefit. A section 51 order was made against them when the defence failed. In *Chapman (TGA) and Another* v. *Christopher and Another*[36] the plaintiff's factory was damaged by a fire begun by the action of the first defendant, Mr Christopher, who threw a match into a tin of beeswax. Mr Christopher had no assets, but was able to take

33. (1995) 44 Con. L.R. 30 (C.A.).
34. *Thistleton* v. *Hendricks* (1992) 70 B.L.R. 112; *Symphony Group Plc* v. *Hodgson* [1993] 4 All E.R. 143 (C.A.).
35. *The Times*, 27 August 1997.
36. *The Times*, 21 July 1997 (C.A.).

advantage of an insurance policy held by his mother that covered him for the first £1 million of accidental damage to property. His defence was taken over and funded by the insurer. The defence failed completely.

The insurers raised two arguments, neither of which impressed the court. The first was that this was not an exceptional type of case. The Court of Appeal agreed that it was not exceptional for insurance purposes, but said that it was exceptional in the general context of litigation. The second argument was that the effect of the decision would be to raise premiums. The court said that there was no reason why the premiums should not properly reflect the insurer's exposure to costs.

The court can also order disclosure of documents where there is a genuine doubt whether a party is paying personally the costs of an action, or is being funded by another.[37]

A defendant's attempt to have a section 51 order made against a legal expenses insurer failed in *Murphy* v. *Young & Co.'s Brewery plc.*[38] The Court of Appeal held that the insurers, the Sun Alliance, had no interest in the litigation as such, and had not initiated it or exercised any particular control over it. It was also irrelevant that the insured's limit of indemnity for costs under the policy (£25,000) had been exceeded.

To summarise the above, insurers must now deal with the risk of section 51 orders being made directly against them, albeit that this will only happen in exceptional cases. They should be particularly careful not to be seen to be actively initiating, pursuing or controlling litigation on their insured's behalf.

8.3. CONTRIBUTION

If a court finds two or more defendants liable for a plaintiff's damage it will often be required to consider further the liability of the defendants amongst themselves. This apportionment will not affect the plaintiff. If and insofar as he has proved his whole losses against *any* defendant, he is entitled to enter judgment, and if necessary enforce it, against that defendant. The apportionment

37. *Abraham and Another* v. *Thompson and Another*, *The Times*, 15 May 1997.
38. [1997] 1 All E.R. 518 (C.A.).

simply means that any defendant can then in turn obtain the appropriate contribution from one or more of his co-defendants.

It has been said that such rules can cause injustice.[39] For example (so the argument runs), if a court holds that the apportionment as between two co-defendants is to be that defendant A is 1 per cent responsible and defendant B 99 per cent, and if defendant B subsequently becomes insolvent, defendant A is left to pay the plaintiff's full loss without being able to recover any contribution. Concern at this sort of scenario led to the "net contribution" or "fair contribution" clauses to be found in the standard architect and engineering appointment forms discussed earlier,[40] and in the Latham-backed NEC Engineering and Construction Contract.

However, there are many counter-arguments to the above. If both defendants have been found *fully* liable for the plaintiff's loss, the 1 per cent/99 per cent apportionment discussed above goes only to the contribution between the two defendants. Why should the plaintiff lose his right to recover damages from a party who has been found liable to pay them, merely because some other party has also been found liable, and has subsequently become insolvent? (Different considerations apply where one defendant, for example, is liable only for some of the plaintiff's losses whereas other defendants are liable for all of them. In such a case of course the defendant who is only liable for some of the losses can never be found obliged to pay for the whole, whatever happens to those other defendants.)

Whatever the merits of the above arguments, it is clearly often important for a defendant to ensure that any other party who is or might be liable for the plaintiff's losses is brought into the action, so that the court can make an apportionment. The Civil Liability (Contribution) Act 1978 provides in section 1(1):

> "Subject to the following provisions of this section, any person liable in respect of any damage suffered by another person may recover contribution from any other person liable in respect of the same damage (whether jointly with him or otherwise)."

The apportionment can be made by the court on its own initiative. It has been held that a claim for restitution may be for "the same

39. See, e.g., "Constructing the Team" (the Latham Report) (HMSO, 1994) at paras. 11.9–11.15.

40. Ch. 3, para 3.2.

damage" within section 1.[41] Conversely, the Court of Appeal has confirmed that liability in respect of the "same damage" means that both of the potentially contributing parties must be liable to the same *person*. Thus, where an employer sued its contractor, and the contractor joined its sub-contractor, the sub-contractor was not entitled to draw into the proceedings an engineer that it alleged was liable to the employer.[42]

It is difficult to extract any principles about apportionment from the case law, since cases typically depend on their own facts. *Holland Hannen and Cubitts* v. *WHTSO*, discussed above,[43] is an example of the re-apportionment by the Court of Appeal of liability towards the employer's design team and away from the nominated sub-contractor. One principle for which there does seem to be some authority is that the architect or engineer supervising a badly-performed job should pay a lesser contribution than the contractor who actually carried out the work. In *Eames* v. *North Hertfordshire Borough Council*[44] Judge Fay Q.C. said that "the blameworthiness of a policeman who fails to detect the crime is less than that of the criminal himself" and that in typical cases involving negligent passing of defective foundations by local authorities he had previously tended to hold the local authority to be about 25 per cent to blame and the builder 75 per cent. The Canadian Supreme Court gave short shrift to a supplier of defective concrete seeking a contribution from the main contractor's supervisor:[45]

> "How could it be fairly heard to say . . . because you failed to supervise me properly, and you were bound to do so by your undertaking to the contractor, you must share with me the burden of making compensation and, to that extent, relieve me of it."

In *Oldschool* v. *Gleeson*[46] the judge refused to allow a contractor to pass the blame for incompetent work onto the consulting engineer on the argument that he had failed to intervene to prevent it.

41. *Friends Provident Life Office* v. *Hillier Parker May and Rowden Estates and General plc*, unreported 3 April 1995.
42. *Birse Construction Ltd* v. *Haiste Ltd* (1995) 76 B.L.R. 26 (C.A.).
43. Ch. 3, para 3.4.2. The case is at (1985) 35 B.L.R. 1 (C.A.).
44. (1980) 18 B.L.R. 50.
45. *Bilodeau* v. *Bergeron* (1974) 2 S.C.R. 345 at 341, *per* Fauteux C.J.
46. (1976) 4 B.L.R. 103.

CHAPTER 9

DISPUTE RESOLUTION UNDER THE HOUSING GRANTS CONSTRUCTION AND REGENERATION ACT 1996

9.1. INTRODUCTION

The Housing Grants Construction and Regeneration Act 1996 ("the HGCR Act") is likely to have far-reaching effects on dispute resolution for construction professionals and their insurers. Part II of the Act, which affects the construction industry, came into force on 1 May 1998. There is no effect on contracts entered into before then.

The Act puts into effect many of the recommendations of the Latham Report of July 1994 ("Constructing the Team"). The aims of that report included trying to change the confrontational atmosphere prevalent in the construction industry; introducing "partnering" and negotiated (rather than tendered) contracts; and making various suggestions that, it was hoped, would achieve a 30 per cent saving in construction costs by the year 2000. The passage of the Act through Parliament was attended by lobbying from various contractors' and sub-contractors' interest groups.

The resultant legislation is intended to promote "fairer" construction contracts. "Pay when paid" clauses are banned (except where the primary paying party is insolvent). Rights to set off against payment otherwise due are restricted. There is a right to suspend work for non-payment. Machinery is put into place for establishing interim payment dates and amounts. Most important of all, a party to a "construction contract" (as defined) has a right to demand that *any* dispute under that contract be referred to adjudication for a decision within 28 days that will be temporarily binding until any later court or arbitration proceedings are concluded.

What, one might ask, has any of this to do with contracts of engagement for construction professionals and their clients? The answer is that the Act defines "construction contracts" in such a way as to catch such contracts. It is not clear why these contracts were brought under the provisions of the Act. The Latham Report did not recommend this, and it seems unlikely that the professional bodies lobbied for it.[1] Nevertheless, the contracts of architects engineers and surveyors, unlike those of doctors, lawyers and other professionals, are now subject to statutory control.

9.2. WHICH PROFESSIONALS' CONTRACTS ARE AFFECTED?

Two types of contract are wholly excluded from the Act:

(a) Oral contracts. A contract is "in writing" not only where there is a document signed by both parties but also where the contract is comprised in an exchange of letters or is otherwise evidenced in writing.[2] It is likely that where the professional writes to the client setting out his proposed terms of engagement, and work begins without any dissent from the client on those terms, the contract will be caught by the Act. However, this is not certain, and the Act does not fully tackle the difficulties of part oral-part written contracts, nor contracts where the offer is accepted by conduct.

(b) Contracts relating to a house or flat where the client occupies, or intends to occupy, the dwelling as his residence (it is unclear whether work to second homes is excluded from the Act).

1. See article by Mr G. Stringer reproduced in Uff Q.C., "Contemporary Issues in Construction Law Vol II—Construction Contract Reform: a plea for sanity" (Construction Law Press), 85 at 287, in which he asks "What business is it in the last years of the twentieth century for Parliament to introduce for these professionals alone statutory terms of engagement?" In the same book Professor Uff Q.C. notes (p. 53) that while the Construction Industry Council "apparently representing the interests of professional groups within the UK construction industry, appears to have acquiesced by becoming full members of the Latham implementation group, there is no evidence that the [professional] Institutions represented are supportive of these changes".

2. S. 107(2).

To discover whether a contract comes under the Act, one has to consider the type of project that it relates to. "Construction operations" is defined in section 105 to cover six types of project. The following is a summary of those operations that are specifically included in, and those specifically excluded from, the Act, but reference should be made to the words of section 105 where appropriate.

"Construction operations" specifically included in the Act	*"Construction operations" specifically excluded from the Act*
Construction, alteration, repair, maintenance, extension, demolition or dismantling of "buildings" "structures" or "works" (including roadworks) forming part of the land (and related preparatory work).	Drilling for oil or natural gas.
Fit-out works, e.g. installation of services such as heating and ventilation.	Mineral extraction (and associated works).
Cleaning and painting of buildings, whether external or internal.	Certain work where the main activity is nuclear processing, power generation, water or effluent treatment; or processing/storage of chemicals, steel or food and drink.
	"Supply only" contracts.
	Repair of artistic works, e.g. sculptures and murals.

These definitions can cause anomalies. A professional is caught by the Act if he designs an industrial plant to incinerate waste, but not where the main activity at the plant is power generation. He is caught if he advises in relation to construction work on a plant for producing steel, but not in relation to a plant for producing other metals or alloys.[3] Regard should also be had to the Construction Contracts (England and Wales) Exclusion Order 1998, which exempts from the Act certain statutory agreements, PFI projects, some finance agreements (including bonds and guarantees) and development agreements as defined.

Insurers and professionals should adopt the working hypothesis that most construction professionals' contracts will be covered by the Act.

3. On this point generally see Ian W. Menzies, "Adjudication under the HGCR Act 1996—an engineer's viewpoint", reproduced in *Contemporary Issues in Construction Law*, at 21.

9.3. THE STATUTORY REQUIREMENTS

Although matters referred to above such as "pay when paid", set-off and interim payments will affect professionals, the most significant effect is likely to be in section 108(1) which states:

"A party to a construction contract has the right to refer a dispute arising under the contract for adjudication under a procedure complying with this section."

Section 108 then goes on to provide eight points that must be included in all "construction contracts". These eight points, with comments, are shown separately in Appendix A to this chapter. If these terms are not included, a statutory provision called the Scheme for Construction Contracts ("the SCC") operates to impose them on the parties. It is important to note that even if a construction contract contains seven out of the eight mandatory points, the *whole* scheme descends on the parties. The scheme is now contained in "The Scheme for Construction Contracts Regulations 1998". Its provisions go beyond simply inserting the eight points referred to above. In particular, there are provisions as to how the adjudication is to be conducted.

Claims in tort do not come under the provisions of the Act. This could lead to anomalous situations where only part of a claim is adjudicable. It is likely that many construction contracts will be amended to allow an Adjudicator to consider such matters as misrepresentation and other tortious claims.

9.4. ADJUDICATION

Although standard form building contracts such as JCT 81 and DOM/1 have incorporated adjudication machinery for many years—in relation to limited areas (such as set-off disputes)—adjudication has no established legal framework in the way that arbitration has. It is intended to be a speedy procedure. Decisions may take place while the contract is ongoing. The adjudicator is to be appointed within seven days of the dispute arising, and makes a decision within 28 days of appointment. He may make his own investigations. Often there will be no hearing or trial in any sense, and the dispute may be resolved on documentation alone. The decision will usually not be reasoned and is likely to be almost unchallengeable. Costs orders will be limited. The decision will be temporarily binding on the parties, i.e. until litigation or arbitration proceedings are concluded.

The precise procedure will depend upon what, if any, terms as to adjudication the parties have incorporated into their contract. There are broadly three possibilities:

(a) A formal set of adjudication rules such as the Commission Industry Council (CIC) Model Adjudication Procedure (February 1998), the Institution of Civil Engineers (ICE) Adjudication Procedure (1997) or the Official Referees' Solicitors Association (ORSA) Adjudication Rules (1998).
(b) "Home made" rules drafted by one or other party to the construction contract. So long as these contain the eight mandatory requirements referred to above (and other mandatory matters under the Act), there is no reason they cannot be used.
(c) The SCC, which will apply *in its totality* if the construction contract does not contain all of the eight mandatory requirements referred to above (the SCC also "fills gaps" where the parties have failed to incorporate certain mandatory matters relating to such matters as set-off etc.).

9.4.1 The SCC Procedure

This contains the following points (summary only):

1. The referring party serves a notice of dispute with a brief description of the dispute, redress sought etc.

2. If an adjudicator is named in a contract, the referring party approaches him. If none is named, the parties can try to agree one, alternatively the referring party applies to the appointing body named in the contract (if there is none, he applies to the "adjudicator nominating body", i.e. a body holding itself out publicly as appointing adjudicators, e.g. RIBA, ICE, CIArb, ORSA). It is important to note that it is only the referring party who has the power to make the relevant applications.

3. Appointing bodies must appoint within five days. Adjudicators must agree to act (or otherwise) within two days. The objective is to achieve the Act's aim of getting an adjudicator in place within

seven days of the dispute arising. There is a cogent argument that if these times limits are not met, any subsequent appointment is not "in accordance with paragraphs 2, 5 or 6" (paragraph 7 of the SCC) so that any appointment is in fact invalid.

4. Within seven days of the notice of dispute the referring party serves a notice of referral on the adjudicator and any other party(ies) to the contract, together with the main contractual documents and any other documents that he relies on.

5. Thereafter, it is up to the adjudicator to set the timetable and any directions, to take the initiative as required under the Act, and to reach his decision within 28 days of referral of the dispute to him.

6. The losing party must pay up on the decision immediately or within such time as the adjudicator directs unless the adjudication followed a validly-served set-off notice under section 111(4) of the Act (in which case payment will usually be due within seven days of the Adjudicator's Decision).

9.5. WHAT THE ACT MEANS FOR PROFESSIONALS AND THEIR INSURERS

The Act is likely to mean more bad than good for professionals, and certainly for their insurers. In theory a client can now, if it wishes, refer a multi-million pound professional negligence claim to an adjudicator and demand a decision within 28 days of the adjudicator's appointment, and payment very shortly thereafter. The professional may still proceed with litigation or arbitration proceedings, but of course those may take months to come to trial, and in the meantime the professional or his insurer will be out of pocket. It seems unlikely that the Act was ever intended to cover this situation. It has been queried whether clients really will refer such decisions to adjudication (bearing in mind that adjudication is not mandatory). However, from the client's point of view there may be little to lose. Costs will be relatively small and even if the claim is only partly successful, it may be possible to obtain early payment of monies that would at least provide a fighting fund for later litigation/arbitration, together with a negotiating weapon in the meantime.

The main advantage of the Act for the professional is that where he is the claimant—e.g. in an action for his fees—it is *he* who obtains the benefits of the speedy procedure outlined above.

For the insurer, the only real merit of the Act is that *if* a matter which would otherwise have gone to arbitration/litigation is resolved by adjudication (i.e. assuming that the claimant loses the adjudication and decides to take the matter no further) the overall costs will inevitably be less than in full-scale proceedings.

9.6. STEPS THAT PROFESSIONALS AND INSURERS CAN TAKE

Professionals should start by considering their contracts. What follows is only an outline of relevant considerations and legal advice should be sought in specific circumstances.

The professional should not necessarily adopt institutional rules or those in the SCC. Appendix B to this chapter contains a comparison of the SCC, CIC, ICE and ORSA rules. In particular, a professional may wish to consider the following:

(i) A provision that the adjudicator has power to make costs orders for *inter partes* costs. In particular, this may operate as a disincentive to claimants using the adjudication system because there is nothing to lose. There is certainly merit in considering a provision that the adjudicator can make costs orders in cases involving claims above a certain financial level, or where the adjudicator considers that one side's case was particularly poor and should not have been run.

(ii) Joinder provisions for adjudication (and/or for arbitration). This will be so if he anticipates wishing to bring others into any professional negligence action against him, e.g. in contribution proceedings. In practice it will usually be the *client* that wants joinder provisions, and the professional will be better off without them (so as to avoid the expense of multi-party proceedings).

Professionals should also consider the following points:

1 There is a danger of an "ambush" whereby the client spends many months preparing a meticulous and detailed claim

complete with expert evidence that becomes virtually unanswerable within 28 days or less, thus almost forcing the adjudicator to give a decision in the claimant's favour. One possible tactic to counter this is the "pre-emptive strike" whereby the professional *himself* serves a notice of adjudication (which could be done as soon as it is clear that there is a dispute), thus forcing the claimant to put his claim immediately.

2 There is likely to be legitimate scope for attacking a claimant who fails to follow the procedural requirements of the Act and SCC (or any applicable rules), and these should always be investigated (see point 3 in paragraph 9.4.1 above, for example).

3 Arbitration (or litigation) could be started immediately an adjudication notice is served in order to save time (admittedly, not very much time, but even serving a notice of arbitration would start the process of getting an arbitrator appointed. Interestingly, the losing professional in an adjudication will then become the claimant or plaintiff in subsequent legal proceedings, which raises questions about the onus of proof and how pleadings are to be formulated).

4 If a decision goes against the professional, he needs to consider what can be done about it. There is no appeal against a decision. The decision of an adjudicator is likely to be regarded by the courts as akin to that of an expert under "expert determination clauses". These can generally only be challenged for:
—Fraud or collusion.
—The adjudicator exceeding his jurisdiction.
—The adjudicator having not answered the question that he was asked.

Of these, the third may offer some possibilities based on *Mercury* v. *Director General of Communications*[4] where it was said that an expert who makes a determination but misinterprets phrases in an agreement does not do what he was asked to do by the parties (and see also *Jones* v. *Sherwood Computer Services Ltd*[5]).

4. [1996] 1 All E.R. 575 (H.L.).
5. [1992] 2 All E.R. 170.

Apart from these limited possibilities, the respondent professional can legitimately make what he may of the much-criticised provisions under the Act for enforcement of adjudicators' decisions. The major difficulty has already been dealt with in Chapter 8, namely that if there is an arbitration clause, the claimant may be unable to enforce the decision in the court. Further, unless the parties have specifically so agreed, the arbitrator cannot make a provisional award under section 39 of the Arbitration Act 1996 (this is one reason why a professional should think carefully before incorporating section 39 into his contract or engagement).

There are potentially further possibilities for avoiding payment if set-offs can validly be raised against the decision.

Insurers will bear in mind many of the above points as part of their own strategy. Assuming, as appears likely, that professional indemnity insurers will cover adjudication risks, they need to consider such matters as limitations on cover and whether deductibles should be increased. In particular, they will wish to tighten the requirements so as to demand immediate notification of claims, and make this a condition precedent to coverage. With only 28 days between appointment and the adjudicator's decision, every day will count.

Upon a claim being made, insurers may also need to write to the insured specifically reserving their rights as to coverage, since the short timetable will often not allow issues of coverage to be fully worked out before substantive work has to be carried out in the adjudication.

APPENDIX A TO CHAPTER 9

EIGHT PROVISIONS THAT MUST APPEAR IN "CONSTRUCTION CONTRACTS" IF THE SCHEME FOR CONSTRUCTION CONTRACTS IS NOT TO APPLY

1 The contract shall enable a party to give notice at any time of his intention to refer a dispute to adjudication. [*Note*: the words are "at any time" so that an adjudication could be started many months after a contract is concluded, and even during later legal proceedings.]

2 The contract shall provide a timetable with the object of securing the appointment of the adjudicator and referral of the dispute to him within seven days of such notice. [*Note*: this raises the issue whether the adjudicator should be named in the contract, as Latham envisaged. However, two possible problems with this are that an adjudicator may be unavailable or unsuitable to the particular dispute that arises.]

3 The contract shall require the adjudicator to reach a decision within 28 days of referral or such longer period as is agreed by the parties after the dispute has been referred. [*Note*: it seems unlikely that the adjudicator is able to give a decision along the lines of "my decision is that I make no decision because I cannot do so in the timetable available".]

4 The contract shall allow the adjudicator to extend the period of 28 days by up to 14 days, with the consent of the party by whom the dispute was referred. [*Note*: the referring party would usually be the claimant, i.e. the person who is actually seeking money, but this is not necessarily so.]

5 The contract shall impose a duty on the adjudicator to act impartially.

APPENDIX A TO CHAPTER 9

EIGHT PROVISIONS THAT MUST APPEAR IN "CONSTRUCTION CONTRACTS" IF THE SCHEME FOR CONSTRUCTION CONTRACTS IS NOT TO APPLY

1 The contract shall enable a party to give notice at any time of his intention to refer a dispute to adjudication.
[*Note*: the words are "at any time" so that an adjudication could be started many months after a contract is concluded, and even *during* later legal proceedings!]

2 The contract shall provide a timetable with the object of securing the appointment of the adjudicator and referral of the dispute to him within seven days of such notice.
[*Note*: this raises the issue whether the adjudicator should be named in the contract, as Latham envisaged. However, two possible problems with this are that an adjudicator may be unavailable, or unsuitable to the particular dispute that arises.]

3 The contract shall require the adjudicator to reach a decision within 28 days of referral or such longer period as is agreed by the parties after the dispute has been referred.
[*Note*: it seems unlikely that the adjudicator is able to give a decision along the lines of "my decision is that I make no decision because I cannot do so in the timetable available".]

4 The contract shall allow the adjudicator to extend the period of 28 days by up to 14 days, with the consent of the party by whom the dispute was referred.
[*Note*: the referring party would usually be the claimant, i.e. the person who is actually seeking money, but this is not necessarily so.]

5 The contract shall impose a duty on the adjudicator to act impartially.

6 The contract shall enable the adjudicator to take the initiative in ascertaining the facts and the law.
[*Note*: it seems that the contract must *positively* mention these two points, if the SCC is not to apply.]

7 The contract shall provide that the decision of the adjudicator is binding until the dispute is finally determined by legal proceedings, by arbitration (if the contract provides for arbitration or the parties otherwise agree to arbitration) or by agreement.

The parties may agree to accept the decision of the adjudicator as finally determining the dispute.
[*Note*: it is unlikely that the parties will wish to adopt the second paragraph, except in cases of small dispute.]

8 The contract shall also provide that the adjudicator is not liable for anything done or omitted in the discharge or purported discharge of his functions as adjudicator unless the act or omission is in bad faith, and that any employee or agent of the adjudicator is similarly protected from liability [*Note*: this mirrors the protection for arbitrators in the Arbitration Act 1996, but it should be noted that the adjudicator of course is not himself a party to the "construction contract" and it would need one of the two parties to step in to his aid if he were sued in negligence.]

APPENDIX B TO CHAPTER 9

A COMPARISON OF FOUR SETS OF ADJUDICATION RULES

	ISSUE	SCC (Scheme for Construction Contracts)	CIC (Construction Industry Council) Model Adjudication Procedure 1st edition (Feb 1998)	ICE (Institution of Civil Engineers) Adjudication Procedure (1997)	ORSA (Official Referees' Solicitors Association) Adjudication Rules 1998 version 1.2
1	Identity of Adjudicator	Must be an actual person. Cannot be an employee of either party. Must declare financial or other interest (r. 4).	—	—	Cannot be "any person named in the contract whose readiness or willingness is in question" (r. 7). Cannot act if conflict of interest (r. 21).
2	Adjudicator-appointing body in default of agreement	An "adjudicator nominating body" being a body holding itself out publicly as a body that will select adjudicators (r. 2).	CIC (r. 10).	ICE (r. 3.3).	ORSA (r. 7).
3	Separate fee agreement for Adjudicator?	No.	Yes (r. 12).	Yes (r. 3.4).	No. However Adjudicator's fees are limited to £1,000 per day or part plus VAT (r. 25).

	ISSUE	SCC (Scheme for Construction Contracts)	CIC (Construction Industry Council) Model Adjudication Procedure 1st edition (Feb 1998)	ICE (Institution of Civil Engineers) Adjudication Procedure (1997)	ORSA (Official Referees' Solicitors Association) Adjudication Rules 1998 version 1.2
4	After Notice of Adjudication to the other party, what is the procedure for referring the case to the Adjudicator?	Referring party serves referral notice, together with the contract and other documents that he intends to rely on (r. 7).	Referring party sends Statement of Case together with contract, evidence etc. (r. 14).	Referring party serves Statement of Case including "information upon which he relies" and supporting documents (r. 4.1, 4.2). Other party serves a response within 14 days of date of referral (of the Statement of Case) to the Adjudicator (r. 5.4).	Procedural matters are for the Adjudicator to decide (r. 19).
5	Joinder of adjudications?	Yes, with consent (r. 8).	Yes, with consent (r. 22).	Yes, with consent (r. 5.7).	—
6	Scope of matters that the Adjudicator must decide (apart from those in the Notice of Adjudication)	Adjudicator decides "matters in dispute". He may also take into account other matters "necessarily connected" with the dispute, or those that the parties agree he can deal with (r. 20).	Only agreed matters (r. 20).	—	Agreed matters, and those that the Adjudicator decides "must be included in order that the adjudication may be effective and/or meaningful" (r. 11).
7	Can the Adjudicator appoint legal or technical advisers?	Yes, without leave—so long as he notifies the parties (r. 13).	As SCC (r. 19).	As SCC (r. 5.6).	Yes, if at least one party requests this (r. 19).
8	Adjudicator's powers in relation to law/evidence	The Adjudicator must apply the law in relation to the contract (r. 12).	The Adjudicator is not obliged to observe the rules of evidence (r. 17) but must apply the law in relation to the contract (r. 12).	The Adjudicator is not obliged to follow court procedures or rules of evidence (r. 5.5). There is power to make separate decisions in respect of different aspects of the dispute (r. 6.1). The Adjudicator does not act as an expert or arbitrator (r. 1.4).	The Adjudicator may come to a "fair and reasonable" view, if it is impossible to reach a view on the legal entitlements within the relevant timescale (r. 15).

9	What can the Adjudicator do if there is a procedural default by one party?	The Adjudicator has power to draw inferences from default or (for example) attach less weight to evidence submitted outside time limits that he has issued (r. 15).	The Adjudicator has power to proceed in spite of the default (r. 17).	As CIC (r. 5.5).	If the Adjudicator requires a bundle of documents from one party, he may then draw such inference as seems proper from any imbalance in any bundle provided (r. 19).
10	Confidentiality	Documents are only confidential if the party supplying the document indicates this—and even then a document may lose its confidentiality if disclosure is "necessary" for the adjudication (r. 18).	—	—	All matters in the adjudication are confidential unless otherwise necessary for enforcing the Adjudicator's decision or for subsequent proceedings (r. 30). The Adjudicator cannot require to see documents that would be privileged in court proceedings (r. 19).
11	The Decision	Reasoned, if at least one party wants this (r. 22).	The Adjudicator shall not be required to give reasons (r. 24).	The Adjudicator shall not be required to give reasons (r. 6.1). There is power to correct clerical mistakes, errors or ambiguities in the decision (r. 6.9).	The decision shall not be reasoned (r. 27).
12	What is the effect of a late decision?	Either party can serve a fresh notice of adjudication (r. 19).	The decision is still effective unless the dispute is referred to a new Adjudicator (r. 25).	Either party can give seven days notice of intention to refer to a replacement Adjudicator, but the decision is still effective so long as the dispute has not actually been so referred (rr. 6.3, 6.4).	—

ISSUE	SCC (Scheme for Construction Contracts)	CIC (Construction Industry Council) Model Adjudication Procedure 1st edition (Feb 1998)	ICE (Institution of Civil Engineers) Adjudication Procedure (1997)	ORSA (Official Referees' Solicitors Association) Adjudication Rules 1998 version 1.2
13 Enforcement	Court may enforce decision. Arbitration Act 1996 s. 42 is incorporated into the contract, subject to modifications (r. 24).	Parties are entitled to summary enforcement (r. 30).	Parties are entitled to summary enforcement (r. 6.7).	Parties entitled to summary enforcement without set off, counterclaim or abatement (r. 28).
14 Costs	No general costs power. Apparently power to order apportionment of Adjudicator's fees (r. 25).	No general power to apportion cost, but the Adjudicator can apportion his fees (rr. 28, 29).	As CIC (r. 6.5).	The Adjudicator cannot make a costs order (r. 21) but can apportion his own fees (r. 24).
15 Interest	Adjudicator may award simple or compound interest "having regard to any terms of the contract relating to the payment of interest" (r. 20).	Power to award simple or compound interest (r. 27).	As CIC (r. 6.2).	As CIC (r. 26).
16 Adjudicator's position in subsequent arbitration	—	Adjudicator cannot be arbitrator in subsequent arbitration (unless the parties agree) nor can he be called as a witness (r. 32).	As CIC (r. 7.1).	Adjudicator cannot be required to give evidence in arbitration (r. 31).

APPENDIX 1

APIA—RIBA/95 WORDING

1. Definitions and Interpretation

1.1 **"Assured"** shall mean:

(a) Any person or Firm for whom indemnity has been requested in the proposal form;

(b) Any other person who has been or during the Period of Insurance becomes a partner director or principal of the Firm;

provided that liability arises directly out of Professional Business carried out by that person in the name of the Firm.

1.2 **"Firm"** shall mean the Assured Firm described in the Schedule.

1.3 **"Professional Business"** shall mean the business described in the Schedule.

1.4 **"Geographical Limits"** shall mean any territory within the European Union, Isle of Man and the Channel Islands or such additional territory described in the Schedule.

1.5 **"Period of Insurance"** shall mean the period shown in the Schedule.

1.6 **"Limit of Indemnity"** shall mean the sum shown in the Schedule. The liability of Insurers under Section 3 shall not exceed the Limit of Indemnity in respect of each and every claim (or series of claims from the same originating cause) but where any claim circumstance or event is notified to Insurers which is the same as or arises out of or is connected with any claim circumstance or event notified at the same time or previously such claim circumstance or event shall not be separate for the purposes of assessing the Limit of Indemnity available to the Assured.

The liability of Insurers under Section 4 shall not exceed in the aggregate the sum shown in the Schedule.

1.7 **"defence costs"** shall mean all costs and expenses incurred with the prior written and continuing consent of the Insurers in the investigation defence or settlement of any claim circumstance or event and the costs of representation at any inquiry or other proceedings, whether civil or criminal, which have a relevance to any claim circumstance or event which (but for the Excess) is likely to form the subject of indemnity by Insurers.

1.8 **"Excess"** shall mean the first amount of each claim (or series of claims from the same originating cause) shown in the Schedule, which is to be borne by the Assured.

1.9 **"document"** shall mean deeds, wills, agreements, maps, plans, records, written or printed books, letters, certificates or written or printed documents or forms of any nature whatsoever (excluding any bearer bonds or coupons, bank or currency notes or other negotiable paper) and/or magnetic tape or other like means of recording information for use with any computer record system.

1.10 **"claim"** shall mean any claim made against the Assured.

1.11 **"claimant"** shall mean the party making such claim.

1.12 **"circumstance or event"** shall mean any circumstance or event which is likely to give rise to a claim.

1.13 **"United Kingdom"** shall mean England, Wales, Scotland, Northern Ireland, Isle of Man and the Channel Islands.

Any marginal note is for information purposes only and shall not be incorporated in or construed as part of the Policy.

Words in the singular include the plural and words in the plural include the singular.

2. Basis of Contract

The Assured having made to Insurers a written proposal on the date stated in the Schedule which together with any other related particulars and statements that have been supplied in writing are the basis of the contract, and having paid to Insurers the premium stated in the Schedule, is indemnified subject to the Policy terms and conditions for any claim made during the Period of Insurance arising only out of the exercise and conduct by or on behalf of the Assured of the Professional Business within the Geographical Limits.

3. Professional Liability

3.1 The Assured is indemnified against any claim made during the Period of Insurance for which the Assured shall become legally liable to pay compensation together with claimant's costs, fees and expenses in accordance with any judgment award or settlement made within the Geographical Limits (or any order made anywhere in the world to enforce such judgment award or settlement in whole or in part) in consequence of:

3.1.1 Any breach of the professional duty of care owed by the

Assured to the claimant which term is deemed to include a breach of warranty of authority;

3.1.2 Any libel, slander or slander of title, slander of goods or injurious falsehood;

3.1.3 The loss, destruction of or damage to any document in the care, custody and control of the Assured or for which the Assured is responsible (except to the extent insured by Section 4).

3.2 **Costs Clause**

In addition to the Limit of Indemnity the Insurers will pay defence costs provided that if a payment greater than the Limit of Indemnity available from Insurers has to be made to dispose of a claim, Insurers' liability for defence costs associated with such claim shall be that proportion of the defence costs as the Limit of Indemnity available from Insurers for such claim bears to the amount required to be paid to dispose of the claim.

4. Additional Protection

The Assured is indemnified for reasonable and necessary costs and expenses first incurred during the Period of Insurance by the Assured arising out of the Professional Business in the United Kingdom and with the prior written consent of Insurers:

4.1 in replacing, restoring and reconstituting any document which is the property of the Assured or for which the Assured is responsible;

4.2 in the prosecution of any injunction and/or proceedings for compensation arising out of infringement of any copyright vested in the Assured provided always that there is no indemnity hereunder in respect of any costs that may be awarded against the Assured.

5. General Exclusions

The Policy shall not indemnify the Assured in respect of:

Excess

5.1 The Excess.

Consortium

5.2 Any claim arising out of the Professional Business carried out by the Assured for and/or in the name of any consortium or joint venture of which the Assured forms part unless specifically endorsed hereon.

Transport Property etc

5.3 Any claim arising out of the ownership, possession or use by or on behalf of the Assured of any aircraft, watercraft, hovercraft or motor vehicle or trailer, or any buildings, premises or land or that part of any building leased, occupied or rented by the Assured, or any property of the Assured.

Disclosed Circumstance

5.4 Any claim arising out of any circumstance or event which has been disclosed by the Assured to any insurer prior to the inception of this Policy.

Employment

5.5 Any claim arising out of injury, disease, illness or death of the Assured or any person working under a contract of employment apprenticeship or service with the Assured, or any claim arising out of any dispute between the Assured and any present or former employee or any person who has been offered employment with the Assured.

Trading Liability

5.6 Any claim arising out of or in connection with any trading loss or trading liability incurred by any business managed by or carried on by or on behalf of the Assured.

Fraud and Dishonesty

5.7 Any claim directly or indirectly contributed to or caused by any dishonest, fraudulent, criminal or malicious act or omission of any partner director or principal of the Assured.

Warranties, Penalties

5.8 Any claim arising out of performance warranties, penalty clauses or liquidated damages clauses unless the liability of the Assured to the claimant would have existed in the absence of such warranties or clauses.

Non-Contribution

5.9 Any claim for which the Assured is or but for the existence of this Policy would be entitled to indemnity under any other insurance except in respect of any amount which exceeds that which would have been payable under such other insurance had this Policy not been effected.

Nuclear and War Risks

5.10 Liability for any claim:

5.10.1 directly or indirectly caused by or contributed to by or arising from (a) ionising radiations or contamination by radioactivity from any nuclear fuel or from any nuclear waste from the combustion of nuclear fuel, (b) the radioactive toxic explosive or other hazardous properties of any explosive nuclear assembly or nuclear component thereof;

5.10.2 directly or indirectly occasioned by or happening through or in consequence of war, invasion, acts of foreign enemies, hostilities (whether war be declared or not), civil war, rebellion, revolution, insurrection, military or usurped power.

Penal Damages

5.11.1 Any penal, punitive, exemplary or aggravated damages whenever identifiable as such.

5.11.2 Any additional damages under Section 97(2) of the Copyright, Designs & Patents Act 1988 or any statutory successor to that Section.

5.11.3 Any fines or penalties of a criminal nature.

6. General Conditions

Surveys

6.1 No indemnity is provided by Section 3.1.1 for claims arising out of any survey and/or valuation report carried out by or on behalf of the Assured unless the Assured has complied with the following conditions:

6.1.1 the report is made in writing and;

6.1.2 the survey and/or valuation is made by

6.1.2.1 a partner director or principal in the Firm or a member of the Assured's staff who is a Fellow or Professional Associate or Member of the Royal Institute of British Architects or of the Royal Institution of Chartered Surveyors or is a Registered Architect who has not less than one year's experience in undertaking structural surveys and/or valuation work such experience being related to the subject matter of the report or

6.1.2.2 any member of the Assured's staff who has not less than five years' experience in undertaking structural surveys and/or valuation work such experience being related to the subject matter of the report and;

6.1.3 except in the case where a report is provided to a Building Society, Insurance Company Bank or other such institutional lender upon a standard report form provided to the Assured for that purpose the Assured has incorporated in the report the following reservation:

"We have not inspected woodwork or other parts of the structure which are covered, unexposed or inaccessible and we are therefore unable to report that any such part of the property is free from defect."

6.1.4 Where the Assured considers that High Alumina Cement may be present in a building the following paragraph is also to be added:

"Furthermore, we must stress that we have not carried out any investigation to determine whether High Alumina Cement was used during the construction of the building inspected and we are therefore unable to report that the building is free from risk in this respect. In view of the possible potential danger connected with High Alumina Cement we strongly recommend that the appropriate investigations, inspections and tests be carried out immediately by a suitably qualified engineer."

6.1.5 any report and/or test made subsequent to the date of this Policy in connection with High Alumina Cement is carried out only by a suitably qualified engineer and presented in writing.

Notification Procedures

6.2 The Assured shall as a condition precedent to their right to be indemnified under:

6.2.1 Section 3 of this Policy, give notice in writing to Insurers as soon as possible during the Period of Insurance of any claim or of the receipt of notice from any person of an intention to make a claim.

6.2.2 Section 4.1 of this Policy, give notice in writing to Insurers as soon as possible during the Period of Insurance if during such Period of Insurance they shall discover that any document has been destroyed or damaged or lost or mislaid.

6.2.3 Section 4.2 of this Policy, give notice in writing to Insurers as soon as possible during the Period of Insurance when a situation comes to their notice which requires or may require any steps to be taken to protect their own or Insurers' interests.

6.3 The Assured shall give during the Period of Insurance full details in writing as soon as possible of any circumstance or event of which the Assured shall first become aware during the Period of Insurance. Any such circumstance or event notified to Insurers during the Period of

Insurance which subsequently gives rise to a claim shall be deemed to be a claim made during the Period of Insurance.

6.4 Notice to Insurers to be given under this Policy shall be deemed to be properly made if received in writing by RIBA Insurance Agency Limited, at the address shown in the Schedule.

Non Admission of Liability

6.5 The Assured shall not admit liability and no admission, arrangement, offer, promise or payment shall be made by the Assured without Insurers' written consent.

Insurers' Rights

6.6 Insurers shall be entitled, if they so desire, to take over and conduct in the name of the Assured the investigation representation defence or settlement of any claim circumstance or event and shall have full discretion in the conduct of the same. The Assured shall not be required to contest any legal proceedings unless a Queen's Counsel (or by mutual agreement between the Assured and the Insurers a similar authority) shall advise that such proceedings could be contested with the probability of success. It is a condition precedent to the Assured being indemnified by Insurers that the Assured shall give all such assistance as Insurers may reasonably require in the investigation representation defence or settlement of any claim circumstance or event.

6.7 In the event that Insurers shall be advised by their solicitors or on the advice of their solicitors' counsel that it is prudent to do so, Insurers shall be entitled to make a payment of the amount available from Insurers of the Limit of Indemnity or of an amount equivalent to that which any claim can be settled (whichever is the lesser) to the Assured in exoneration and total discharge of any further liability of any kind whatsoever by the Insurers to the Assured under this Policy. It shall be deemed to be proper payment in exoneration and discharge of the Insurers' liability hereunder to the Assured if the Insurers pay these monies to the RIBA Insurance Agency Limited.

6.8 Payment of the Excess by the Assured is a condition precedent to the Assured being indemnified by Insurers.

Applicable Law

6.9.1 This contract is governed by the laws of England.

6.9.2 Any dispute or difference arising hereunder between the Assured and Insurers shall be referred to a Queen's Counsel of the English Bar to be mutually agreed between Insurers and the Assured or in the event of disagreement by the Chairman of the Bar Council. The Assured must give written notice within forty-five days of receipt of the Insurers' decision with which he is in dispute or difference.

Subrogation Against Employees

6.10 Insurers shall not exercise any right of subrogation that may exist against any employee or former employee of the Assured unless Insurers shall have made a payment brought about or contributed to by the act or omission of the employee or former employee which was dishonest, fraudulent, criminal or malicious.

Additional Insurance

6.11 The Assured shall not effect insurance for any sum that exceeds the Limit of Indemnity without the prior written consent of the RIBA Insurance Agency Limited.

Fraud

6.12 If any request for indemnity is made and the same is false or fraudulent as regards the amount or otherwise this Policy shall become void and any indemnity hereunder shall be forfeited.

7. *Special RIBA Conditions*

7.1 Insurers will not exercise their right to avoid the Policy nor will Insurers reject a request for indemnity when it is alleged that there has been:

7.1.1 Non-disclosure of facts; or

7.1.2 Misrepresentation of facts; or

7.1.3 Incorrect particulars or statements; or

7.1.4 Late notification of a claim; or

7.1.5 Late notification of intention to make a claim; or

7.1.6 Late notification of a circumstance or event.

Provided always that the Assured shall establish to Insurers' satisfaction that such alleged non-disclosure, misrepresentation or incorrect particulars or statements or late notification was innocent and free of any fraudulent conduct or intent to deceive.

7.2 When Insurers are so satisfied the following conditions shall apply:

7.2.1 In any case of a claim and the Assured were previously aware of the claim or a circumstance or event, or in any case of the Assured being previously aware of an intention to make a claim or of a circumstance or event and the Assured could have notified the claim circumstance or event under any preceding policy of indemnity, then if the indemnity available from Insurers under this Policy is greater or wider in scope than that to which the Assured would have been entitled under such preceding policy of indemnity, Insurers shall only be liable to indemnify the Assured for such amount and on such terms as would have been available to the Assured under such preceding policy of indemnity; save that nothing in this clause shall entitle the Assured to indemnity wider or more extensive than is available to the Assured under this Policy (notwithstanding the terms of this clause).

7.2.2 Where the Assured's conduct or breach of or non-compliance with any condition of this Policy has resulted in prejudice to the handling or settlement of any claim, the indemnity afforded by this Policy in respect of such claim (including defence costs) shall be reduced to such sum as in Insurers' opinion would have been payable by them in the absence of such prejudice.

7.2.3 No indemnity shall be available for any claim circumstance or event notified to Insurers after the Period of Insurance.

In the event of any disagreement by the Assured regarding the application of these Special Conditions, such disagreement shall at the Assured's request be referred to the person nominated by the President for the time being of the Royal Institute of British Architects for his consideration and intercession on the Assured's behalf if the facts are considered to warrant this by the person so nominated, and the Insurers agree to give due and proper consideration to any such intercession.

APPENDIX 2

SURVIS-PI 3

IN CONSIDERATION of the Insured named in the Schedule hereto having paid the premium set forth in the Schedule to the Insurers who have hereunto subscribed their Names (hereinafter referred to as "the Insurers").

THE INSURERS HEREBY SEVERALLY AGREE each for the proportion set against its name to indemnify the Insured (as defined herein) in accordance with the Terms and Conditions contained hereunder or endorsed hereon.

PROVIDED THAT:
1 the total liability of the Insurers shall not exceed the limits of liability expressed in the said Schedule or such other limits of liability as may be substituted therefore by memorandum hereon or attached hereto signed by or on behalf of the Insurers,
2 the liability of each of the Insurers individually to the Insured in respect of any claim for indemnity and any contribution towards the Insured's costs shall be limited to the proportion set against each Insurer's name.

For the avoidance of doubt it should be noted that the limit of indemnity and the excess applies to all the Insureds jointly and for this purpose only the Certificate is a joint Certificate.

Definitions

1 "PROFESSIONAL BUSINESS" shall mean:

a) those services which are normally undertaken by members of the Royal Institution of Chartered Surveyors or as otherwise declared to Insurers hereto and performed in the conduct of business by or on behalf of the Firm(s) named in the Schedule,

b) advice given or services performed by any Insured whilst holding an individual appointment but if as a Director or officer of a company only in relation to services performed in connection with buildings and/or property and/or land, such services being of the same nature as in a) above being services normally performed by that Director or officer for clients of the Firm(s) named in the Schedule providing the fees (if any) relating to those services undertaken by any Insured holding an individual appointment are taken into account in ascertaining the gross earnings of the Firm(s).

In the event of any dispute or disagreement arising between the Insured and the Insurers as to the correct interpretation of the definition of Professional Business the facts shall be submitted to the President for the time being of The Royal Institution of Chartered Surveyors or his nominee whose decision shall be final and binding on both parties.

2 "THE INSURED" shall mean any of the following:

a) those Partner(s)/Director(s) of the Firm(s) named in the proposal form dated as shown in the Schedule and any other person or persons who may at any time during the period of this Certificate become Partner(s)/Director(s) in the Firm(s),
b) any former Partner(s)/Director(s) of the Firm(s) for services performed for and on behalf of the Firm(s) including retired Partner(s)/Director(s) remaining as Consultants to the Firm(s),
c) those persons named as consultants in the proposal form dated as shown on the Schedule,
d) any person who is or has been under a contract of service for and/or on behalf of the Firm(s),
e) the Estates and/or legal representatives of any of the persons noted under a), b), c) or d) hereof in the event of their death, incapacity, insolvency or bankruptcy,
f) any Firm(s) named in Item 1 of the Schedule.

3 "FIRM(S)" shall mean the Firm(s) named in the Schedule or the predecessors in business of the said Firm(s) as disclosed to Insurers.

4 "DOCUMENTS" shall mean deeds, wills, agreements, maps, plans, records, books, letters, certificates, computer system records, forms and documents of whatsoever nature whether written, printed or reproduced by any other method (other than bearer bonds, coupons, bank notes, currency notes and negotiable instruments).

5 "CERTIFICATE PERIOD" shall mean the Period of Insurance specified in the Schedule.

Whereas the Insured, as defined herein, have made to Insurers a written proposal bearing the date stated in the Schedule containing particulars and statements which it is hereby agreed are the basis of this Certificate and are to be considered as incorporated herein:

Insuring Clauses

NOW WE, THE INSURERS TO THE EXTENT AND IN THE MANNER HEREINAFTER PROVIDED, HEREBY AGREE:

1 Civil liability

To indemnify the Insured against any claim or claims first made against them or any of them during the Certificate Period in respect of any civil liability whatsoever or whensoever arising (including liability for Claimants' costs) incurred in the course of any PROFESSIONAL BUSINESS carried on by the Insured.

Where a series of such claims arise from a breach of or repeated breaches of a single duty or identical duties owed and arising from a single engagement all claims within that series shall for the purpose of the limit of indemnity (Condition 7) and the excess (Condition 8) under this Certificate be treated as a single claim.

Provided that any and all such claims arising from a single survey and/or valuation shall for the like purpose be treated as a single claim under this Certificate.

2 Fidelity

To indemnify the Insured against their own direct loss or losses which, during the Certificate Period, they shall discover they have sustained by reason of any dishonesty or fraud of any past or present Partner, Director or Employee of the Firm(s) named in the Schedule provided always that:

a) such dishonest or fraudulent act(s) are carried out by the person(s) concerned with the manifest intent to cause such loss to the Insured or to obtain improper personal gain either for themselves or in collusion with others,
b) no indemnity shall be afforded hereby to any person committing or condoning such dishonesty or fraud,
c) the annual accounts of the Insured have been prepared and/or certified by an Independent Accountant or Auditor,
d) any dishonesty or fraud committed by a person or persons acting in concert shall for the purposes of this Certificate be treated as giving rise to one loss,
e) such loss or losses shall include Accountants' fees incurred as a result of such loss up to £15,000 or such amount as agreed by the Insurers,
f) any monies which but for such dishonesty or fraud would be due to such person from the Insured or any monies of such person held

by the Insured, shall be deducted from any amount payable under this Certificate.

3 Loss of documents

To indemnify the Insured against reasonable costs and expenses of whatsoever nature incurred by the Insured in replacing or restoring DOCUMENTS either the property of or entrusted to or lodged or deposited with the Firm(s), having been discovered during the Certificate Period to have been damaged, lost or mislaid and which after diligent search cannot be found.

Special institution conditions

1 a) Insurers will not exercise their right to avoid this Certificate where there has been non-disclosure or misrepresentation of facts or untrue statements in the proposal form, provided always that the Insured shall establish to Insurers' satisfaction that such non-disclosure, misrepresentation or untrue statement was free of any fraudulent intent,

b) however, in the case of a claim first made against the Insured during the period of this Insurance where

i) they had previous knowledge of the circumstances which could give rise to such claim, and

ii) they should have notified the same under any preceding Insurance,

then, where the indemnity or cover under this Certificate is greater or wider in scope than that to which the Insured would have been entitled under such preceding Insurance (whether with other Insurers or not), Insurers shall only be liable to afford indemnity to such amount and extent as would have been afforded to the Insured by such preceding Insurance.

2 Where the Insured's breach of or non-compliance with any Condition of this Certificate has resulted in prejudice to the handling or settlement of any claim Insurers shall be entitled to reduce the indemnity afforded by this Certificate in respect of such claim (including costs and expenses) to such sum as in Insurers' reasonable opinion would have been payable by them in the absence of such prejudice.

3 In the event of any dispute or disagreement between the Insured and Insurers regarding the application of these Special Institution Conditions, such dispute or disagreement shall be referred by either party for arbitration to any person nominated by the President for the time being of the Royal Institution of Chartered Surveyors.

Exclusions

The Certificate shall not indemnify the Insured against:

1 any claim or loss where the Insured are entitled to indemnity under any other Insurance(s) except in respect of any excess beyond the amount which would have been payable under such Insurance had this Certificate not been effected,

2 any claim or circumstance that may give rise to a claim which has been notified to any Insurance Intermediary or Insurer pursuant to any other Policy or Certificate of Insurance attaching prior to the inception of this Certificate or disclosed on the completed proposal form that shall form the basis of this contract,

3 any claim or loss arising out of any dispute between the Insured and any present or former Employee or any person who has been offered employment with the Insured,

4 any claim or loss arising out of the death or bodily injury or disease of an Employee under a contract of service with the Firm(s) whilst in the course of employment for or on behalf of the Insured,

5 any claim brought by a Firm, company or organisation controlling the Insured Firm(s) or of which any Partner(s)/Director(s) of the Firm(s) have control unless such claim or claims originates from an independent third party,

6 any claim or loss arising out of the use of any motor vehicles by the Insured in circumstances in which provisions of the Road Traffic Acts apply,

7 any claim or loss arising out of the ownership by the Insured of any buildings, premises or land or that part of any building leased, occupied or rented by the Insured,

8 any claim or loss arising out of any dishonesty or fraud of any person after discovery by the Insured, in relation to that person of reasonable cause for suspicion of fraud or dishonesty,

9 any claim or loss arising out of any trading losses or trading liabilities incurred by any business managed or carried on by the Insured including loss of any client account or business,

10 any liability for any amount of liquidated damages or penalties which arises out of any express guarantee assumed by the Insured under a contract or agreement which would not otherwise have attached in the absence of such contract or agreement,

11 any claim or loss (including loss of value) arising directly or indirectly from pollution. This Exclusion shall not apply where such claim or loss arises from the Insured's negligent structural design or specification or failure to report a structural defect in a property but cover shall only extend to that part of any claim or loss which relates to the cost of

re-designing, re-specifying, remedying and/or rectifying the defective structure but shall not include the cost of remedying and/or rectifying any loss or damage to the land.

For the purposes of this Exclusion, pollution shall mean pollution or contamination by naturally occurring or man-made substances, forces or organisms or any combination of them whether permanent or transitory and however occurring.

12 any claim or loss arising out of the enforcement of any judgment originally obtained in any Court of the United States of America/Canada or any territories which come under the jurisdiction of the United States of America/Canada,

13 any claim or loss arising out of survey/inspection and/or valuation reports of real/leasehold property unless such surveys/inspections and/or valuations shall have been carried out by:

a) A Fellow or Professional Associate of the Royal Institution of Chartered Surveyors (RICS); or
A Fellow or Associate of the Incorporated Society of Valuers and Auctioneers (ISVA); or
A Fellow or Associate of the Faculty of Architects and Surveyors (FAS); or
A Fellow or Associate of the Royal Institute of British Architects (RIBA); or
A Fellow or Associate of the Royal Incorporation of Architects in Scotland (RIAS); or

b) anyone who has not less than five years experience of such work; or

c) any other person delegated by the Insured to execute such work as part of their training subject always to:
   i) supervision of such work by a person qualified in accordance with a) above; or
   ii) agreement in writing having been obtained from the Insurers prior to cover being granted,

14 any claim or loss whether directly or indirectly caused by, or contributed to by, or arising from:

a) ionising radiation or contamination by radioactivity from any nuclear fuel or from any nuclear waste from the combustion of nuclear fuel or the radioactive toxic explosive or other hazardous properties of any explosive nuclear assembly or nuclear component thereof; or

b) war, invasion, acts of foreign enemies, hostilities (whether war be declared or not), civil war, rebellion, revolution, insurrection, military or usurped power or confiscation or nationalisation or requisition or destruction of or damage to property by, or under the order of, any government or public or local authority.

General conditions

1 The Insured shall not admit liability for, or settle any claim, or incur any costs or expenses in connection therewith, without the written consent of the Insurers who shall be entitled at any time to take over and conduct in the name of the Insured or the said Firm(s) as the case may be, the defence or settlement of any such claim. Nevertheless neither the Insured nor the Insurers shall be required to contest any legal proceedings unless a Queen's Counsel (to be mutually agreed upon by the Insured and the Insurers) shall advise that such proceedings should be contested.

2 The Insured shall give to the Insurers as soon as possible details in writing of:

a) any claim or claims made against them,

b) the discovery of any loss to them which may be the subject of indemnity hereunder.

3 The Insured shall give to Insurers notice in writing as soon as possible during the Certificate Period of:

a) any circumstance of which the Insured shall first become aware during the Certificate Period which may give rise to a claim against them,

b) the discovery of a reasonable cause for suspicion of dishonesty or fraud on the part of a present Partner, Director or Employee of the Firm(s) whether giving rise to a claim or loss under this Certificate or not,

c) any threatened or actual proceedings under the Property Misdescriptions Act 1991.

Provided notice has been given in accordance with this Condition then any subsequent claim made against the Insured or any loss discovered by the Insured shall be deemed to have been made or discovered during the Certificate Period.

4 Where notice has been given in accordance with General Condition 2 or 3 the Insured shall give such full co-operation to Insurers as they shall reasonably require.

5 If any payment is made under this Certificate in respect of a claim and the Insurers are thereupon subrogated to the Insured's rights of recovery in relation thereto it is agreed that the Insurers shall not exercise such rights against any Employee of the Insured unless such claim has been brought about or contributed to by the dishonest, fraudulent, criminal or malicious act or omission of the Employee.

6 If the Insured shall make any claim under this Certificate fraudulently or knowing the same to be fraudulent as regards amount or otherwise this Certificate shall become void and all claims hereunder shall be forfeited.

7 The liability of the Insurers shall not exceed for any one claim by the

Insured under this Certificate the sum specified in Item 3 of the Schedule except that their liability for or in respect of the replacing or restoring of computer system records shall not exceed £50,000 any one claim and £150,000 in the aggregate.

Insurers shall in addition indemnify the Insured in respect of all costs and expenses incurred with their written consent in the defence or settlement of any claim which falls to be dealt with under Insuring Clause 1 of this Certificate, provided that if a payment in excess of the amount specified in Item 3 of the Schedule to this Certificate has to be made to dispose of such a claim, the Insurers' liability for such costs and expenses shall be of such proportion hereof as the amount specified in Item 3 of the Schedule to this Certificate bears to the amount paid to dispose of that claim.

Insurers may in addition indemnify the Insured in respect of 80% of costs and expenses incurred with their prior written consent in the defence of any proceedings brought under the Property Misdescriptions Act 1991 but only where the Insurers believe that defending such proceedings could protect the Insured against any subsequent or concurrent civil action arising from professional services undertaken by the Insured giving rise to such proceedings. Any subsequent or concurrent civil action arising out of any proceedings notified hereunder shall be deemed to be notified hereunder.

8 If an amount is specified under Item 4 of the Schedule this amount shall be borne by the Insured at their own risk, and Insurer's Liability shall only be in excess of this amount.

The amount specified under Item 4 of the Schedule shall not be applicable to:

a) claims or losses falling under Insuring Clause 3 of the Certificate,
b) claims arising out of any libel or slander,
c) costs and expenses incurred with Insurers' written consent such consent not to be unreasonably withheld.

9 The proper law for the interpretation of this Certificate is English Law. The Courts of England and Wales alone shall have jurisdiction for hearing and determining any litigation arising out of or in connection with the interpretation of this Certificate and any arbitration proceedings shall be heard and determined solely in England in accordance with English Law and procedure.

10 The subscribing Underwriters' obligations under certificates to which they subscribe are several and not joint and are limited solely to the extent of their individual subscriptions. The subscribing Underwriters are not responsible for the subscription of any co-subscribing Underwriter who for any reason does not satisfy all or part of its obligations.

11 THE INSURED SHALL GIVE IMMEDIATE NOTICE IN WRITING, with full particulars, of the happening of any occurrence likely to give rise to a claim under this Certificate, of the receipt by the

Insured or notice of any claim and of the institution of any proceedings against the Insured, together with the Certificate number to the address shown in Item 10 of the Certificate Schedule.

12 Where a retroactive date is specified in the Schedule this Certificate will not respond in respect of any claim or loss otherwise falling for indemnity under this Certificate where the cause of such claim or loss occurred or was alleged to have occurred prior to the said retroactive date.

APPENDIX 3

CoWa/F WARRANTY AGREEMENT

Warranty Agreement CoWa/F

Note

This form is to be used where the warranty is to be given to a company providing finance for the proposed development. Where that company is acting as an agent for a syndicate of banks, a recital should be added to refer to this as appropriate.

THIS AGREEMENT

(In Scotland, leave blank. For applicable date see Testing Clause on page 5)

is made the .... day of .... 19 ....

BETWEEN:-

(insert name of the Consultant)

(1) ....

of/whose registered office is situated at ....

.... ("the Firm");

(insert name of the Firm's Client)

(2) ....

whose registered office is situated at ....

.... ("the Client"); and

(insert name of the financier)

(3) ....

whose registered office is situated at ....

("the Company" which term shall include all permitted assignees under this agreement).

WHEREAS:-

A. The Company has entered into an agreement ("the Finance Agreement") with the Client for the provision of certain finance in connection with the carrying out of

(insert description of the works) ....

....

(insert address of the development) at ....

....

.... ("the Development").

(insert date of appointment) (delete/complete as appropriate)

B. By a contract ("the Appointment") dated ....
the Client has appointed the Firm as [architects/consulting structural engineers/consulting building services engineers/ surveyors] in connection with the Development.

(insert name of building contractor or "a building contractor to be selected by the Client")

C. The Client has entered or may enter into a building contract ("the Building Contract") with

....

....

....

for the construction of the Development.

3rd Edition

NOW IN CONSIDERATION OF THE PAYMENT OF ONE POUND (£1) BY THE COMPANY TO THE FIRM (RECEIPT OF WHICH THE FIRM ACKNOWLEDGES) IT IS HEREBY AGREED as follows:-

(delete "and care" or "care and diligence" to reflect terms of the Appointment)

1. The Firm warrants that it has exercised and will continue to exercise reasonable skill [and care] [care and diligence] in the performance of its duties to the Client under the Appointment. In the event of any breach of this warranty:

   (a) the Firm's liability for costs under this Agreement shall be limited to that proportion of the Company's losses which it would be just and equitable to require the Firm to pay having regard to the extent of the Firm's responsibility for the same and on the basis that ......

   (insert the names of other intended warrantors)

   ....

   ....

   ....

   ....

   ....shall be deemed to have provided contractual undertakings on terms no less onerous than this Clause 1 to the Company in respect of the performance of their services in connection with the Development and shall be deemed to have paid to the Company such proportion which it would be just and equitable for them to pay having regard to the extent of their responsibility;

   (b) the Firm shall be entitled in any action or proceedings by the Company to rely on any limitation in the Appointment and to raise the equivalent rights in defence of liability as it would have against the Client under the Appointment;

(delete where the Firm is the quantity surveyor)

2. [Without prejudice to the generality of Clause 1, the Firm further warrants that it has exercised and will continue to exercise reasonable skill and care to see that, unless authorised by the Client in writing or, where such authorisation is given orally, confirmed by the Firm to the Client

in writing, none of the following has been or will be specified by the Firm for use in the construction of those parts of the Development to which the Appointment relates:-

(a) high alumina cement in structural elements;

(b) wood wool slabs in permanent formwork to concrete;

(c) calcium chloride in admixtures for use in reinforced concrete;

(d) asbestos products;

(e) naturally occurring aggregates for use in reinforced concrete which do not comply with British Standard 882: 1983 and/or naturally occurring aggregates for use in concrete which do not comply with British Standard 8110: 1985.

(further specific materials may be added by agreement)

(f)

]

3. The Company has no authority to issue any direction or instruction to the Firm in relation to performance of the Firm's services under the Appointment unless and until the Company has given notice under Clauses 5 or 6.

4. The Firm acknowledges that the Client has paid all fees and expenses properly due and owing to the Firm under the Appointment up to the date of this Agreement. The Company has no liability to the Firm in respect of fees and expenses under the Appointment unless and until the Company has given notice under Clauses 5 or 6.

5. The Firm agrees that, in the event of the termination of the Finance Agreement by the Company, the Firm will, if so required by notice in writing given by the Company and subject to Clause 7, accept the instructions of the Company or its appointee to the exclusion of the Client in respect of the Development upon the terms and conditions of the Appointment. The Client acknowledges that the Firm shall be entitled to rely on a notice given to the Firm by the Company under this Clause 5 as conclusive evidence for the purposes of this Agreement of the termination of the Finance Agreement by the Company.

6. The Firm further agrees that it will not without first giving the Company not less than twenty one days' notice in writing exercise any right it may have to terminate the Appointment or to treat the same as having been repudiated by the Client or to discontinue the performance of any services to be performed by the Firm pursuant thereto. Such right to terminate the Appointment with the Client or treat the same as having been repudiated or discontinue performance shall cease if, within such period of notice and subject to Clause 7, the Company shall give notice in writing to the Firm requiring the Firm to accept the instructions of the Company or its appointee to the exclusion of the Client in respect of the Development upon the terms and conditions of the Appointment.

7. It shall be a condition of any notice given by the Company under Clauses 5 or 6 that the Company or its appointee accepts liability for payment of the fees and expenses payable to the Firm under the Appointment and for performance of the Client's obligations including payment of any fees and expenses outstanding at the date of such notice. Upon the issue of any notice by the Company under Clauses 5 or 6, the Appointment shall continue in full force and effect as if no right of termination on the part of the Firm had arisen and the Firm shall be liable to the Company and its appointee under the Appointment in lieu of its liability to the Client. If any notice given by the Company under Clauses 5 or 6 requires the Firm to accept the instructions of the Company's appointee, the Company shall be liable to the Firm as guarantor for the payment of all sums from time to time due to the Firm from the Company's appointee.

8. The copyright in all drawings, reports, models, specifications, bills of quantities, ca culations and other similar documents provided by the Firm in connection with the Development (together referred to in this Clause 8 as "the Documents") shall remain vested in the Firm but, subject to the Firm having received payment of any fees agreed as properly due under the Appointment, the Company and its appointee shall have a licence to copy and use the Documents and to reproduce the designs and content of them for any purpose related to the Premises including, but without limitation, the construction, completion, maintenance, letting, promotion, advertisement, reinstatement, refurbishment and repair of the Development. Such licence shall enable the Company and its appointee to copy and use the Documents for the extension of the Development but such use shall not include a licence to reproduce the designs contained in them for any extension of the Development. The Firm shall not be liable for any such use by the Company or its appointee of any of the Documents for any purpose other than that for which the same were prepared by or on behalf of the Firm.

9. The Firm shall maintain professional indemnity insurance in an amount of not less than

(insert amount) pounds (£)

for any one occurrence or series of occurrences arising out of any one event for a period

(insert period) of years from the date of practical completion of the Development for the purposes of the Building Contract, provided always that such insurance is available at commercially reasonable rates. The Firm shall immediately inform the Company if such insurance ceases to be available at commercially reasonable rates in order that the Firm and the Company can discuss means of best protecting the respective positions of the Company and the Firm in respect of the Development in the absence of such insurance. As and when it is reasonably requested to do so by the Company or its appointee under the Clauses 5 or 6, the Firm shall produce for inspection documentary evidence that its professional indemnity insurance is being maintained.

10. The Client has agreed to be a party to this Agreement for the purposes of acknowledging that the Firm shall not be in breach of the Appointment by complying with the obligations imposed on it by Clauses 5 and 6.

(delete if under Scots law)

[11. This Agreement may be assigned by the Company by way of absolute legal assignment to another company providing finance or re-finance in connection with the carrying out of the Development without the consent of the Client or the Firm being required and such assignment shall be effective upon written notice thereof being given to the Client and to the Firm.]

(delete if under English law)

[11S. *The Company shall be entitled to assign or transfer its rights under this Agreement to any other company providing finance or re-finance in connection with the carrying out of the Development without the consent of the Client or the Firm being required subject to written notice of such assignation being given to the Firm in accordance with Clause 12 hereof.*]

12. Any notice to be given by the Firm hereunder shall be deemed to be duly given if it is delivered by hand at or sent by registered post or recorded delivery to the Company at its registered office and any notice given by the Company hereunder shall be deemed to be duly given if it is addressed to "The Senior Partner"/"The Managing Director" and delivered by hand at or sent by registered post or recorded delivery to the above-mentioned address of the Firm or to the principal business address of the Firm for the time being and, in the case of any such notices, the same shall if sent by registered post or recorded delivery be deemed to have been received forty eight hours after being posted.

(complete as appropriate)

13. No action or proceedings for any breach of this Agreement shall be commenced against the Firm after the expiry of   years from the date of practical completion of the Premises under the Building Contract.

(delete if under Scots law)

[14. The construction validity and performance of this agreement shall be governed by English Law and the parties agree to submit to the non-exclusive jurisdiction of the English Courts.

(alternatives: delete as appropriate)

[**AS WITNESS** the hands of the parties the day and year first before written.

Signed by or on behalf of the Firm ....

(for Agreement

in the presence of: ....

(executed under hand and NOT as a Deed)

Signed by or on behalf of the Client ....

in the presence of: ....

Signed by or on behalf of the Company ....

in the presence of: ....]

(this must only apply if the Appointment is executed as a Deed)

[**IN WITNESS WHEREOF** this Agreement was executed as a Deed and delivered the day and year first before written.

by the Firm

....

....

by the Client

....

....

by the Company

....

....

....]]

(delete if under English law) [14S. *This Agreement shall be construed and the rights of the parties and all matters arising hereunder shall be determined in all respects according to the Law of Scotland.*

***IN WITNESS WHEREOF** these presents are executed as follows:-*

SIGNED by the above named Firm at ....

on the .... *day of* .... *Nineteen hundred and* ....

as follows:-

.... *(Firm's signature)*

Signature .... *Full Name* ....

Address ....

.... *Occupation* ....

Signature .... *Full Name* ....

Address ....

.... *Occupation* ....

SIGNED by the above named Client at ....

on the .... *day of* .... *Nineteen hundred and* ....

as follows:-

For and on behalf of the Client

.... *Director/Authorised Signatory*

.... *Director/Authorised Signatory*

SIGNED by the above named Company at ....

on the .... day of .... Nineteen hundred and ....

as follows:-

For and on behalf of the Company

.... *Director/Authorised Signatory*

.... *Director/Authorised Signatory*]

APPENDIX 4

CoWa/P&T WARRANTY AGREEMENT

Warranty Agreement CoWa/P&T

(In Scotland, leave blank. For applicable date see Testing Clause on page 4)

THIS AGREEMENT

is made the ....day of 199

BETWEEN:-

(insert name of the Consultant)

(1) ....

of/whose registered office is situated at ....

.... ("the Firm"), and

(insert name of the Purchaser/the Tenant)

(2) ....

whose registered office is situated at ....

....

(delete as appropriate)

("the Purchaser"/"the Tenant" which term shall include all permitted assignees under this Agreement).

WHEREAS:-

(delete as appropriate)

A. The Purchaser/the Tenant has entered into an agreement to purchase/an agreement to lease/a lease with

....

.... ("the Client") relating to

(insert description of the premises)

....

....

....("the Premises") (delete as appropriate) [forming part of ....

(insert description of the development) ....

....

(insert address of the development) at ....

.... ("the Development").]

(delete as appropriate) ["The Premises" are also referred to as "the Development" in this Agreement.]

(insert date of appointment) (delete/complete as appropriate)

B. By a contract ("the Appointment") dated .... the Client has appointed the Firm as [architects/consulting structural engineers/consulting building services engineers/ surveyors] in connection with the Development.

C. The Client has entered or may enter into a contract ("the Building Contract") with

(insert name of building contractor or "a building contractor to be selected by the Client")

....

....

....

for the construction of the Development.

NOW IN CONSIDERATION OF THE PAYMENT OF ONE POUND (£1) BY THE PURCHASER/THE TENANT TO THE FIRM (RECEIPT OF WHICH THE FIRM ACKNOWLEDGES) IT IS HEREBY AGREED as follows:-

(delete as appropriate to reflect terms of the Appointment)

1. The Firm warrants that it has exercised and will continue to exercise reasonable skill [and care] [care and diligence] in the performance of its services to the Client under the Appointment. In the event of any breach of this warranty:

(a) subject to paragraphs (b) and (c) of this clause, the Firm shall be liable for the reasonable costs of repair renewal and/or reinstatement of any part or parts of the Development to the extent that

- the Purchaser/the Tenant incurs such costs and/or
- the Purchaser/the Tenant is or becomes liable either directly or by way of financial contribution for such costs.

The Firm shall not be liable for other losses incurred by the Purchaser/the Tenant.

(insert the names of other intended warrantors)

(b) the Firm's liability for costs under this Agreement shall be limited to that proportion of such costs which it would be just and equitable to require the Firm to pay having regard to the extent of the Firm's responsibility for the same and on the basis that ....

....

....

....

.... shall be deemed to have provided contractual undertakings on terms no less onerous than this Clause 1 to the Purchaser/the Tenant in respect of the performance of their services in connection with the Development and shall be deemed to have paid to the Purchaser/the Tenant such proportion which it would be just and equitable for them to pay having regard to the extent of their responsibility;

(c) the Firm shall be entitled in any action or proceedings by the Purchaser/the Tenant to rely on any limitation in the Appointment and to raise the equivalent rights in defence of liability as it would have against the Client under the Appointment;

(d) the obligations of the Firm under or pursuant to this Clause 1 shall not be released or diminished by the appointment of any person by the Purchaser/the Tenant to carry out any independent enquiry into any relevant matter.

(delete where the Firm is the quantity surveyor)

2. [Without prejudice to the generality of Clause 1, the Firm further warrants that it has exercised and will continue to exercise reasonable skill and care to see that, unless authorised by the Client in writing or, where such authorisation is given orally, confirmed by the Firm to the Client in writing, none of the following has been or will be specified by the Firm for use in the construction of those parts of the Development to which the Appointment relates:-

(a) high alumina cement in structural elements;

(b) wood wool slabs in permanent formwork to concrete;

(c) calcium chloride in admixtures for use in reinforced concrete;

(d) asbestos products;

(e) naturally occurring aggregates for use in reinforced concrete which do not comply with British Standard 882: 1983 and/or naturally occurring aggregates for use in concrete which do not comply with British Standard 8110: 1985.

(further specific materials may be added by agreement)

(f)

In the event of any breach of this warranty the provisions of Clauses 1a, b, c and d shall apply.]

3. The Firm acknowledges that the Client has paid all fees and expenses properly due and owing to the Firm under the Appointment up to the date of this Agreement.

4. The Purchaser/the Tenant has no authority to issue any direction or instruction to the Firm in relation to the Appointment.

5. The copyright in all drawings, reports, models, specifications, bills of quantities, calculations and other documents and information prepared by or on behalf of the Firm in connection with the Development (together referred to in this Clause 5 as "the Documents") shall remain vested in the Firm but, subject to the Firm having received payment of any fees agreed as properly due under the Appointment, the Purchaser/the Tenant and its appointee shall have a licence to copy and use the Documents and to reproduce the designs and content of them for any purpose related to the Premises including, but without limitation, the construction, completion, maintenance, letting, promotion, advertisement, reinstatement, refurbishment and repair of the Premises. Such licence shall enable the Purchaser/the Tenant and its appointee to copy and use the Documents for the extension of the Premises but such use shall not include a licence to reproduce the designs contained in them for any extension of the Premises. The Firm shall not be liable for any use by the Purchaser/the Tenant or its appointee of any of the Documents for any purpose other than that for which the same were prepared by or on behalf of the Firm.

6. The Firm shall maintain professional indemnity insurance in an amount of not less than
(insert amount) pounds (£)
for any one occurrence or series of occurrences arising out of any one event for a period
(insert period) of years from the date of practical completion of the Premises under the Building Contract, provided always that such insurance is available at commercially reasonable rates. The Firm shall immediately inform the Purchaser/the Tenant if such insurance ceases to be available at commercially reasonable rates in order that the Firm and the Purchaser/the Tenant can discuss means of best protecting the respective positions of the Purchaser/the Tenant and the Firm in the absence of such insurance. As and when it is reasonably requested to do so by the Purchaser/the Tenant or its appointee the Firm shall produce for inspection documentary evidence that its professional indemnity insurance is being maintained.

(insert number of times)

(delete if under Scots law)

[7. This Agreement may be assigned by the Purchaser/the Tenant by way of absolute legal assignment to another person taking an assignment of the Purchaser's/the Tenant's interest in the Premises without the consent of the Client or the Firm being required and such assignment shall be effective upon written notice thereof being given to the Firm. No further assignment shall be permitted.]

(insert number of times)

(delete if under English law)

[7S. *The Purchaser/the Tenant shall be entitled to assign or transfer his/their rights under this Agreement to any other person acquiring the Purchaser's/the Tenant's interest in the whole of the Premises without the consent of the Firm subject to written notice of such assignation being given to the Firm in accordance with Clause 8 hereof. Nothing in this clause shall permit any party acquiring such right as assignee or transferee to enter into any further assignation or transfer to anyone acquiring subsequently an interest in the Premises from him.*]

8. Any notice to be given by the Firm hereunder shall be deemed to be duly given if it is delivered by hand at or sent by registered post or recorded delivery to the Purchaser/the Tenant at its registered office and any notice given by the Purchaser/the Tenant hereunder shall be deemed to be duly given if it is addressed to "The Senior Partner"/"The Managing Director" and delivered by hand at or sent by registered post or recorded delivery to the above-mentioned address of the Firm or to the principal business address of the Firm for the time being and, in the case of any such notices, the same shall if sent by registered post or recorded delivery be deemed to have been received forty eight hours after being posted.

(complete as appropriate)

9. No action or proceedings for any breach of this Agreement shall be commenced against the Firm after the expiry of years from the date of practical completion of the Premises under the Building Contract.

(delete if under Scots law)

[10. The construction validity and performance of this Agreement shall be governed by English law and the parties agree to submit to the non-exclusive jurisdiction of the English Courts.

(alternatives: delete as appropriate)

(for Agreement executed under hand and NOT as a Deed)

[**AS WITNESS** the hands of the parties the day and year first before written.

Signed by or on behalf of the Firm ....

in the presence of: ....

Signed by or on behalf of the Purchaser/the Tenant ....

in the presence of: ....]

(this must only apply if the Appointment is executed as a Deed)

[**IN WITNESS WHEREOF** this Agreement was executed as a Deed and delivered the day and year first before written.

by the Firm

....

....

....

....

by the Purchaser/the Tenant

....

....

....

....]]

(delete if under English law)

10S. *This Agreement shall be construed and the rights of the parties and all matters arising hereunder shall be determined in all respects according to the Law of Scotland.*

***IN WITNESS WHEREOF** these presents are executed as follows:-*

SIGNED by the above named Firm at ....

on the .... *day of* .... *Nineteen hundred and* ....

as follows:-

.... *(Firm's signature)*

Signature .... *Full Name* ....

Address ....

.... *Occupation* ....

Signature .... *Full Name* ....

Address ....

.... *Occupation* ....

SIGNED by the above named Purchaser/Tenant at ....

on the .... *day of* .... *Nineteen hundred and* ....

as follows:-

For and on behalf of the Purchaser/the Tenant

.... *Director/Authorised Signatory*

.... *Director/Authorised Signatory*]

INDEX